THE ISLAND

AMERICA READS

Rediscovered Fiction and Nonfiction from Key Periods in American History

THE GREAT DEPRESSION

Little Napoleons and Dummy Directors (1933)
Being the Narrative of the Bank of United States

The Barter Lady (1934)
A Woman Farmer Sees It Through

The House of Dawn (1935)
A Novel

WORLD WAR II

The Island (1944)
A History of the First Marine Division on Guadalcanal

Robinson Crusoe, USN (1945)
The Adventures of George R. Tweed Rm1c on Japanese-Held Guam

The Bismarck Episode (1948)

THE ISLAND

A History of
the First Marine Division on

GUADALCANAL

August 7 – December 9, 1942

HERBERT LAING MERILLAT

WESTHOLME
Yardley

Originally published in 1944 by Houghton Mifflin Company.

Westholme Publishing, LLC
904 Edgewood Road
Yardley, Pennsylvania 19067
Visit our Web site at www.westholmepublishing.com

First Printing: March 2010
10 9 8 7 6 5 4 3 2 1

ISBN: 978-1-59416-113-1

Printed in United States of America.

To George...Who Did It

Preface

I N AREA COVERED and numbers engaged the Battle of
Guadalcanal is small compared with the titanic struggles
in Russia or even in North Africa. But in the history of the
Pacific war it will assume the symbolic import that Verdun
did in the last war, and Stalingrad in this war.' In those
words the *New York Times* appraised the place of Guadalcanal in history. As the first major battle in which American
forces met and vanquished the Japanese enemy, it has ac-
quired a special significance in the minds of Americans.

In this book I have tried to tell, as accurately as I can, the
story of the Marines who fought in the Battle of Guadalcanal
more than four months, as I saw the story develop. It is
offered as an account of what the First Marine Division, Reinforced, gave and took in the long struggle with the Japanese
for the possession of Henderson Field, the key to the southern
Solomons. Only incidentally is it a story of individual ex-
ploits or a record of personal reactions and experiences.

After the Marines under Lieutenant General A. A. Vandegrift (then Major General) in the second week of August, 1942,
had seized the airfield area on Guadalcanal and the small
islands guarding Tulagi Harbor, the Japanese made four determined efforts in as many months to recapture what they
had lost in their first setback in the islands of the Pacific. Each
attempt was on a larger scale than the last, and the small, almost unknown islands of the Solomons in the South Pacific
became the setting for a struggle of major proportions between
the United States and Japan. I have sought in this book to

show the development of the fighting, which continued in crescendo until the crisis in mid-November was resolved in favor of the American forces.

The Guadalcanal campaign continued two months after the first units of the First Marine Division left the island. During that period United States ground forces consisting principally of United States Army units, with some Marine units attached, under the command of Major General Alexander M. Patch, United States Army, pushed forward along the beaches, across the ridges, and through the jungles of Guadalcanal to drive the Japanese from the island.

February 10, 1943, it was announced that organized Japanese resistance had ended on Guadalcanal. Six months after the first landing the victory was at last complete. The final drive, undertaken when forces on Guadalcanal were at last large enough both to defend the airfield and at the same time to pursue the remnants of the Japanese army on the island, constitutes a campaign in itself and doubtless will be told by others who were on the scene. I have limited my story to the campaign fought by the First Marine Division, Reinforced, from the original landings on August 7, 1942, until Lieutenant General Vandegrift turned over his command to Major General Patch on December 9, 1942 — the period during which I was on the island.

In a sense, the forces of both belligerents were under siege during the last four months of 1942. Both had to depend on long and uncertain supply lines (ours being longer and more uncertain than the Japanese) subject to the hazards of air, surface, and underwater warfare. Both at times became desperately short of critical supplies. Both were subject to heavy and sustained pounding by bombs and shells during long periods. Although we had the advantage of definite air superiority (in quality if not quantity) during most of the campaign, the Japanese had, for a long period, the advantage of greater numbers and weight in naval surface craft.

The campaign revealed, with unusual clarity, the interplay

and interdependence of sea, air, and land power. The tide of battle shifted as we or the Japanese brought to bear a preponderance in one or another of these categories. At last a strong team of all types of power decisively defeated the Japanese and drove them from the island.

I was attached to the Marine ground forces under the command of Lieutenant General Vandegrift and my account will be concerned primarily with the ground fighting on Guadalcanal and the work done by aviation units based on Henderson Field. The naval phases of the campaign, however, must be described by others more competent to speak. Some important engagements were fought far from the island's shores. Even those taking place close to Guadalcanal (five major naval engagements were fought within sight of our beachhead) were confused pictures of gun-flashes and burning ships to the Marines who saw them from the shore. We watched breathlessly, acutely aware of their importance to the outcome of the campaign, but our knowledge of the results came largely from official communiqués.

For similar reasons I have not tried to tell the story of distant aerial actions, sometimes taking place hundreds of miles from Guadalcanal, which contributed to the success of the campaign. United States Army bombers based in New Guinea, for example, maintained a steady and cumulatively effective pressure against the enemy bases in New Britain and the northern Solomons that threatened our position on Guadalcanal.

This is principally a story of the Marine infantry who manned the defenses of Henderson Field and tracked the Japanese through the jungle. Theirs were the drama and the danger of close-quarter combat with a clever and determined enemy. But many others, not so often mentioned in these pages, shared with the rifleman, the machine-gunner, and the mortar crew the heat, dirt, disease, mosquitoes, hunger, the long months of strain and hardship, and the repeated poundings by enemy bombs and shells.

Their work was less dramatic, but no less important. There were artillerymen, whose guns, under their skillful handling, were among our most effective weapons. There were men in tanks, men who manned the anti-aircraft guns, men who unloaded ships and moved supplies, men who worked on the airfield, bridges, roads, and installations, men who laid telephone wires through shellings and battles, men who drove jeeps, trucks, and amphibian tractors, men who clerked and baked and cooked, men who guarded prisoners. Almost all, being Marines first and specialists second, had to take up positions in the firing line at some time or other.

There were the doctors and medical corps men of the Navy, who brought the wounded from the front lines and cared for them. There were the officers and crews of motor torpedo boats who stalked the Japanese ships at night. There were men of the Navy and Coast Guard who maintained and operated the boats, chaplains of the Navy, and naval construction men, the Sea Bees, who helped develop the island as a powerful base.

And there were the airmen, to whom too much praise cannot be given. They were magnificent — the men who flew the fighters and bombers, manned the guns, and repaired shattered planes on the ground. Their bivouacs and working places were the primary targets of Japanese bombs and shells. The field from which they operated was the principal objective of the enemy's determined drives against Guadalcanal.

When Admiral Halsey visited Guadalcanal shortly after assuming command of the South Pacific area, he remarked that he could scarcely tell who belonged to the Army, Navy, Marine Corps, or Coast Guard. All looked alike in their dirty khaki and bearded faces — or in their lack of khaki. All worked together as a team inside the defense perimeter around Henderson Field. Ground forces, air forces, naval forces — all shared in the ordeal and in the final victory. Who can say there was a hierarchy of heroes on Guadalcanal?

Some of those heroes are mentioned by name — men whose

deeds won them the highest decorations awarded by our nation or who occupied positions of great responsibility. But those named are few compared to the numbers who fought and worked, and sometimes died, in anonymity.

I am greatly indebted to many officers and men for their assistance and encouragement in the preparation of this record. Lieutenant General Alexander A. Vandegrift, then a Major General commanding the First Marine Division, and his Chief of Staff, Colonel (now Brigadier General) Gerald C. Thomas, gave all possible assistance and co-operation, and without their great interest in having a record of the campaign which would be available to the men who fought on Guadalcanal, this work could not have been undertaken.

Lieutenant Colonel Merrill B. Twining, Operations Officer of the First Marine Division after Colonel Thomas became Chief of Staff, Lieutenant Colonel Edmund J. Buckley, the Intelligence Officer, Major James C. Murray, Jr., Adjutant and later Personnel Officer, and the officers and men of their staff sections, were also most helpful.

The Marine Combat Correspondents attached to units operating on Guadalcanal have provided some of the material used in this book through stories which they wrote on the spot. Second Lieutenant James W. Hurlbut, who landed on Guadalcanal as a Sergeant correspondent on the first day of the attack, has made the largest contribution of that sort. I have also drawn on the stories of Second Lieutenant Edward J. Burman, a Sergeant correspondent when he first went to Guadalcanal, and Master Technical Sergeant Richard H. Venn. Engaging in pioneer work in the Marine Corps, as Marine reporters living and fighting with the units whose stories they told, those men maintained a high standard of work which has resulted in a unique contribution to war-reporting. It was a great pleasure to work with them on Guadalcanal.

Turning from the field to Headquarters in Washington, I want to thank Brigadier General Robert L. Denig, Director of Public Relations for the Marine Corps, and his executive officer, Lieutenant Colonel George T. Van der Hoef, for their help and encouragement. They instituted the plan to send Public Relations Officers and Combat Correspondents into the field with combat units, providing the opportunity for facts used in records like this to be collected. Since my return to the United States they have made possible my continued work on the history.

Technical Sergeant Richard T. Wright, who served as a Combat Correspondent in the Pacific for more than a year, has helped me at Headquarters in a multitude of ways.

In the time that has elapsed since the Guadalcanal campaign, many of those mentioned by name in this account have been advanced above the ranks held by them at the time of the battle. Because of difficulties in keeping pace with such promotions, I have, with few exceptions, given all ranks and grades as of the relevant times in the narrative.

Anyone who has been through a battle will appreciate the difficulties of getting an accurate picture of what happened. From the welter of conflicting reports, personal adventures, rumors and alarms, it is exceedingly difficult to reconstruct an accurate record of events. Men's memories are particularly unreliable when they refer back to the excitement of battle and men's imaginations incline them to make a good story better. I have seen some stories issuing from Guadalcanal, repeated in print, so encrusted with dramatic fictions that the original kernel of truth is almost hidden. Simply by virtue of being often repeated many such fictions undoubtedly will pass into history as truths. I have tried, in these pages, to avoid statements which could not be checked against personal observation or a report from a source I considered reliable. But he is a rash man who comes out of a military campaign and says, 'This is exactly what happened,' and I make no such pretensions. The opinions expressed are my own and do not necessarily represent those of the Marine Corps or the Naval Service at large.

H. M.

Contents

Illustrations

Maps

PART ONE

Chapter 1

Into the Pacific

O NE MIDNIGHT in May, 1942, ten tugs strained at a
converted luxury liner at Norfolk, Virginia, maneuver-
ing the big ship away from the dock. Slowly she slid out into
the channel, then began her progress toward the open sea,
past the dimmed-out city and naval base, out of the safety of
the harbor into waters infested with German submarines.
It was a solemn moment for those on board. They were seeing
the last of the United States for many months, perhaps years.
If they had known where the long journey ahead of them
would end, the occasion would have seemed even more impressive, but few of them realized that they were destined to
be the first American land forces to undertake offensive action
against the enemy in the Pacific.

The United States had been at war five and a half months.
They had been months full of disaster for the United States
and her allies — Pearl Harbor, Guam, Wake, Bataan, Hong-
kong, Malaya, Singapore, Burma, the Netherlands East
Indies, and Corregidor. The nation's new war heroes were
men who had shown skill and valor in adversity, who had
fought a losing battle gamely. We had no victories to boast
of except the Battle of Coral Sea and no conquering heroes
to acclaim. The nation, despite official caution and warnings

against optimism, insisted on regarding the Coral Sea battle as a great victory, perhaps the turning-point which everyone so eagerly awaited. The man in the street clung to a belief that Australia was swarming with the khaki of a new United States Army, that the island continent had been saved for all time from the threat of invasion, and that the United Nations would soon strike out at the Japanese. He would have been surprised and disappointed if he had known that the blacked-out transport which pulled out of Norfolk early in the morning of May 20 carried only the vanguard of assault troops for operations in the South Pacific.

That ship was the *U.S.S. Wakefield*, formerly the trans-Atlantic liner *S.S. Manhattan*. The fighting men she carried were the Advance Echelon of the First Marine Division under Major General A. A. Vandegrift. Their immediate destination was Wellington, New Zealand.

Years of training and planning had gone into the creation of the unit then heading for the South Pacific. Most of the enlisted men and junior officers were young men in their late teens or early twenties, who had joined the Marines as war grew imminent, but they were led by officers and noncommissioned officers who had long experience in amphibious operations. In the nineteen-thirties the Navy and Marine Corps had begun a series of joint fleet exercises in the Caribbean to experiment in landing operations. At a time when the armies and navies of the world were skeptical of the feasibility of amphibious operations, when military thought on the subject was dominated by the British failure at Gallipoli, the United States Navy and Marine Corps worked out methods of seizing and holding island bases from potential enemies.

The early exercises provided a body of experience and learning which became crystallized in landing operations doctrine destined to serve as the blueprint for successful amphibious operations in the Second World War. The Marine Corps Schools at Quantico devoted more and more attention to the peculiar problems of amphibious warfare and by the time the Japanese attacked Pearl Harbor, a group of thoroughly schooled officers and a body of well-trained men was ready to undertake the mission of wresting Japan's island bases from her.

In 1935 the Fleet Marine Force was established as an integral part of the United States Fleet, to be available for immediate action on call of the Commander-in-Chief. Units of that force were trained as specialists in landing operations, forming a mobile, heavily armed, seaborne striking force. By the end of 1941 two Marine Divisions had been organized within the Fleet Marine Force. One, based on the West Coast, was the Second Marine Division. The other, based on the East Coast, was the First Marine Division, whose Advance Echelon departed on the *Wakefield* for the Pacific in May, 1942.

The Fifth Marines, one of the two Marine infantry regiments which won fame at Belleau Wood, Blanc Monte, Soissons, St. Mihiel, and Meuse Argonne in the First World War, formed the backbone of the Advance Echelon. The Fifth Marines were reinforced by a battalion of artillery — the Second Battalion, Eleventh Marines — and detachments of Division Special and Service Troops.

Advance elements of the Echelon left earlier in May, one group under the command of Major James G. Frazer, leaving from Norfolk May 10, and another under Lieutenant Colonel John D. Macklin, leaving from New Orleans May 12. The movement of the main body from New River, North Carolina, to Norfolk began May 16, and embarkation of all units and loading of supplies and equipment were completed on the 19th.

That day there were unmistakable signs that the *Wakefield* was about to 'shove off.' There was a last-minute haste in the pace of loading, orders were issued for a strict black-out on the big transport, and thin wisps of smoke from the funnel told that the boilers were getting up steam. Major General Vandegrift and his Staff Officers came aboard. Colonel W. C.

James (Chief of Staff), Lieutenant Colonel F. B. Goettge (Division Intelligence Officer), Lieutenant Colonel G. C. Thomas (Division Operations Officer), Lieutenant Colonel R. McC. Pate (Division Supply Officer), and Captain J. C. Murray, Jr. (Division Adjutant), accompanied the General.

Just after midnight the *Wakefield* got under way. Under heavy escort the big ship made the dangerous trip through the Atlantic and Caribbean to the Panama Canal. Although at times the escorting ships laid patterns of depth charges on suspicions that enemy submarines were near-by, the transport made the Canal safely. Two days later we crossed the Equator and the next day was taken up with the traditional ceremonies of introducing thousands of polliwogs to the mysteries of the Kingdom of Neptunus Rex and qualifying them as shellbacks.

In the next week we began to hear reports of the Battle of Midway, a victory which was to have a very direct effect on the fate of the First Marine Division. That distant engagement meant that the Marines aboard the *Wakefield* were to see action much earlier than they had expected. Japanese losses paved the way for the United Nations offensive in the Solomons two months later.

A day in June we awoke to find we had made a landfall. The mountains of New Zealand towered near-by, and in the distance we soon could make out a city sprawling on the hills which turned out to be Wellington. Spirits were high as the ship tied up to the dock, greeted by local dignitaries and a snappy performance by the Royal New Zealand Air Force Band. The Marines looked forward to liberty in this new land, but first came the serious business of unloading and getting established in camps.

Lieutenant Colonel M. B. Twining and Quartermaster Clerk Harry E. Detwiler had flown to New Zealand before the Advance Echelon left the United States, to make arrangements for camps to receive the Marines on their arrival and for storage space for supplies and equipment. As soon as he arrived in Wellington, May 5, Lieutenant Colonel Twining started on a reconnaissance of possible camp sites near the city. He completed his selection on the 9th and construction of the camps began May 16, under the supervision of the New Zealand Public Works Department. They stopped work on all other projects to concentrate on the Marine camps. Bad weather, a scarcity of labor, and shortages of materials harassed the construction work, but it proceeded at good speed. Nothing could be done about the weather, but the labor shortage was made up in part by using women and New Zealand troops, and the Dominion was combed for building materials to use on the project. Lumber used in the camps was, on the average, only three to five days out of New Zealand forests. Nearly everything available in the islands in the way of plumbing was used in the camp projects. In spite of the difficulties, enough construction had been completed by June 10 to house the entire Advance Echelon of the First Marine Division.

Meanwhile, Quartermaster Clerk Detwiler searched the city of Wellington and vicinity for empty warehouses and other available storage space. He, too, ran into difficulties in a city where such space was already at a premium, but succeeded in finding enough room in the upper stories of wool warehouses and elsewhere to meet immediate needs.

The task immediately confronting the Advance Echelon upon its arrival in Wellington was to unload the ships, disembark the troops, and establish itself in the camps. The two ships which arrived in Wellington June 8, a week ahead of the *Wakefield*, were already partly unloaded when the main group arrived. There were difficulties with local labor, however, and unloading went very slowly. After the *Wakefield* arrived, the Marines took over the unloading of ships and thereafter it proceeded much faster.

Disembarkation of troops began June 15 and was completed on the 19th. On that date Division Headquarters was set up at the Hotel Cecil, an old hotel near the main railroad station where the bars and fixtures of a British public house gave way to bunks and office equipment of the Headquarters group. The troops of the Advance Echelon moved to seven camps near Wellington. Ammunition, gasoline, and vehicles were dispersed at various points near the waterfront outside Wellington.

The Advance Echelon, promptly after its arrival, took steps to organize a defense of the beaches near the main camps. June 15 the Commanding General received a letter from Vice Admiral Ghormley, Commander of the South Pacific Area with headquarters at Auckland, instructing him to report to the New Zealand authorities in regard to defensive measures in New Zealand, and Major General Vandegrift immediately called upon Lieutenant General Puttick, General Officer in Command of the New Zealand Army. Discussions led to the issuance of instructions designating the Fifth Marines and supporting troops, under the command of Colonel Hunt, as a beach defense group to provide for defense against possible enemy raids and landings on a long strip of beach considered particularly vulnerable to enemy attack. This protection was destined to be short-lived, however, for as events developed the beach defenses were secured July 2 when the Fifth Marines re-embarked at Wellington.

NEWS OF A MISSION

While the Marines were still getting squared away in their new camps and enjoying their first shore liberty in a remarkably hospitable land after a month at sea, the Commanding General and his Staff learned that the Division might be called upon for a combat mission much earlier than anyone had supposed when the Advance Echelon sailed from Norfolk.

June 26, Major General Vandegrift, accompanied by Lieutenant Colonel Goettge, Lieutenant Colonel Thomas, and Major E. W. Snedeker (Division Communications Officer), flew to Auckland for conferences with Vice Admiral

Ghormley and his Staff, to discuss plans for training the First Marine Division. Upon their arrival, however, they learned that matters of much greater import and urgency were on the agenda. At a conference called by the Admiral, which Major General Vandegrift and Lieutenant Colonel Thomas attended as representatives of the First Marine Division, the Admiral informed all those present that an important directive had been received concerning plans to seize Japanese-held areas in the Solomon Islands.

Late in the spring of 1942, the Japanese had moved into southeastern Solomons, taking over Tulagi with its excellent harbor and apparently intending to establish air bases in the area. From such bases the Japanese could have threatened our line of communications with Australia and New Zealand. The new enemy positions were uncomfortably close to new United Nations bases in the New Hebrides and New Caledonia. It was a period when both Japan and the United States were grabbing up islands on the perimeter of Japan's newly seized empire.

The Solomons, a chain of islands extending from northwest to southeast for a distance of six hundred miles, lie about eight hundred miles from the northeast coast of Australia. Guadalcanal, destined to be the first objective in the Solomons operations, lies directly east of Port Moresby, at a distance of about eight hundred miles.

All the Solomon Islands except Bougainville were placed under British Mandate after the First World War, with the seat of government at Tulagi. Bougainville, with New Britain and New Ireland to the northwest and part of the huge island of New Guinea, were under Australian mandate.

The Marine officers informed Vice Admiral Ghormley of the situation in the First Division — that the Advance Echelon was still busy preparing camps and handling stores and that the Rear Echelon, consisting of more than half of the Division, was en route to Wellington, but the date of its arrival was uncertain. After further discussion it was decided that the Ad-

vance Echelon would be embarked immediately at Wellington. Thus it happened that the First Marine Division began
preparing for combat operations less than a fortnight after its
arrival in New Zealand. Major General Vandegrift, Lieutenant Colonel Thomas, and Major Snedeker returned to Wellington on the 27th and Lieutenant Colonel Goettge flew directly from Auckland to Australia to get information concerning the area of future operations and secure the services of
persons familiar with the Guadalcanal–Tulagi area.

June 27 and 28 the Staff was busy developing plans and
writing orders for the embarkation of the Advance Echelon.
The Fifth Marines, Reinforced, were ordered to embark on
transports July 2, with equipment and supplies cut down to
the bare essentials needed to fight and live. All overnight
liberty was cancelled, effective June 30. July 2 the trains
which so recently had taken the Marines to their camps began
bringing them back to Wellington and the Marines began
embarking on transports and combat-loading the ships. 'Combat-loading,' as the term indicates, means loading supplies for
actual combat, according to an intricate and exacting plan
whereby those items most urgently needed in landing shall be
quickly available for unloading during landing operations.

As the long lines of Marines moved aboard the transports,
the atmosphere was very different from that of the embarkation in Norfolk. The official 'word' was that the Fifth Marines were to engage in training exercises, but few really believed that was the purpose of this new movement. The men
were sober and little inclined to joke as they filed up the gang-
planks. Somehow they sensed that they would soon be off to
the wars in earnest.

While the real objective of the Marines then embarking was
a carefully guarded secret in Wellington, an item appearing
in a local paper caused consternation in Marine Headquarters
at the Hotel Cecil. July 4 the *Dominion*, a Wellington daily,
carried a story with a New York dateline which expressed a

'hope' that United States Marines would soon strike against Japanese outposts in the Pacific.

HOPE OF COMING U.S. THRUST
South Pacific Marines
INTENSIFIED RAIDS IN NORTH
(Received July 3, 7 p.m.)

New York, July 2.

Operations to seize Japanese-held bases, such as Rabaul, Wake Island, and Tulagi, are advocated by the military writer of the New York *Herald-Tribune*, Major Eliot. One of the signs which suggest that the United Nations may be getting ready to capitalize on the naval advantage gained on the Coral Sea and Midway battles is the recent American bombing of Wake Island, he says. The other signs include the intensified raids on the Timor and New Guinea areas.

'Bombing alone is not enough, because at best it can only prevent the enemy from using the bases,' he continues. 'What is needed is to drive the Japanese out of their positions and convert them to our own use. The only way to take positions such as Rabaul, Wake Island, and Tulagi, is to land troops to take physical possession of them.'

The *New York Times* suggests that Wake Island may be retaken 'not only to avenge the Marines who died defending it but also because if we could take hold of the island our lines would be advanced more than 1000 miles.'

[Following paragraphs in bold type]

The newspaper adds: 'It may also be significant that the censor passed the news of the arrival of the completely equipped expeditionary force of American Marines at a South Pacific port recently, as Marines are not usually sent to bases where action is not expected.

'It may well be that we are preparing to reap the fruits of the Coral Sea and Midway victories. Sooner or later the present stalemate in the South Seas will be broken on a battlefield of our own choosing.'

The remarkable thing about the story is that it names Tulagi, a pin-point on the map of which few Americans had ever heard, as a possible and likely objective. It looked as though there might have been a leakage of information in America. The Marine Command fervently hoped that the Japanese would not conclude that the sudden appearance of Tulagi in the public prints indicated an immediate official interest in the little island.

To newspaper readers such an item in the press would mean only a momentary spurt of interest in a strange island which they would have to look up on the map. To the Marines then embarking far away in the Pacific the item might mean more barbed wire on the beaches where they must land, more Japanese soldiers to oppose them, more spilled blood and torn flesh in their own ranks.

FINAL PREPARATIONS

While the Fifth Marines, Reinforced, were disembarking, then re-embarking, unloading, then reloading, in Wellington, the Rear Echelon of the Division was on its way from New River to New Zealand. The first elements left in cargo ships carrying small groups of Marines and the main body embarked at San Francisco in three transports. The Rear Echelon consisted of the First Marines, commanded by Colonel Clifton B. Cates, and elements of the Eleventh Marines (Colonel Pedro A. del Valle) and of Division Special and Service Troops not already in the Pacific. Brigadier General William H. Rupertus, Assistant Division Commander, was in command of the Rear Echelon. Lieutenant Colonel Robert C. Kilmartin, the Division Personnel Officer (D–1), served as his Chief of Staff.

The transports and cargo ships made the long voyage to New Zealand without incident. The first cargo ship arrived in Wellington July 7 and the other cargo ships and the transports from San Francisco arrived four days later. Officers and men, who had looked forward to shore liberty after the long sea voyage, found that they must begin immediately to re-embark and reload on ships of the South Pacific Amphibious Force headed for 'landing exercises.'

The following week was one of feverish activity along the Wellington waterfront. The docks and quays were piled high with supplies and equipment being transferred from one ship to another. Marine working parties labored day and night combat-loading ships. Torrential rains set in during the week, turned the quay into a lake, and drenched the working parties of Marines who labored around the clock in three shifts. Equipment and stores not absolutely essential to combat were taken off the ships that had come in from the United States and trunks and seabags were sent to storage. Headquarters groups reduced equipment to a bare minimum and the various personnel sections, with their records, debarked to remain ashore.

Meanwhile, officers of the First Marine Division were carrying out missions in preparation for operations in the Solomons and for a rehearsal of the proposed landings. Lieutenant Colonel Goettge had flown to Australia from Auckland June 30 to get in touch with United States Army and Navy and Australian personnel acquainted with the Tulagi–Guadalcanal area and to get guides and pilots to serve with the task force which was to operate in that area. When the Japanese occupied the Solomon Islands, almost all the white population of the islands evacuated to Australia and Lieutenant Colonel Goettge interviewed many of those people.

July 9 he returned to Auckland after arranging for eight Australian officers to accompany unit commanders and to act as guides, advisers, and pilots in areas which they thoroughly knew from personal experience. This group of former planters, traders, civil servants, and ships' officers in the Solomons reported at Wellington July 15 and embarked with the First Marine Division.

July 9 two groups of Marine officers left Wellington on reconnaissance missions. Lieutenant Colonel Twining and Major W. B. McKean were to make an aerial reconnaissance over the future theater of operations; Major I. W. Fuller, Captain L. A. Ennis, and Captain C. R. Schwenke were to fly to a near-by island group and there select a suitable site for landing exercises in rehearsal of the Tulagi–Guadalcanal operation.

The latter group accomplished their mission without incident. They flew from Auckland to Noumea, New Caledonia, and thence to an island being considered as a training area. From there they made flights over several islands investigating possible sites for the landing exercises. After finding a suitable area, they made arrangements with the civil and military authorities in the island group selected to evacuate the population temporarily from the location, to provide maps, and to co-operate in the conduct of the exercise. They then returned to New Zealand.

The other mission ran into incidents aplenty. Lieutenant Colonel Twining and Major McKean flew by transport plane to Noumea, then Brisbane, then Townsville, to find a combat plane to take them over the southeastern Solomons. In Townsville they arranged for an Army B–17 to take them on their mission. July 16 they flew to Port Moresby and took off at dawn the next day for a flight over the Tulagi–Guadalcanal area. Shortly after noon they reached Tulagi, where they reconnoitered the beaches, harbor, landing area, and defensive installations. While they were over the island, three Zero float-plane fighters took off from Gavutu in pursuit. The B–17 continued on to the north coast of Guadalcanal, where they reconnoitered the beaches and landing area. When the Flying Fortress was five miles southwest of Lunga Point, it was attacked by the three Zeros. Again and again the Japanese fighters ran on them and for twenty minutes the Fortress engaged the enemy planes, losing altitude all the time in order to maintain its speed. The American plane sent one Zero crashing to the ground in flames, another fell away smoking, and the third made off. The B–17 was hit by a twenty-millimeter shell from the Zero which exploded inside the fuselage, but no one was hurt. Lieutenant Colonel Twining, later Operations Officer on Guadalcanal, and Major McKean, thus could claim the distinction of being the first members of the First Marine Division to draw enemy blood in the Solomons after this bout with the Zeros.

By the time the remaining fighter plane broke off contact, the Flying Fortress was ten minutes short of enough gas for the return trip to Port Moresby, but a tail wind helped them on their way. Night fell, they got off their course, and for an hour they were lost in the darkness over New Guinea. At last they called for a radio beam and searchlights to lead them in and they landed at Port Moresby in the nick of time, all gasoline gone. Lieutenant Colonel Twining and Major McKean then reported back to the First Marine Division, returning by way of Townsville, Brisbane, Sydney, Auckland, and Suva. They arrived in the islands selected for training July 25 and joined the Division.

July 15 Major General Vandegrift and Lieutenant Colonel Thomas went to Auckland to confer with Vice Admiral Ghormley and Rear Admiral R. K. Turner, Commander of the South Pacific Amphibious Force who was to arrive in Auckland that day from the United States. The conferees discussed the entire field of operations in which the Division was to participate and the Commanding General learned exactly what forces would be at his disposal. At this conference it was decided to sortie from Wellington on the 22d instead of the 18th, the date previously set. The delayed arrival of the ships of the Rear Echelon, nearly all of which were commercially loaded and had to be reloaded for combat, made the postponement necessary. Moreover, the limited port facilities in Wellington and the torrential rainfall during the week after the Rear Echelon arrived interfered with and delayed the loading.

July 16 the Amphibious Force, South Pacific Area, was

formally established and two days later Rear Admiral Turner assumed command. The same day he arrived in Wellington, and the Staffs of the Amphibious Force and the First Marine Division continued to develop plans for the forthcoming operations. Final decisions were reached on such questions as whether the attacks on Guadalcanal and Tulagi should be made on the same day and whether any of the landings should be made under cover of darkness.

ON TO THE SOLOMONS

The morning of July 22, twenty-four ships of the task force assigned to the Solomons operation sortied from Wellington Harbor. In column the cruisers, destroyers, transports, and cargo ships filed past the headlands outside the harbor and at noon they took up their positions in convoy and proceeded out to sea. On the fourth day the monotony of the slow progress toward the north through heavy seas was interrupted by an impressive rendezvous at sea with the powerful task forces which were to support the landing operations. It was a beautiful day, and fairly calm after three days of heavy seas. At one-thirty in the afternoon some ships appeared on the horizon, and as excited Marines crowded the rails the number of approaching ships steadily grew. Throughout the afternoon more and more ships appeared, three different forces, each with an aircraft carrier looming in its midst, each coming from a different point of the compass. More transports, too, were included in this concentration of naval power. They brought the Second Marines, Reinforced (Colonel J. M. Arthur), the Third Defense Battalion (Colonel R. H. Pepper), and the First Raider Battalion (Colonel Merritt A. Edson). By nightfall almost every variety of naval ship was in sight, from battleship and aircraft carrier to destroyer-transport and minesweeper. It was a thrilling sight which none who saw it will ever forget. We slept that night with the peace that comes with believing such strength cannot fail to achieve its objective.

The task forces moved on toward the island selected for training, and on the 28th that peaceful little island faced an invasion by the strongest amphibious force ever sent out by the United States up to that time. The inhabitants had been moved off the southern shore and mountain slopes. The island stood undefended except for a girdle of coral reef, but that proved defense enough, and at the end of four days the island stood unviolated. When the first wave of landing boats hit the coral on the first day of the landing exercises, it became apparent that landings could not continue as scheduled without serious damage to landing craft which must be kept intact for the operation in the Solomons. The coral ripped the bottoms of boats and twisted their propellers. For this reason it was decided that no more boats should be sent all the way to the beach.

For four days, however, the exercises continued. Each Marine unit rehearsed going over the side and down the cargo nets into landing boats with its essential gear, learning to time its movements according to the intricate schedule worked out for the landing operation in the Solomons. Boat crews practiced assembling in formations for taking on their loads and moving to the beach. The movement to the shore was coordinated with naval gunfire and aerial attacks against 'enemy' positions.

July 31 the exercises were concluded, and late in the afternoon the force got under way for the Solomons. Final orders for the attack on Tulagi and Guadalcanal were issued by the Commander of the Task Force. In general, the order called for the capture and occupation of Tulagi, Gavutu, and Guadalcanal Islands, and the subsequent destruction of minor enemy forces in outlying positions on Florida and near-by islands. Fifteen minutes before sunrise, naval aircraft were to attack and destroy enemy aircraft and shipping in the area. Beginning at daylight, naval gunfire from cruisers and destroyers was to be directed at enemy forces and installations in the vicinity of the beaches on which the Marines would land.

Throughout the day naval aircraft and gunfire from surface vessels were to support the landing forces in their operations. D–Day was tentatively set for August 7.

The operations plan called for landings on Guadalcanal by Combat Group A (the Fifth Marines, Reinforced), commanded by Colonel Leroy P. Hunt, less the Second Battalion under Lieutenant Colonel H. A. Rosecrans, which was to land on Tulagi. After Combat Group A had secured an initial beachhead west of the Ilu River, four miles east of the airfield which was the Marines' main objective, Combat Group B (First Marines, Reinforced), commanded by Colonel Clifton B. Cates, was to land and advance in a southwesterly direction toward Grassy Knoll behind the airfield, to cut off a possible Japanese withdrawal into the hills. The Support Group, consisting of elements of the Eleventh Marines and Division Special and Service Troops not attached to other task groups, commanded by Colonel Pedro A. del Valle, were then to land, and all artillery units would then revert to Colonel del Valle's command.

Tulagi was to be seized by the First Raider Battalion (Colonel Merritt A. Edson) and Combat Team 2 (Second Battalion, Fifth Marines, under Lieutenant Colonel Rosecrans), and Gavutu and Tanambogo were to be taken by the First Parachute Battalion commanded by Major R. H. Williams. The Third Defense Battalion was to land on order and provide anti-aircraft defenses for the beachheads.

Major General Vandegrift planned to direct the Guadalcanal operations from the flagship while Brigadier General Rupertus co-ordinated the operations in the Tulagi–Gavutu area. H–Hour, the time of the first landing on Tulagi, was tentatively set for eight in the morning, and Zero-hour, the time the first wave of boats was to hit the beach on Guadalcanal, was to be half an hour later, at eight-thirty.

The days passed quietly as we moved through the Coral Sea. Officers pored over the final operations plans and instructed their men on details of the terrain where they would operate and the type of enemy resistance they were likely to meet. Weapons were cleaned, packs put in order. August 5 we turned northward. An officer remarked, 'For a week we've been looking at the Japs out of the corner of our eyes. Now we are staring them in the face.' The enemy, however, did not see us. All day on the 6th we were hidden from enemy eyes by low-lying clouds and mist. Japanese search planes never found us and the assault which was launched the next morning was a complete surprise.

Chapter 2

D-Day and After[1]

TO AN EYE not too distorted by memories of the battles that have bloodied its soil or the men and ships that lie beneath the waters off its shores, Guadalcanal is an island of striking beauty. Blue-green mountains, towering into a brilliant tropical sky or crowned with cloud masses, dominate the island. The dark green of jungle growth blends into the softer greens and browns of coconut groves and grassy plains and ridges. Much of the shoreline is rough with coral that cuts men's feet and rips the bottoms of landing boats, but there are also good beaches of soft sand. The water is always warm. It is clear and clean, too, except when flotsam from wrecked ships — oil, crates, stinking bloated sides of beef, papers — washes ashore.

In three distinct ranges, the central one reaching heights of eight thousand feet, the mountains cut across the island. They rise steeply from the southern coast, fill the central part of the island from one end to the other, then diminish toward the north. From Cape Esperance to Marau Sound, ninety miles away, they form the backbone of Guadalcanal.

On the northern side of the island is a coastal plain, broad enough and flat enough for many airfields. From the high

[1] 'D-Day' was the day on which the attack started.

20

jagged mountains to the south fingers of coral ridges, many of them grass-covered, reach into the plain. The plain, too, is covered with tall grass, about the height of a man's shoulders, except where coconut palms have been planted near the shore and where swift-flowing streams and their many tributaries feed lush tropical growth and groves of great trees. In the dense jungle of such lowlands and coral ridge slopes the most bitter fighting of the Guadalcanal campaign took place.

The northern coastal plain is the most important part of Guadalcanal in both war and peace. There the peaceful life of the Melanesian natives centered. Its military significance derives from its suitability for airfields. From the Matanikau River eastward to Taivu Point, a distance of about twenty miles, there are grassy fields on the plain ideal for the construction of airfields. Farther east the plain is swampy or covered with dense jungle.

Native villages dot the shoreline — little groups of fiber huts and gardens where the natives of Guadalcanal lived a simple life, before the war reached them, on the fertile alluvial soil. The natives also grow fruit — bananas, limes, oranges, and pawpaws. Unfortunately none of these fruit trees grew inside the tiny airfield area first occupied by the Marines and fresh fruit was a rarity in Marine messes. Occasionally, however, a patrol or scouting party going far down the coast would bring back a bunch of bananas or helmetful of limes given them by friendly natives. At Headquarters we looked forward to the British District Officer's visits to his old station at Aola. Such trips usually meant fresh limeade in the mess.

When the Japanese first came to the island early in the summer of 1942, they made friendly advances to the natives. As in other Pacific islands they had taken over, the Japanese told the natives that the day of the white man was past, that the yellow men came as their friends and saviors. Here is a sample of the propaganda used by the Japanese in the Solomons. The placard, written in English, was found in a Japanese camp near Henderson Field when we first landed.

Nippon has declared war against United States of America and England, and is going to the glorious war with them to keep the independence and honour of the Yellow Race.

Already Navy of Nippon is winning a victory everywhere, and occupied all Bismarck Archipelago. Therefore you don't belong to the sovereignty of England but the sovereignty of Nippon.

See your circumstances in past time!

There is nothing but oppression and squeeze of the White Race!

Follow us!

— and happiness and wealth will be given.

NAVY OF NIPPON

The friendship, however, was short-lived, for when the Japanese began looting the gardens and stealing the natives' pigs, the natives turned against them. Whenever the Japanese appeared in a new part of the island, the natives abandoned their villages and withdrew to the hills to live as best they could. The native villages along the northern coast were deserted as the war spread over the island.

Large coconut plantations, the chief economic asset of the island, line the shore for many miles. They are scattered from one end of the island to the other, and extend in some cases a mile or two inland. The many rivers, flowing swift and clear from the mountains, become sluggish and muddy as they approach the sea. Some are almost shut off from the sea, except in flood, by sand bars across their mouths. These streams provided ample water for the natives who lived along their banks, for the Japanese invaders who frightened them out, and for the Americans who drove the invaders out.

A traveler skirting the northern coast of Guadalcanal on a ship, southeastward from Cape Esperance, sees a succession of points reaching out into the sea, many of them formed by the deltas of rivers. The points are barely distinguishable against the dark, dominating background of soaring mountains, but a man familiar with the coastline can pick them out for the newcomer. Each point and each river along that quiet green coast has its story to tell of men fighting against each other and the jungle.

Rounding the northwest end of Guadalcanal and heading southeastward, as the Marines did early in the morning of August 7, the traveler sees Savo Island — rugged, high, and almost circular — about ten miles off Cape Esperance. Savo became a name rich in sinister connotation for the Marines on Guadalcanal. All things grim, dangerous, and forbidding seemed to be associated with the little island. The deep water around Savo is the graveyard of the three American cruisers and the Australian cruiser sunk by the Japanese in the night battle of August 9. Later night battles between American and Japanese surface forces, and bombing attacks, have added to the list of blasted ships that lie beneath these waters. Savo pointed the way to Japanese bases in the northern Solomons. It served as a landmark for countless Japanese ships that slipped into the waters off Guadalcanal by night. Enemy planes approaching to bomb Henderson Field often flew over Savo. 'Gun flashes off Savo,' 'Flares near Savo,' 'Twenty-seven Jap bombers coming from the direction of Savo' — these frequent reports added to the island's unenviable reputation.

At one time we noticed that smoke columns arose from Savo about noon, the favorite time of day for Japanese air raiders. The smoke seemed to be associated with those raids in some mysterious way. Perhaps it was a signal. In any event, it seemed that the Japanese would not overlook such an ideal spot for setting up an observation post.

Later we learned the origin of the mysterious smoke columns. The natives were accustomed to burn off the grass and brush from plots of land they had picked as the sites of new gardens when old gardens lost their fertility. The smoke came from the grass and brush fires. To avoid any more confusion on the matter, arrangements were made with the natives to burn off the ground for new gardens only on Wednesdays and Saturdays.   After adhering to the agreed schedule for several weeks, the natives requested that the day for burning off the grass be changed to Fridays and Tuesdays.   Here is their request and report, submitted in the incomparable English of their spokesman Johnson:

11/10/42   This Savo reports
from *Johnsen*

1) Please we beg you sir if you can you will let this two days for us for the fire in our garden Friday and Tuesday please.

2) Dayly fire is every day if you see it smoking in a buhish that is our cooking fire that is for every day and also at home.   Only for two days for big fire working in our gardens around this island Friday and Tuesday.

3) And also for our fishing at sea it is right for us to fishing or not? and going by a native boat around this Island at Savo please tel us what you think is right.

4) For the people we are all in bush now what you think is right please let us know it and do flow what you *think*
from Johnes Savo let you know the Savo report with kindly regards and good wishes
136 people were gatherd.

From Cape Esperance to Taivu Point, forty miles away, the shore now is littered with the wrecks of landing boats and barges.   Some are American, especially in the central area, but most are Japanese.   Between Esperance and Tassafaronga — a stretch of coast which was a Japanese beachhead on the island for five months — are the wrecks of Japanese transports and cargo ships, gutted by fires and explosions and run up on the beach by men desperate to save anything they might from the hulls that had fallen victims to our bombers.   Farther east are beached American ships, the victims of Japanese torpedoes.

Still going southeastward, beyond Tassafaronga, the traveler sees the unmistakable outline of Point Cruz, a growth-covered coral spit reaching out into the sea. It was once a vantage-point for Japanese observers watching activities at the United States Naval Operating Base at Kakum across the bay and a forward position for Japanese guns.

Just east of Point Cruz, between the coral spit and the mouth of the Matanikau River, is a half-mile of beach, coconut palms, and jungle that was once upturned, burned, and blasted as few spots on this earth have been. By now surely the quick-growing jungle plants have thrown a coat of green over those scars of battle, inflicted by the concentrated fires of both belligerents on this most fought-over spot on all Guadalcanal. For more than four months the Americans and Japanese surged back and forth over this bit of land. They made the name 'Matanikau' a memorable one in Marine history.

The river itself is muddy and deep. A sand bar extends across the river's mouth and, except when the river runs high, only a little water trickles through a narrow shallow channel to reach the sea. Across this sand bar the Japanese launched a tank attack late in October, the first thrust in the crucial land fighting of that month. Their shattered tanks can still be seen on the sand bar and shore to the west.

The Japanese planned to receive the surrender of Major General Vandegrift on the banks of the Matanikau in October. The General, accompanied only by an aide, was to walk along the beach toward the west until he came to the mouth of the Matanikau, where the Japanese Commanding General would receive him. The enemy's surrender demand was never delivered. Instead of overrunning the airfield, the Japanese forces attacking in October were driven back with shattering losses, and Major General Vandegrift never made the mournful journey to the river's mouth.

From the Matanikau the shoreline sweeps seaward again toward Lunga Point. The seaborne traveler scanning the island with his glasses is approaching Henderson Field, the heart of the original Marine position and the prize of all the fighting that raged on Guadalcanal. Just west of Lunga Point is Kukum, a native village where the Japanese had built primitive landing facilities and which the American forces used as a naval operating base in the early weeks of the campaign, before Japanese artillery drove them out.

Lunga Point is formed by the delta of the Lunga River, which was as important to the Marines on Guadalcanal as the Nile is to Egypt. In its swift waters, flowing through the center of our position just west of Henderson Field, the Marines found some respite from the strain of battle and the heat and dirt of Guadalcanal. The river was drinking fountain, bath, and laundry. In the early days all our drinking water came from the river above the bridge which the Japanese had built half a mile inland from the mouth of the river. Below that point the Marines swam and washed their clothes.

About three miles east of Lunga Point is the Tenaru River, another sluggish stream with a sand bar across its mouth. The coconut palms all along the shore from Kukum to the Tenaru and a bit beyond are shattered and ripped by shell-fire. The grove of coconuts just east of the river and the sandy beach were the scene of the bloody battle of the Tenaru River when more than seven hundred Japanese were encircled and annihilated August 21.

The next river the traveler sees is the Ilu.[1] The Marines first landed on the beach just east of the Ilu. Our traveler, looking at 'Beach Red' where the Marines swarmed ashore on that historic day, can see a large hill rising above the line of palms that fringe the shore. A grove of trees on the hillside otherwise covered with grass, describes a rough 'L' and makes the hill a familiar landmark. This is Mount Austen, or 'Grassy Knoll' as it was known among the Marines. It ap-

---

[1] On the crude maps of Guadalcanal which served the landing force, the names of some rivers were confused. The principal river reaching the sea on the western boundary of the Marines' original beachhead is actually the Tenaru River. The Ilu is one of its tributaries. The river marked on our maps as the Tenaru is actually Alligator Creek (or Snake River). Throughout this book, however, 'Tenaru' is used as the name of the stream properly known as Alligator Creek, and 'Ilu' is used as the name of the river which is actually the Tenaru.

pears deceptively close, but actually it is about four miles from the beach. In the early days, when the Japs were free to roam the jungle around the tiny area where the Marines had dug in behind defensive lines, new arrivals on the island occasionally asked, with mixed heartiness and anxiety, 'Where are the Japs?' The old-timers took delight in pointing to Grassy Knoll, which appears to rise almost from the very edge of the airfield, and saying, 'There they are.' The inquiring newcomer usually was unbelieving — and noticeably more nervous.

On a dry day, if planes have been taking the air, a cloud of dust lying over the ground beyond the coconut palms, in the direction of Grassy Knoll from Beach Red, will mark the location of the original Henderson Field, little over a mile from the beach.

From Beach Red the coastline again sweeps out toward the sea forming Koli Point where the deep Malimbiu River joins the sea. This is the scene of several actions. Beyond lies a succession of other points jutting out into the sea and the green mass of coconut palms and tropical trees continues on, broken occasionally by the mouth of a stream. Togama Point, the Metapona River, Berande Point, the village of Tasimboko, Taivu Point, Gorabusu, Aola — all are sites of landings by American or Japanese forces or of battles between the two. Taivu Point, twenty-five miles along the shore from Lunga Point, was a Japanese beachhead during the first six weeks of the Guadalcanal campaign. Aola is the Government Station of the British Administration. It is the main settlement on the island and lies about thirty-five miles east of Henderson Field. Beyond Aola there is little of interest connected with the Guadalcanal campaign.

THE LANDING ON GUADALCANAL

When we first saw Guadalcanal, from the decks of our invasion fleet slipping along the coast of the island early in the morning of August 7, it was a black shadow barely distinguishable against a sky only slightly less dark. We had turned out about two in the morning, to make our final preparations for landing and to eat a big breakfast — our last substantial meal for many days. No one's appetite seemed to be much affected by the imminence of action. It was much like any other morning aboard the transports during the days we had been approaching Guadalcanal. Packs were put in order, weapons were checked, and officers and men put on the green 'utility suits' that had been laid aside for this day of days.

Some of us went topside, making our way through dim companionways to the blacked-out weather decks, to get our first glimpse of the island that would become a battlefield in a few short hours. As the ships approached Savo, they split into two groups, one veering off to port to approach Tulagi, the larger force continuing on toward the southeast along the northern shore of Guadalcanal.

A shadow loomed up to port. It was Savo Island. By now there was tension in the air and complete silence save for the steady throbbing of engines, the gentle splash of ships' prows cutting through the water, and the hushed movements of men on the open decks.

It was a solemn moment. Back in San Francisco the streets were crowded with men and women going to work. In New York they were beginning to think of knocking off for lunch. Very few of those millions going about their daily work knew that a strong force of United States and Australian warships and transports bearing thousands of Marines was about to launch an attack on an unknown Pacific island. Some of us thought of those crowds as we stood on the deck of the transport, watching the outline of Guadalcanal come into bolder relief as our eyes grew accustomed to the darkness.

The situation seemed unreal. Here we were, after weeks at sea and years of preparation, ready to make the first big landing operation of the war against Japanese opposition. There, on that strange island, were the Japanese, probably just beginning to stir after a quiet night. Yonder was the airfield they had built, which we meant to take from them. Had they spotted us yet? Sparks spouted from the funnel of the *McCawley*, flagship of the Amphibious Force, sunk by the Japanese ten months later in the American attack on New Georgia. We thought surely the enemy must have seen them from the coast, but there was no sign of activity on those dark shores. Later we learned that the enemy knew nothing of our approach.

As the sky began to brighten, 'General Quarters' sounded and the ships' crews took battle stations. About six o'clock the order came to stand by to lower boats. Then, at quarter past six, came the sound we had been waiting tensely to hear. The guns of an American cruiser opened up and a salvo of shells went crashing shoreward. The bombardment of Guadalcanal had begun. Thereafter our warships maintained a steady rain of fire, raking the Japanese positions around the airfield as the Marines prepared to land. At the same time Navy dive-bombers and fighter planes attacked the airdrome, wharves, enemy camps and concentrations in the Kukum–Lunga–Tenaru–Tetere area. From the transports we saw the red tracers cut the darkness over Guadalcanal and the flashes of high explosive from bombs and shells. I remember thinking at the time it must be hell to be caught in such a bombardment. We couldn't then foresee the future when we, in our turn, would spend the nights in foxholes and dugouts while Japanese warships returned the compliment.

About seven o'clock came the order to lower boats. With no opposition from shore batteries or enemy aircraft, the process of lowering and loading the boats proceeded methodically. The boat crews of Navy men and Coast Guardsmen lowered them away and they began to circle in the rendezvous areas. The First Battalion, Fifth Marines, Reinforced, under Lieutenant Colonel W. E. Maxwell was to be the first unit to land on Beach Red, east of the Ilu River, and the transport carrying the men of that unit was soon surrounded by Higgins boats,[1] ramp boats, and tank lighters. Amphibian tractors began their churning progress toward the beach carrying engineering supplies.

By now the sun was up and we scanned the shoreline of this strange island with our field glasses, looking for signs of enemy activity. A pall of smoke and dust had settled over the beach where shells and bombs had ripped through the coconut plantations. From Kukum a huge column of black smoke and occasional flashes of fire reaching high into the sky told that a gasoline dump had been hit.

Zero hour, when the first unit was to hit the beach, had been set for nine-ten o'clock. On schedule the boats carrying Lieutenant Colonel Maxwell's troops took on their loads of men and equipment and circled in their rendezvous area. The line of departure was marked by two destroyers lying off shore. Soon after the first wave of boats sped across the line toward the beach, the destroyers laid down a concentrated barrage on the beach area. It was lifted just before the first boat hit the beach.

The landings proceeded smoothly — with a smoothness that appears remarkable, in fact, in light of the hasty organization of the combined attack force and the physical condition of the men called upon to perform the landings. The operations plans had been very quickly drawn up and had not been completed until the attack force had actually started the approach to Guadalcanal. Officers less thoroughly schooled in the principles of amphibious warfare could scarcely have developed and mastered the plans so quickly. The attack force had never had an opportunity for full rehearsal of the impending operation. The exercises off Koro Island had provided valuable lessons, but could not be regarded as a satisfactory rehearsal.

[1] Higgins boats are landing boats long used by Marines and named after their designer and builder, Andrew J. Higgins. When the boat hits the beach, men jump over the side and wade through the water. Newer type ramp boats have ramps in the bow which let down on the beach, allowing direct passage of men from boat to shore.

The men of the First Marine Division had spent long weeks in crowded transports. One reinforced regiment, the First Marines, had been at sea thirty-nine of the previous fifty days and had spent the remaining eleven days in the cramped quarters of troop ships. The Fifth Marines had been at sea a month and a half of the previous three months, had been on troop ships in port three more weeks of that period, and had had only two and a half weeks on land in the camps of New Zealand.

Thorough training, however, carried the First Marine Division through. They demonstrated that they were, in fact as well as on paper, a mobile striking force ready to move and to operate with the fleet on the shortest notice.

I went ashore with the Advance Echelon of Division Headquarters. Colonel W. C. James, Chief of Staff to Major General Vandegrift, Commander W. T. Brown (M.C.U.S.N., Division Surgeon), Lieutenant Colonel Merrill B. Twining and Major William Buse, of the Operations Section, Lieutenant Colonels Randolph M. Pate and F. B. Geraci, of the Supply Section, Captain J. C. Murray, Jr., Division Adjutant, and Second Lieutenant Fred Kidde, of the Intelligence Section, made up this group. We went over the side and down the net about nine o'clock. A message from an observation plane, that no enemy movement toward Beach Red could be seen, cheered us on our way. We sped toward the beach with the boats bearing the last elements of the Fifth Marines, Reinforced, under Colonel Leroy P. Hunt. Buffeted and sprayed by the choppy waters, we got further encouragement when Lieutenant Colonel Twining, watching the shore with his glasses, announced, 'There goes the signal from Hunt's boys. "Landing unopposed." '

When we jumped ashore from the Higgins boat, we saw a busy scene. Medical dressing stations had been set up on the beach. Signs marked the gathering points for various units and supply dumps that steadily grew as the landing boats shuttled back and forth, between the beach and the ships in the transport area. Already tanks and amphibian tractors were crawling up on the beach. There were scattered rifle shots to the south and west as Marines fanned out through the coconuts and tall grass.

Although the landing was unopposed, seizure of the beach-head was a slow job because of the thick vegetation and the narrow but deep feeders of the Ilu River. About a hundred yards south of the beach the coconut palms ended and a field of high grass extended to the south. Beyond that a branch of the Ilu runs roughly parallel to the shoreline. Along it and the lesser streams feeding the Ilu there is dense tropical growth. We didn't know where we might encounter enemy opposition, so the advance was cautious. Within two hours, however, enough of the beachhead had been secured to speed up the landing of supplies and equipment. The First Pioneer Battalion (Lieutenant Colonel George R. Rowan) was princi-pally responsible for the ship-to-shore movement of supplies and equipment, and they worked day and night during the period of unloading, trying to keep up with the stream of material moving ashore.

Later in the morning the First Marines, Reinforced, under Colonel Clifton B. Cates began to land and to pass through the Fifth Marines, whose mission was to secure the beachhead. Colonel Cates's regiment struck out toward the southwest, in the direction of Grassy Knoll, while the First Battalion, Fifth Marines, moved forward along their right, toward the Tenaru. Shortly after noon units of the support group under the com-mand of Colonel Pedro A. Del Valle, of the Eleventh Marines — the remaining elements of artillery and detachments of special and service troops not attached to the infantry regi-ments — began to land.

Throughout the day, as the Marines poured ashore and secured the beachhead, all was silent in the west where the Japanese were encamped. Our bewilderment at this develop-ment increased. It seemed incredible that the Japanese were going to let us take over the airfield without a fight. The next day or perhaps that night, would tell whether the enemy had organized a defensive line farther west or was preparing to attack our foothold on the island.

Division Headquarters came ashore at four o'clock in the afternoon after spending the day aboard ship directing the widely scattered operations in the Guadalcanal and Tulagi areas. The Command Post was set up in the coconut grove south of the branch of the Ilu running parallel to the beach. There we bivouacked for the night. General Vandegrift summoned the regimental commanders and received them at the base of a palm tree where his staff had gathered — our first command post on Guadalcanal. After hearing their reports, the General remarked, 'I'm beginning to doubt whether there's a Jap on the whole damned island.' Then he told them of plans for continuing the operation on the following day. The First and Fifth Marines were to advance to the airfield area and seize the line on the Lunga River, the Fifth on the right along the beach and the First on the left, farther inland.

That night disturbing news came from Tulagi. Just after midnight General Vandegrift received a message telling him of heavy casualties in that area. The message — which fortunately turned out to exaggerate our losses — reported twenty-two per cent casualties suffered by the First Raider Battalion on Tulagi and fifty to sixty per cent casualties in the First Parachute Battalion on Gavutu. The Assistant Division Commander, Brigadier General Rupertus, requested that additional units be sent to the Tulagi area by daylight. Captain Murray, the Division Adjutant, went out to the flagship to place the request before Rear Admiral Turner, Commander of the Amphibious Force, South Pacific Area, and the next morning two battalions of the Second Marines landed in the Tulagi area.

During the first day of the landing we had our first taste of bombing from the air. About noon officers trying to guess at Japanese counter-moves began keeping an eye on the sky. It was to be expected that the enemy would strike from the air, probably with planes based on Rabaul, as soon as possible after learning of our attack against his new base in the southeastern Solomons. The Japanese planes would probably reach us about noon. The guess was not far off. At three-thirty in the afternoon the sound of bombs at sea, geysers of water, and a sky full of anti-aircraft bursts announced the bombers' arrival to those of us who were on shore. The Japanese ignored the Marines' busy and crowded beachhead and concentrated on the shipping off shore. But they didn't score any hits. Half an hour later the Japanese struck again, this time with dive-bombers. They hit the stern of one destroyer, knocking out her after gun and the auxiliary radio.

August 8 the Marine forces on Guadalcanal pushed westward to take possession of the airfield and to occupy and defend the Lunga area according to the plans developed the previous night. The Fifth Marines crossed the Tenaru River and moved westward along the beach. As the long lines of green-clad men moved up, Colonel Hunt had a nod and a word of encouragement for each. We still couldn't believe that the Japanese would abandon their new airfield without a struggle and no one knew what lay beyond the Tenaru in the way of Japanese defenses. The advance continued unopposed, however, and by one o'clock in the afternoon the Fifth Marines had reached the position north of the airfield where they were to assemble. The First Marines, moving over more difficult terrain farther inland, were making slow progress and a change in plan was necessary. The Fifth Marines continued on toward Kukum and word was sent to the First to advance up to the Lunga River, but not to cross it.

The Fifth encountered no opposition until they passed through Kukum. Then they were fired upon by snipers and machine guns manned by Japanese in dugouts. The area was quickly mopped up, however, and patrols were sent to the south. The First Marines came up and occupied the line of the Lunga River and the airfield was in our hands.

At noon the Japanese bombers had returned, this time bent on a daring low-level torpedo attack. As our transports and their escort warships dispersed out to sea toward the west, the bombers swooped in from the east, almost skimming the waves. They lunged straight into a wall of anti-aircraft fire from our ships and many burst into flames and plunged into the sea. Watching from the shore we lost count of the hits as the bombers were shot down one after another. One Japanese plane escaped the anti-aircraft fire and made off, at low level, toward Savo Island. A Navy Grumman, patrolling overhead, spotted him, swooped down, and sent him crashing into the sea in flames. For a few minutes after the raid, many columns of smoke and flame rose from the sea between Guadalcanal and Florida. From the shore it looked as though many of our ships on the horizon had been hit, but as the smoke began to clear away, we saw that only one transport had been set afire. A Japanese bomber shot down by anti-aircraft fire had plunged into the forward hold of the transport *U.S.S. George Elliott*. She was abandoned and later sunk. All the other smoke over the transport area had come from the wrecks of Japanese planes.

With our uncontested occupation of Henderson Field, it became certain that the Japanese had abandoned the important position they had been developing so feverishly during the previous weeks. The small military garrison and the force of laborers had taken to the hills or withdrawn along the shore of the island to the west as the Marines advanced from the east. The Japanese either left so hastily that they hadn't time to destroy valuable installations or thought that they might soon again be in possession of the airfield area. Whatever their reasons, they didn't bother to destroy any installations, supplies, or equipment. The enemy's precipitate flight from the airfield violated the proud boasts of Japanese combat doctrine, which emphasizes aggressiveness and last-ditch resistance. The Japanese were greatly outnumbered on Guadalcanal on D–Day, but even so it was hardly to be expected they would abandon valuable installations without even a pretense of resistance.

Ammunition dumps, some anti-aircraft guns and artillery pieces, gasoline dumps, radio equipment, trucks, cars, refrigerating equipment, road-rollers, tractors, electric power plant — all were found unharmed except for the damage done by our naval shells and bombs. Tinned food, beverages, tents, huge stocks of straw mats and sandbags, left behind by the Japanese, were quickly put to use by the Marines. Two radio direction-finder systems, set up on a mound overlooking the airfield, were almost ready for use. The biggest prize of all was the airfield with its 3778-foot runway almost completed.

General Vandegrift, as he watched the uncontested progress of the Marines into the airfield area and realized that the Japanese had withdrawn to the hills, nodded toward the ridges and jungle to the west where the enemy had taken refuge and remarked, 'It looks like Nicaragua all over again.' We had taken our objective, but were faced with the long, difficult task of scouring the jungle all over the island to clean out the detachments of enemy troops.

Up to the night of August 8–9 the only opposition offered by the Japanese had been in the form of three ineffective air raids and scattered sniping. Soon, however, they were to contest our landing operation with a much mightier weapon.

There were certain nights on Guadalcanal — the 'purple nights' — that Marines then there will long remember. One of these was the night of August 8–9. It was a night of wild alarms and tension on Guadalcanal and heavy fighting at sea. We learned later that fighting was still continuing across the straits in the Tulagi area. On Guadalcanal it was a night to be remembered for other reasons.

First the rains came, shortly after dark. A drizzle turned into a downpour. We were bivouacked beneath the coconut palms without tents, and soon everyone and his gear were thoroughly drenched. Men who had not yet had the experience of actual contact with the enemy were firing at shadows, as they were to do for many nights. With rain pouring down and rifles cracking throughout our position, sleep seemed out of the question. There was a peculiar thunder in the sky which, with the help of a little imagination, sounded like airplane engines. I recall lying in a puddle at the foot of a palm tree, listening to the thunder and wondering if a Japanese plane was cruising back and forth over our position. After midnight I realized that there *was* an enemy plane overhead. About two o'clock it began to drop flares over Beach Red, over Lunga, and in the transport area. This was the first visit of 'Louie the Louse,' the name the Marines gave the Japanese night-flyer who became a familiar figure during later weeks on Guadalcanal.

As the flares floated down, a thunderous bombardment began out at sea. To those of us watching from our bivouacs on the island, the flashes and explosions seemed to be on the very shoreline. Our first thought was that we were being bombed. Then it dawned on us that a naval battle was in progress out toward Savo Island. We realized that our fate might depend on the outcome. The naval gunfire boomed steadily for half an hour, and at intervals thereafter. Occasionally brilliant red flashes filled the sky and told of mortal hits on warships. Gradually the sound of battle receded and it seemed to the tense watchers on Guadalcanal that the enemy ships had been turned back.

It was a long time before we realized how serious were the consequences of the battle we had witnessed. The ships we had seen exploding and burning were the United States cruisers *Quincy*, *Vincennes*, and *Astoria*, and the Australian cruiser *Canberra*.

Three and a half years earlier, the *Astoria* had brought to Japan the ashes of her popular emissary in Washington, Ambassador Saito. Tokyo, touched by this friendly gesture of the United States, had enthusiastically received the *Astoria* and her commanding officer, Captain R. K. Turner. American flags flew on the Ginza and signs in the department stores said: 'Welcome *Astoria*.' Now, off Savo Island, the *Astoria* was blasted and shattered by Japanese guns. Rear Admiral R. K. Turner saw her death from his flagship.

After the noise of battle had died down, rumors flew thick that the Japanese were attempting to land at Beach Red and on the beach two hundred yards north of the Division Command Post, which had been set up in the coconuts just west of the Tenaru River. The flares dropped by Japanese planes and the scattered small-arms fire throughout our position gave a ring of truth to the alarm. In the blackness and rain our own landing boats, carrying supplies along the beach, had been mistaken for the enemy. The Japanese made no effort to land on our beachhead that night.

After daybreak the hot sun quickly dried out wet Marines and wet gear. Regimental and battalion commanders gathered at the Division Command Post to hear Lieutenant Colonel Gerald C. Thomas, Division Operations Officer, outline the organization of defensive lines around Henderson Field. During the day we continued the job of preparing defensive positions and moving supplies from ship to shore and shore to unit areas. Twice that day the transports and cargo ships dispersed out to sea on alarms of enemy attacks, and the unloading proceeded slowly. Late in the afternoon as we watched from the beach, the ships began to withdraw toward the southeast, leaving Guadalcanal behind.

We were on our own.

LANDINGS ON TULAGI, GAVUTU, AND TANAMBOGO

Meanwhile, the Marines operating in the Tulagi area had been meeting fierce resistance. The Japanese there — cut off from escape, well dug in, and strongly armed — fought to the death. The determined resistance upset the timetable which had been set for the operation and it took three days to wipe out the last organized resistance.

Operations in the Tulagi area were under the immediate

command of Brigadier General W. H. Rupertus, Assistant Division Commander, whose Chief of Staff was Colonel R. C. Kilmartin.

Tulagi, Gavutu, Tanambogo, and other smaller islands are about twenty miles north of the Lunga area, just off the coast of Florida Island. The little islands guard Tulagi and Gavutu Harbors, an indentation in the Florida Island coast, from the open sea.

Tulagi, about two miles long from northwest to southeast and half a mile wide, was the seat of the administration of the British Solomon Islands Protectorate. A ridge extends its length, three hundred and fifty feet high in the northwest end of the island, lower in the southeastern end. Tulagi Settlement is located in the southeastern end of the island, on the northern side. There the British had built wharves, unloading facilities, and government buildings. Tulagi Harbor, with the adjoining Gavutu Harbor, affords a secure anchorage for ships and seaplanes.

Gavutu Island lies a mile and three-quarters to the east of Tulagi. This island is connected with Tanambogo Island to the north by a stone causeway. These two islands, one hundred and forty-eight and one hundred and ten feet high respectively, form the western side of Gavutu Harbor. The Japanese had developed facilities for a seaplane base in Gavutu Harbor and fifteen aircraft were caught on the surface before they could take off when the United Nations' attack was launched August 7.

TULAGI

The main assault on Tulagi began at eight o'clock in the morning, but the honor of being the first to land in the entire Solomons campaign fell to Company B, Second Marines, under the command of Captain E. J. Crane. At seven-forty they landed from boats near the village of Haleta on a Florida Island promontory overlooking the island fortress of Tulagi which the First Raider Battalion was to assault half an hour later. Their purpose was to deny this point, commanding the landing beach on Tulagi, to the enemy. They met no opposition at this point, but later in the day were to see lively action.

The remainder of the First Battalion, Second Marines, under Major Robert E. Hill, landed on another foreland of Florida Island at the opposite end of the harbor and proceeded along a trail to the high ground overlooking the village of Halavo. They encountered no opposition and after reconnoitering the shoreline, to make certain there were no enemy detachments that could harass the Marine landings on Gavutu and Tanambogo, were withdrawn.

At eight o'clock the first wave of the First Raider Battalion, under the command of Colonel Merritt A. Edson, hit the beach on the southwest slope of the northern ridge on Tulagi. It is a hilly wooded area and the Marines expected tough going. The Japanese, however, offered no opposition at this point. One man was lost to a sniper's bullet; the rest landed safely. Avoiding the trails along the shore, which are commanded by steep cliffs, the Raiders made their way along both sides of the central ridge of the little island, pushing through to the phase line *OA*.[1] (See Map.)

Companies B and D landed in the first wave. Company B advanced straight across the ridge and secured the settlement at Sasapi. Company D also crossed the ridge and started advancing down the northeastern slope toward the government area. Companies C and A landed in the second wave. Company C secured the left flank of the beachhead and Company A advanced down the central ridge on the right slope. No opposition was met on this side of the ridge until the Raiders reached the phase line. Company B, after securing Sasapi, started down the northeastern coast. They ran into enemy

---

[1] The phase line *OA* was the first objective of the Marines. The operations plan called for naval shelling of the southern part of the island after the line *OA* had been reached.

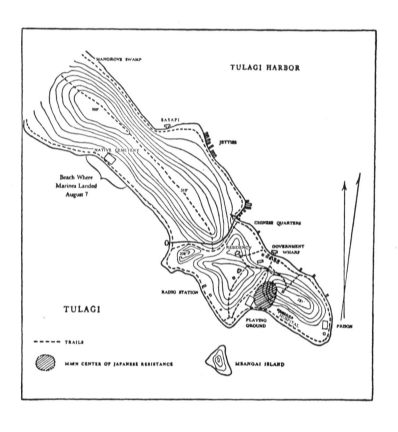

TULAGI HARBOR

MANGROVE SWAMP

BASAPI

JETTIES

NATIVE CEMETERY

Beach Where
Marines Landed
August 7

CHINESE QUARTERS

RESIDENCY

GOVERNMENT
WHARF

RADIO STATION

TULAGI

PLAYING
GROUND

PRISON

----- TRAILS

MAIN CENTER OF JAPANESE RESISTANCE

MBANGAI ISLAND

THE SOLOMONS CAMPAIGN OPENED ON TULAGI ISLAND

outposts near Carpenters' Wharf. Just beyond this point their commanding officer, Major Justice Chambers, was severely wounded by mortar fire.

As the Second Battalion, Fifth Marines, under Lieutenant Colonel H. A. Rosecrans, landed on the beach, all units of the Raiders advanced to the southeast. Company C of the Raiders, coming down the southwestern side of the island, ran into heavy opposition on Hill 208, where a concentration of machine-gun nests held them up for an hour. Gunnery Sergeant Michael J. J. Kennedy's method of dealing with this opposition was typical. When his unit was pinned down by Japanese machine-gun fire, Gunnery Sergeant Kennedy waited for a lull in the fire, charged down the hill road with a grenade in his hand, and threw it at the machine-gun emplacement. The Japanese threw it back at him. Kennedy started back to safety, fell down, and had to crawl back up the hill under heavy fire. After half an hour the Raiders broke through and continued on toward Hill 281. One platoon was left on the ridge east of the playing-field area and two others advanced on toward the end of the island south of Hill 281.

Company D advanced roughly parallel to Company C on the opposite side of the island, and by nightfall, after fighting through heavy opposition, the company was on the north side and ridge line of Hill 281. In that afternoon's fighting the squad of which Private Methodius C. Cecka was a member lost its squad leader. Cecka took over. He grabbed up a Browning automatic rifle from a Marine who had been killed, and opened fire on the Japanese. They shot the Browning out of his hand. He lost one finger and was shot through the elbow, but he continued firing until he ran out of ammunition. Then he used a captured Japanese pistol, firing with his left hand. Although he was wounded about three o'clock in the afternoon, he didn't report to the sick bay until eight o'clock.

At one point, late in the afternoon Company C was held up by machine-gun fire from a dugout built up in a ravine.

Major Kenneth D. Bailey, who distinguished himself then and in every subsequent action he fought in, ran to the top of the dugout and began kicking away the rocks and sandbags on top to give Marines an opening for their fire. Japanese in the dugout shot him through the leg.

Company B of the Raiders took up positions for the first night in the Government Wharf area, with Company A on the hill east of the playing ground.

The Second Battalion, Fifth Marines, had started to land half an hour after the Raiders first hit the beach. Two companies, E and F, cleaned up the northern end of the island where there was scattered opposition. Company G pushed down the west side of the island while Company H took up positions on the central ridge just north of the phase line *OA*. When the Marines reached the phase line they sent up a flare signaling for a naval bombardment of Hill 281, south of the line.

The day's fighting, which grew hottest after the Marines passed the phase line, was at close range. At many points enemy machine guns in dugouts and caves held up the Marines' advance. Many became heroes in eliminating these points of enemy resistance, by charging machine-gun nests with hand grenades, rifles, and Reising guns. In many cases the Japanese allowed the Marines to pass through them, then opened fire from the rear. Snipers in trees, behind rocks, and concealed in buildings and caves harassed the Marines. The enemy's main defenses were concentrated in the ravine west of Hill 281, a precipitous rock covering the southeast end of Tulagi, and on the steep slopes of the hill itself. There the Marines ran into the heaviest opposition. When it appeared that the area could not be taken the first day, a defensive line for the night of the 7th was formed along the ridge north and west of the ravine where the playing ground is located.

That night the enemy counter-attacked. About ten-thirty they sortied from their caves and dugouts, striking toward the summit of Residency Hill. They drove a salient between C and A Companies of the Raiders, isolating Company C near the beach and hill west of the playing ground. At this point, while the Japanese were laying down a flanking fire with two machine guns against A Company, Platoon Sergeant Clifford C. Hills took the situation in hand. On his own initiative he crawled forward to within twenty yards of the Japanese machine guns. He put them out of action with his automatic rifle and relieved the pressure on the flank.

Private First Class Edward H. Ahrens, of Company A, was one of the men protecting the right flank of the battalion. Single-handed he went after a group of Japanese trying to infiltrate through the Marine lines to get in the rear of the Raiders. They cut him down with knives and bayonets, but even though he was mortally wounded he killed the officer in charge of the enemy group and two other Japanese, breaking up the enemy attack.

The Japanese worked their way northward through the ravine and up the ridge. The fighting was at close quarters, with grenades, rifles, and knives. The enemy had several tricks to trap Marines into betraying their positions. A group of Japanese talking in the darkness would draw machine-gun and rifle fire from Marines while others sneaked up on the disclosed machine-gun positions to throw hand grenades. A few enemy rifle shots also would serve to draw heavy Marine fire, giving away the locations of the guns. With such tactics the Japanese succeeded in making their way up Residency Hill almost to the command post. Second Lieutenant John R. Doyle, in a mortar observation post on the brow of the hill, held his exposed position with a small group of men even after they had been ordered to fall back to the reverse slope. As the Japanese scrambled up the steep hill to the outpost, the Marines pushed them back over the cliff.

Company B of the Raiders was ordered up from its bivouac area to help repulse the enemy attack. Private First Class Elmer Hacker was sent from the command post to guide Company B to its assigned position. His path led through heavy enemy fire and small Japanese detachments infiltrating through our lines. A heavy rain added to the confusion and difficulties of the night battle. Hacker got through, however, and succeeded in leading his company back into position to repulse the Japanese.

Meanwhile, the enemy forces in the southern end of the island were trying to work their way northward along both sides of Hill 281. They were held up by Company C of the Raiders on the west side and Company D on the east.

Sergeant Wallace Clark and Private First Class Wilfred A. Hunt together had gone up on Hill 281 to reconnoiter enemy positions. When Hunt came down to bring back his squad, Clark stayed on alone, observing Japanese positions. He was shot through the shoulder and fell over a cliff about fifteen feet high. In great pain, he managed to crawl back to his company's command post and groan out the information he had learned. Meanwhile, Hunt again started up the hill with his squad and ran into heavy fire from enemy machine guns. He charged the Japanese emplacement with hand grenades and silenced the enemy, clearing the way for his squad to continue its advance.

Although the Japanese succeeded in infiltrating into Marine positions during the night, they never made a serious break-through and in the morning of the 8th the Marines resumed their attack. Companies E and F of the Second Battalion, Fifth Marines, who had mopped up the northwest end of the island upon landing the first day, advanced southward. On the second day they lined up east of Hill 281 — Company F on the right and Company E on the left — and advanced over the top of the hill to the west side of the island. F Company now flanked the Japanese concentration on the south, giving the Marines positions for mortars and machine guns on three sides of the main enemy position. About three o'clock in the afternoon, Company G of the Fifth Marines and the Raiders pushed through the ravine, blasted the Japanese out of their principal strongpoint, and completed physical possession of

Tulagi. Many snipers, however, were still concealed in trees, tall grass, and caves, and twice the next day Marines combed the area around Hill 281, finding snipers each time. For days afterward there were occasional snipers' shots — and snipers shot — on the island and some Japanese held out in the caves which honeycombed Hill 281.

August 10, in the course of the mopping-up operations, Gunnery Sergeant Angus R. Goss was severely wounded by a hand grenade thrown by a Japanese soldier in a cave which the Marines were trying to clean out. Goss then charged the cave by himself in the face of machine-gun and rifle fire, entered the cave, and killed the enemy soldiers with his submachine gun.

Only three of the estimated four hundred and fifty Japanese on Tulagi surrendered. The enemy had to be blasted out of each position. Their defense was organized around small groups in dugouts and caves, communicating with each other by radio. In many of the cliffside caves radios were found. In one case, on the third day of fighting, a Japanese was still firing from his cavern after all his comrades had been shot. For two days he had lived with corpses, without food or water. Some caves were manned by thirty or forty of the enemy. When the one manning the machine gun was picked off, another would take his place, and so on until the last man was dead.

Through the narrow ridge connecting the northern and southern hills on Tulagi the British had dug a narrow cut, some ten feet wide and thirty or forty feet deep. The cut leads from the Government Wharf area to the playing ground. The Japanese had dug a cave into the side of the embankment at its base and from this almost unapproachable emplacement commanded the entrances to the narrow cut from both directions. Marines could only fire on the hole from the narrow entrances to the cut or from the summit of the ridge. They had to pick off the enemy gunners one by one as they replaced each other at the mouth of the cave.

GAVUTU

The assault on Gavutu, mile-long island which was the site of the principal Japanese seaplane base in the southeastern Solomons, began at noon on the 7th. In the dawn bombing raid and shelling all the planes based there had been blasted before they could leave the water. One four-engined patrol bomber, nine Zero fighters fitted with floats, and five patrol planes lay wrecked on the beach or under the waves.

As noon drew near, the landing boats bearing the First Parachute Battalion, commanded by Major Robert H. Williams, approached Gavutu. They hugged the shore of Florida Island, formed an assault wave, and moved toward Gavutu. Even before the assault wave had been organized, the Japanese opened up with machine guns from the hill overlooking the seaplane base. The hill, one hundred and forty-eight feet high, forms most of the island. There is a narrow flat strip facing the harbor and most Japanese construction was located there. Concrete docks and seaplane slips extended into the harbor. Machine shops and repair facilities had been built on the docks and near-by shore.

The First Parachutists had expected to land on the concrete seaplane slips, but the naval gunfire and bombing had hurled huge blocks of concrete into the water, blocking the approach. The attacking Marines had to clamber onto a wharf higher than their boats, swept by machine-gun fire. The enemy, in dugouts near the shore and caves in the face of the hill, allowed the first wave of Marines to land, then opened up as the second wave disembarked. Major Williams was badly wounded leading his men in the first wave and had to be evacuated. His executive officer, Major C. A. Miller, took command.

While the Parachutists were coming ashore at the dock, First Lieutenant Walter S. Young, battalion communications officer, found that a dugout near the shore and commanding part of the dock still contained enemy troops firing on the

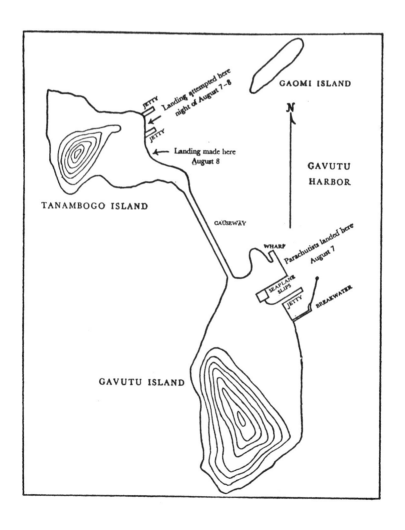

GAOMI ISLAND

N

Landing attempted here
night of August 7–8

JETTY

JETTY

GAVUTU
HARBOR

Landing made here
August 8

TANAMBOGO ISLAND

CAUSEWAY

WHARF

Parachutists landed here
August 7

SEAPLANE
SLIPS

JETTY

BREAKWATER

GAVUTU ISLAND

GAVUTU ISLAND — TARGET OF THE FIRST PARACHUTE BATTALION

Parachutists. Although it was beyond his duties as communications officer to do so, Lieutenant Young voluntarily tried to silence the enemy in the dugout and was killed by a shot from within as he tried to force an entrance.

Platoon Sergeant Harry M. Tully had seen some of his best friends killed in the deadly fire that greeted the Parachutists on their landing. An excellent marksman, Tully set about to avenge his comrades' death. Showing patience that is rare under fire, Tully lay in wait long periods to make sure of snipers' positions, then got them in his sights and killed them. At night some Japanese tried to escape the island by swimming behind logs or oil barrels to near-by Florida Island. Other enemy soldiers tried to reach the island by the same method to join in the fight. Tully posted himself on the beach at night, looking for the telltale disturbances in the water as logs drifted in and out. Matching the Japanese in patience, Tully sometimes waited many minutes as a shadow moved a few inches, then came to rest and waited to move again. When he made sure that the shadow was an enemy, Tully fired. Tully located one sniper firing from Tanambogo, five hundred yards away, took careful aim with his rifle, and killed him.

The Japanese had converted the steep hill into a honeycomb of machine-gun emplacements. Tunnels connected some of these chambers cut out of the rocks. The hill rises steeply from the flat strip near the beach and is difficult enough to climb even when a hail of machine-gun bullets is not beating down from it. A most effective means of closing up the hillside caves was used by the Parachutists, who are experts in demolition work. They hurled charges of TNT into the caves. Captain Harry L. Torgerson perfected the method and closed up many of the holes by himself. When the Japanese threw out the explosive charges hurled at them in their hideaways, the Parachutists tied the TNT charges to boards and thrust them into the cavern mouths. Covered by the fire of only four of his men, Captain Torgerson rushed from cave to cave with these crude but effective bombs and came out of his daring day's work with only a wrist watch broken and his trousers blasted off.

During the day and night of August 7 the Parachutists carried on the attack by themselves. About ten o'clock on the 8th they were reinforced by the Third Battalion, Second Marines, under the command of Lieutenant Colonel R. G. Hunt. Companies L and K assisted the Parachutists in cleaning up enemy forces on Gavutu.

Second Lieutenant Harold A. Hayes led the way into enemy caves in the final mop-up. Many of the cliffside holes were still occupied by Japanese who were armed and resisting to the end. Hayes and his men cleaned them out, killing those who still resisted and taking seven prisoners. Private O. E. Attencio, seeing a corpsman struggling in the water near the beach to rescue a wounded man, ran into the sea with a stretcher to help. The beach was under sniper fire from the cliff and one bullet wounded the corpsman. Attencio stayed with him holding his head above the water until another sniper's bullet killed the corpsman. Attencio stayed on in the exposed spot, crouching in the water for two hours and warning other Marines away from the sniper's nest.

TANAMBOGO

The Third Battalion, Second Marines, was also given the task of taking Tanambogo Island across the causeway from Gavutu. On the night of the 7th, Company B of the First Battalion, Second Marines, had made an unsuccessful attempt to land on Tanambogo.

Company B, under Captain Crane, which had landed on Florida Island before the landings on Tulagi began, was ordered to Gavutu about two o'clock the afternoon of the 7th. The troops embarked immediately from Halavo Peninsula and were guided to Gavutu by Pilot Officer C. E. Spencer, of the Royal Australian Air Force, an officer well acquainted with the Tulagi area who had led them in their landing on Halavo Peninsula. They arrived at Gavutu at dusk. There they were ordered to land on Tanambogo. Heavy fire from that island interdicted the road across the causeway and Company B was to land on the beach north of the causeway.

Naval gunfire preceded the landing of Captain Crane's men. The last shell hit a fuel dump near the beach just as the Marines landed, brilliantly lighting the beach and silhouetting the attackers. The Marines were jammed between two piers, one of which had been built since Pilot Officer Spencer had last seen the area. Heavy machine-gun fire raked them from the hill. Seeing that they were caught in a pocket, unable to peep over the edge of the pier or to set up machine guns without drawing heavy fire from the hill, Captain Crane decided to land farther down the beach. Only two of his landing boats, however, had reached the beach. The coxswain of the third had been killed, his boat had turned back, and the remaining boats followed it back to Gavutu without landing, thinking there had been some change in plans. This left Captain Crane with only two boats and one of these was used to evacuate the wounded. Facing hopeless odds the Marines, after crouching in the water almost four hours, made their way back to Tanambogo in the one remaining boat. Two men, stranded on Tanambogo in the confusion, stripped and swam back to Gavutu during the night.

A second, and successful, attempt to dislodge the Japanese defenders of Tanambogo was made by the Third Battalion, Second Marines, on the 8th. After naval guns and bombs had blasted Tanambogo, the assault began. First, two tanks under Lieutenant R. J. Sweeney were sent ashore at four-fifteen. One tank was to cover the south side of the hill and the other the east slope. One tank got ashore and delivered effective fire into enemy positions, but the Japanese rushed from their dugouts and stalled it by thrusting a heavy iron bar through the tracks and set it afire with rags soaked in oil. The other tank, in which Lieutenant Sweeney was killed trying to get better observation, fired from the beach, then was re-embarked on its lighter and returned to Gavutu.

Company I of the Second Marines followed the tanks to Tanambogo, landing at four-twenty. About half of the landing force worked up the southern slope of the hill while the balance worked around the east and north sides and along the shore. Sniper fire from near-by Gaomi Island harassed the attackers and naval gunfire on that area was requested. A destroyer bombarded Gaomi and silenced all effective fire from that direction.

Then a platoon of Company K crossed the causeway to Tanambogo and took up positions on the south end of the island. By nine o'clock the southeast two-thirds of the island had been secured. Here, as on Gavutu, the Japanese had holed up in caves and dugouts on the hillside. During the night of the 8th the enemy sortied from their dugouts and there was fighting at close quarters with knives and bayonets. But the Marines held the ground they had gained during the day.

Sunday, the 9th, Company I of the Second Marines secured the rest of Tanambogo and mopped up enemy forces in that area. Sergeant Orle S. Bergner by himself blew up the largest enemy pillbox on Tanambogo. One light machine gun covered his approach to the pillbox. As the bullets from his covering gun spattered just a foot over his head, and under enemy fire from a near-by cave, he dug a hole in the ground for the explosive charge, then crawled to cover as the pillbox was blasted. Bergner also led the work of demolishing other caves and dugouts on Tanambogo with TNT and dynamite. At the same time they organized defensive positions.

The other little islands in the area had few Japanese. The Marines encountered no opposition when they occupied Makambo and only slight opposition on Mbangi and Songanangong. Several enemy detachments of twelve to fifteen men were reported on Florida Island and mopping-up operations there extended over several weeks.

Chapter 3

Taking Stock

FEW MARINES realized the seriousness of our situation in the early days on Tulagi and Guadalcanal. The average Marine — we can call him George — going about his daily business of digging emplacements and foxholes and moving supplies from the beach, could not guess what a severe trial lay ahead of him. He knew that a major part of his mission, to wrest the airfield on Guadalcanal from the enemy, had been accomplished. He knew that there were very few Japanese troops on the island. The little enemy detachments were a nuisance, of course, and it would be a tiresome job to hunt them down, but George had no doubt it could be done quickly. He had seen the beaches crowded with mountains of supplies. He worked hard for days carrying them to unit areas. But he could not know that these stacks of stores which looked so impressive were but a small fraction of the supplies and equipment that his commanders had expected to land.

George was still under the impression that the naval battle off Savo Island had been a victory for the United Nations. He thought the big guns that spoke so thunderously that wild night could only have been on one of our mighty new battleships, and if *that* ship had been in the fight the result could only have been a victory for our fleet. His logic in this matter was colored by a deep confidence in Americans' ability to defeat the enemy on land, on the sea, or in the air.

His job had been easier than he thought it would be. The enemy had let him take the airfield without a fight. Well, that was George's good luck. Now he was ready to move on. 'Scuttlebutt' [1] had two favorite topics — the night naval battle off Savo and the next objective. 'Where do we go from here?' He thought of himself as an assault soldier, a specialist in landing operations. When he had successfully taken one objective, he expected to be sent somewhere else to repeat the performance.

There were, on the other hand, little incidents that planted doubts in George's mind. Things happened that should not happen if all is well. He began to gain a sober appreciation of what lay ahead. For example, there was 'Oscar the Submarine.' Japanese underwater craft had appeared off Guadalcanal while our ships were still unloading and for days thereafter they lurked near-by. The Marines called the Japanese submarine, or submarines, Oscar. August 12, when a few of us made the first crossing from Guadalcanal to Tulagi, Oscar came to the surface and started shelling us as we approached Tulagi in Higgins boats. He was overtaking us fast when a battery of seventy-five-millimeter howitzers from Tulagi got his range and forced him to submerge. Thereafter no boats tried to cross from Guadalcanal to Tulagi until they had air coverage.

The next morning, before dawn, Oscar shelled the Marine position around the airfield. Later in the day he brazenly surfaced in full view of the Marines on the shore and resumed his shelling. Thereafter, for many days and nights, the submarines popped up at odd moments of the day or night and shelled us.

---

[1] 'Scuttlebutt' is Navy and Marine slang for 'rumors.' Before the day of modern drinking fountains on Navy ships, the scuttlebutt was a cask of water where the men got their drinking water. Such a gathering-point was naturally the scene of much gossip and exchange of rumors.

Oscar never caused any damage or any casualties and George liked to joke about his pranks, but at the same time Oscar's very presence was a humiliating impertinence. How could a Japanese sub get away with surfacing whenever it chose and shelling Guadalcanal? George knew the answer, and it worried him. He could see the airfield, without a single plane on it. He knew it was ready to receive planes, but none arrived. 'They will be in tomorrow,' according to the scuttlebutt. Many tomorrows passed before the first flight of American planes landed on Henderson Field.

George knew, too, that there was no coast artillery on the beach, that there were no motor torpedo boats to patrol the straits. Only slow, vulnerable Higgins boats were available for anti-submarine patrol. The day before our planes finally arrived, a Japanese destroyer caught two of the helpless craft on patrol and sank them both. The only other opponents we had for Oscar were the half-tracks [1] which ran to the beach and shot at the submarine with their seventy-five-millimeter guns. The submarines then kept at a more respectful distance during the day, but were free to cruise up and down the channel.

Other things bothered George. Japanese planes had complete freedom of the skies over Guadalcanal. In the first two weeks of our occupation of the Lunga area there were no heavy raids — only six or eight bombers at a time came over — but George grew restless and annoyed at the lack of opposition. A ninety-millimeter anti-aircraft battery, the enemy's favorite target, had been set up on the airfield under the command of Major J. S. O'Halloran, of the Third Defense Battalion. The guns kept the bombers high and occasionally shot one down, but could not prevent them from flying over.

Growing a little impatient at holding the line alone, the anti-aircraft gunners wrote the following mock memorandum:

---

[1] 'Half-tracks' are self-propelled tank destroyers, running partly on wheels and partly on crawler-type tractor treads.

From: The Anti-Aircraft Artillery
To: Mr. Piper, Piper Cub Company, U.S.A.
Via: Division Air Officer

Subject: Piper Cub, request for.

1. Dear Mr. Piper. I hate to bring this to your attention, but we would like one of your little Piper Cub airplanes. We forgot to bring ours. We got a pilot but no airplanes. The Japs got both, real big ones (the airplanes, not the Japs).

2. We also got some AA guns, but they is not enough and too late.

3. If you cannot afford a plane for us marines, we compromise easy for one captive balloon and one net section for our AA.

4. If you can't help us out please bring this to the attention of Mr. S. Claus. Xmas is only four months away. The Japs is two hours away.

Signed,
The A.A. Boys

P.S. Do you have any kites?

George began to notice other shortages. He knew he would have to live on iron rations the first few days of the operation. But after the situation had become somewhat stabilized, he thought he might reasonably expect the chow to be a bit better. Substantial quantities of Japanese food had been captured — rice, tinned fruit, tinned meat, tinned milk, and even candy. Even with this loot added to the larder, however, the Marines on Guadalcanal had to go on a schedule of two meals daily. August 12, Division Headquarters passed the word to all units that the most stringent economy must be effected in the use of rations and that the two-meal schedule should be followed. In Tulagi the Marines went on a schedule of one meal daily, to stretch eight days' supply of rations as far as possible. August 13 the Commanding General informed the Commander of the South Pacific Amphibious Force that the Marines had only ten days' rations on the basis of two meals daily. Fewer ships have ever been more welcome than those that began bringing in food August 20.

Even such a routine matter as digging foxholes and making air-raid shelters became a major problem. Few sandbags had been landed, and, if the Japanese had not obligingly left large stocks of straw bags, construction of emplacements and dugouts would have been seriously hampered. There was an acute shortage of spades and digging implements. One of the good results of the action at the Tenaru later in the month was that a considerable quantity of small spades was found on the bodies of Japanese killed in that battle.

Working on the defenses around the airfield, George noticed there wasn't much barbed wire to stretch in front of his lines. His lieutenant took him out one day on a working party to strip some old rusty barbed wire from a coconut-plantation fence. Was this all the wire they could get? Unfortunately, it was. No more than twenty-five rolls had been brought ashore in the original landing operation. Many weeks passed before enough was landed to throw a protective apron all around our position. Meanwhile, the little wire on hand was strung up at a few important points in the defense line. A few strands on the beach at the mouth of the Tenaru were to play an important part in the battle that raged there August 21.

In a hundred little ways George began to feel the impact of the night battle off Savo Island — probably without realizing what lay behind these puzzling shortages and deficiencies. Four cruisers were lost; George began to tighten his belt, learned to know what it is to be shelled and bombed without being able to fight back, crouched in his foxhole with no barbed wire between him and the Japanese.

George was a bit 'trigger-happy' the first few nights. He wanted to fire at palm fronds swaying in the wind, and at cows and lizards. He hadn't yet been in a real fight with the enemy and he was still nervous in the jungle night. He knew the Marine lines were spread very thin around the airfield and it would be a simple matter for enemy patrols to slip through at night until the lines were tightened. Sometimes they did slip through. August 10 two batteries of artillery, used as infantry to fill out the defense perimeter south of the airfield, had not yet finished organizing their lines. Their lines faced each other at one point. A Japanese patrol worked its way between them one night, fired a few rounds, drew a reply from both sides, and withdrew as a spirited fire fight developed between the two lines of Marines firing on each other. Machine-gun and rifle bullets whined over the airfield in an engagement which passed into Guadalcanal legend as the 'Battle of the Arena.' But George quieted down in a few nights and learned that his best protection lay in silence and cold steel.

TRYING TO MOP UP

While George was settling down to a new routine of life near Henderson Field and thinking about some of the puzzling things he noticed, his commanders, fully aware of the seriousness of the situation, set about developing plans for defending the airfield and for rounding up the Japanese forces known to be hiding near-by.

The Marine Command decided upon a 'perimeter' defense around the airfield. A line of men and guns was thrown all the way around our position, ready to meet a Japanese attack at any point. It was a thin line and those who manned it knew it was all that lay between the enemy and the airfield. It was designed to prevent even night infiltration of our position, but until the arrival of another Marine regiment in September there were many gaps in the sector south of the airfield. There three artillery battalions of the Eleventh Marines — Second Battalion (Lieutenant Colonel E. G. Hagen), Third Battalion (Lieutenant Colonel J. J. Keating), and Fifth Battalion (Lieutenant Colonel E. H. Price) — the First Pioneer Battalion (Lieutenant Colonel G. R. Rowan) and the First Engineers Battalion (Major J. G. Frazer) were used as rifle units, in addition to their other duties, to fill out the defenses of Henderson Field during the early weeks of the campaign.

That position was a small one — much smaller than people at home realized for a long time. From the Tenaru River on the east, a sluggish stream barred from the sea by sand, it stretched along the coast to a point about a mile south of Kukum. Then it swung inland in a rough semicircle, south of the airfield, back to the Tenaru River. The entire area was less than fifteen square miles. We faced the sea, with our flanks resting on streams and coconut groves, and the rear line running through the jungle growth and coral ridges that lie back of Henderson Field. Mr. Hanson Baldwin described our position best when he pointed out it was as if the Marines held Jones Beach and the Japanese loosely dominated the rest of Long Island.

After organizing the defense perimeter, the Marine Command turned to the task of seeking out the main Japanese force on the island which had withdrawn to the west along the coast, across the Matanikau River. Two problems vexed them from the outset. First, how many men could be safely detached from the thin line around the airfield to go out to hunt down the enemy? Secondly, how could enough landing boats be obtained to carry out the mopping-up operations on distant points of the island?

Of course the security of the airfield was of paramount importance. If the removal of one small unit from the defense perimeter meant that the airfield might be endangered, then that unit could not be detached. Over the airfield hung a threat that could never be ignored. It was, in a sense, a distant one, but an important and direct one. The day we landed on Guadalcanal there was an impressive concentration of Japanese ships at Rabaul. The concentration persisted throughout the time we were on Guadalcanal. It was there the day we left. Rabaul is only six hundred miles from Guadalcanal, less than two days' sailing time even for slow transports. That concentration and similar concentrations of enemy ships at Buin and Shortlands, even closer to Guadalcanal, dictated the strategy of the ground forces on Guadalcanal. Never could Marines be detached from the defense perimeter and sent out so far that they would be unable to return and man defensive positions in case a large force of Japanese ships should begin to move toward Guadalcanal. We shall see this principle in operation in November.

As early as August 12, General Vandegrift began urging that another infantry regiment, the Seventh Marines, be sent to Guadalcanal to strengthen the defenses of the airfield and make available enough men for operations in other parts of the island. In a letter to Rear Admiral Turner he said: 'I want to suggest that if we are to hold this place that the 7th be sent up. For should they [the Japanese] desire to land a major effort ten or twenty miles away we do not have a sufficient mobile reserve to go after them.'

A second problem was the shortage of landing boats. One consequence of the withdrawal of our transports and supply ships after the Battle of Savo Island was that adequate arrangements could not be made to maintain the necessary number of boats for use by the land forces on Tulagi and Guadalcanal. Lieutenant Commander Dexter, Commanding Officer of the Naval Local Defense Unit, selected Kukum as a potential base for the operation of landing boats and developed what maintenance facilities he could. But the only facilities available were hoists for changing propellers and equipment for making simple engine adjustments. No supplies of gasoline or Diesel oil had been unloaded for the naval unit. The boats had already been hard worked when they were left in the area, and without proper maintenance they deteriorated further at a rapid rate. Of the boats that had been left on the beach when the task force withdrew August 9, a third were inoperative two days later because of mechanical breakdowns or lack of gasoline. All of these inoperative boats were driven onto the beach in a storm. The rest were gathered and moored off Kukum. It was a small supply of run-down boats. Their inadequacy seriously hampered later unloading of ships arriving with supplies and equipment and hindered the planning of mopping-up operations in which landing boats were needed.

Despite these problems, plans were developed for going out after enemy detachments. From Tulagi several small groups were tracked down on Florida Island. On Guadalcanal we knew that most of the Japanese were west of the Matanikau.

Before we landed on Guadalcanal the Japanese forces consisted of about two thousand construction workers in naval construction battalions and three hundred to five hundred officers and men of the Imperial Navy who served as guards for the laborers and manned the anti-aircraft batteries and other defensive installations. Most laborers and Navy personnel were at breakfast when our attack started and they immediately took to the bush. So far as the laborers were concerned, it was every man for himself. Later they began surrendering in groups when they felt the pinch of hunger in the jungle. The naval forces, however, apparently had a prearranged rendezvous area where most of them later gathered.

The first encounter with the Japanese detachment at Matanikau ended in disaster for a Marine patrol led by Colonel Frank B. Goettge, Division Intelligence Officer. Several things had pointed to the village of Matanikau as the concentration point of the Japanese who had fled so ignominiously from the airfield. A large flag, apparently the rising sun on a white background, had been seen flying near the village.[1] Movements of Japanese soldiers had been seen in that neigh-

---

[1] Some stories concerning the Goettge patrol which have appeared in print have said that the Japanese waved a white surrender flag to lure Marine patrols into ambush. Although some who saw the flag from a distance took it for a surrender flag, it was not assumed by those taking part in the Goettge patrol that they would receive the surrender of Japanese. The patrol was purely for reconnaissance purposes. This particular story of Japanese trickery and treachery must be discounted.

borhood through field glasses, and a prisoner captured south of Kukum had confirmed that most of the enemy military personnel had gathered there, adding that they were beginning to suffer from lack of food and many might be willing to surrender.

Acting on such information, Colonel Goettge organized a patrol to scout the area where the Japanese were suspected to be.   Lieutenant Commander Malcolm Pratt (M.C. U.S.N.), medical officer attached to the Fifth Marines, volunteered to accompany them.   Captain Wilfred Ringer, Intelligence Officer of the Fifth Marines, First Lieutenant Ralph Cory, Japanese interpreter attached to the Fifth Marines, First Sergeant Stephen A. Custer, of the Division Intelligence Section, and twenty-two enlisted men of the Division and Fifth Marines Intelligence Sections made up the patrol.

The group shoved off from Kukum in a Higgins boat after dark on August 12 and made their way to Point Cruz where they went ashore and hastily established a defensive line on the beach.   Then Colonel Goettge, Captain Ringer, and First Sergeant Custer started inland to reconnoiter.   They had gone only about twenty-five feet when they were fired upon, and Colonel Goettge fell.   Custer also was wounded and he and Captain Ringer returned to the beach.   From then on throughout the night the little patrol fought it out with Japanese concealed in the darkness of the dense woods.   Platoon Sergeant Frank L. Few and Corporal Joseph Spaulding crawled toward the spot where Colonel Goettge had fallen and found that he was apparently dead.   Spaulding returned to the others to get help to bring the Colonel back and Few, left alone, was attacked by a Japanese.   In the scuffle Few was wounded, but killed his assailant and then he, too, returned to the beach.

One by one, as the fire fight continued, the members of the Marine patrol were wounded.   Captain Ringer decided to send for help and dispatched Sergeant C. C. Arndt to the Lunga area.   But Arndt had gone only a short distance up the beach when he was fired upon, and not knowing whether he had been killed or not, Captain Ringer sent another messenger. This time Corporal Spaulding set out. Both messengers reached camp the next morning after a hazardous journey, partly on foot, partly in the water, during which they both had brushes with Japanese scouts.

Meanwhile, the tiny Marine beachhead was wiped out. Platoon Sergeant Few was the only other member of the patrol to get back to camp. As day began to break, Few, seeing that further resistance was helpless as all his comrades lay about him dead or wounded, swam out into the ocean and made it safely to Kukum.

After this tragic encounter two patrols from the Fifth Marines marched out toward the Matanikau to try to cross the river to the spot where the Goettge patrol had landed. Both ran into strong positions at the mouth of the river and were not able to cross. Accordingly it was decided to send a stronger party into the area, to wipe out the nest of Japanese.

One company (Company L, Third Battalion, Fifth Marines, under Captain Lyman Spurlock) left camp early in the morning of the 18th, cut back through the jungle and crossed the Matanikau River about a mile from its mouth. They bivouacked for the night on a ridge in the rear of the enemy position. Colonel W. J. Whaling, Executive Officer of the Fifth Marines, who directed the operation, and Company I (Third Battalion, Fifth Marines, under Captain B. W. Hardy, Jr.), embarked at Kukum in landing boats and shoved off about five-thirty the morning of the 19th, heading for Kokumbona. About an hour later they landed on the beach a mile west of that village. The third company (Company B, First Battalion, Fifth Marines), commanded by Captain William Hawkins, advanced along the beach road toward the Matanikau and took up positions east of the river. At eight-fifty the Eleventh Marines laid down artillery concentrations on the enemy position, and when it lifted Company B tried to cross the river. But the beach and sand bar across the river mouth were covered by enemy machine-gun fire which pinned the company down. Its left flank lay in thick jungle growth near the river bank. An enveloping movement was attempted through the jungle, to cross the river upstream from its mouth, but this was checked by heavy fire on the opposite bank at the point where the company tried to cross.

Meanwhile, Company L, to the rear of the enemy, had begun to attack. They bore the brunt of the action as it developed in the jungle and coral hills back of Matanikau village. The day before, while getting into position on the ridge south of Matanikau, Company L had encountered enemy groups and had killed several. Now, as the Japanese had started for the hills to the south when our artillery had ceased firing, Company L met them at close quarters. The Marines drove them back in bitter fighting — back toward the village and the river. In this action Lieutenant George Meade lost his life. When his platoon was held up by an enemy sniper, he rushed through the jungle to hunt him down. He shot the sniper with his forty-five pistol and cleared the way for further advance, but only after he had been mortally wounded himself. Twice Company L occupied the enemy camp and twice they were driven out before they succeeded in overrunning it and holding it.

Company I, which had landed west of Kokumbona about six-thirty in the morning, started to advance eastward to take the village. Then they planned to sweep eastward and join the other Marines at Matanikau.

Colonel Whaling and Lieutenant Colonel F. C. Biebush (Commanding Officer of the Third Battalion, Fifth Marines) stayed in their boat and started back along the coast toward Matanikau. Just then the Higgins boats which had engaged in landing the Marines near Kokumbona were fired upon by a Japanese destroyer lying off shore, and the landing boats scattered.

As the last of three salvos was fired by the Japanese warship, Colonel Whaling's boat was fired on from the beach near

Kokumbona, by machine guns and rifles. Farther east they ran into more fire. A Japanese waving a large rising-sun flag appeared on the beach. Colonel Whaling drew a bead on him, hit him, and he rolled over backward. The rising sun did not appear again. The boat continued on to the Matanikau. Lying off shore Colonel Whaling observed the artillery fire at nine o'clock and could·see Company L on the ridge south of the beach, to the left and rear of the enemy.

Colonel Whaling and Lieutenant Colonel Biebush landed and found Captain Hawkins, whose men were still at this point pinned down on the east side of the river. Colonel Whaling suggested a wide enveloping movement on the enemy's right flank, Company B to cross the river well above the Japanese positions, farther up river from the point where their earlier attempt to cross had been stopped by enemy machine-gun fire. The going was too slow through the jungle, however, and Company B remained near the beach. They attempted to dislodge by mortar fire the heavy machine gun that was raking the east bank of the river. The jungle prevented good observation of the mortar fire, but the tenth round apparently rocked the machine gun and killed some gunners. In the lull that followed, Company B brought some machine guns into position to fire on the west bank. Five minutes later they saw the helmets of men from Company L in the Japanese camp across the river and crossed the sand bar to join them after one-thirty.

After his conference with Captain Hawkins, Colonel Whaling returned to his boat, to set out in an attempt to contact Companies I and L. Just as he returned to the boat he got a message directing all companies to return to camp that evening.

Company I had taken the village of Kokumbona as planned and was ready to move eastward, to meet the other companies and mop up the area lying between the two captured villages. The order to return to camp prevented their juncture·and Company I re-embarked in boats near Kokumbona and returned to Kukum.

The three companies had killed about seventy-five Japanese and had entered the two villages, but an unknown number of enemy soldiers had escaped to the hills or remained near the shore between Kokumbona and Matanikau. That evening Company I was fired on as they returned from Kokumbona, showing that the enemy was still there.

Plans for finishing the job in the Matanikau area were developed after the action on the 19th. An entire battalion was to be landed at Kokumbona, move eastward and comb the area thoroughly. This operation was originally scheduled to take place Sunday, August 23, but as it turned out bigger things impended that day and the operation was postponed. A Japanese invasion force was then headed for Guadalcanal and no Marine units could be sent beyond the defense perimeter.

Meanwhile, Marine forces from Tulagi had been mopping up Japanese detachments on near-by Florida Island. Some Japanese had escaped to Florida during the fight for Tulagi, Gavutu, and Tanambogo. Others had been there before our attack, manning lookout stations. Patrols from the First Raiders and from the Third Battalion, Second Marines, operated on Florida almost every day. Haleta, Halavo, Port Purvis, and Bungana Island were the first points to be visited in the clean-up campaign that began August 14. Two companies of the First Raiders raided Tanavola Point on Sandfly Passage, where they killed ten Japanese. Company A of the Raiders went to the interior of Florida Island to round up a detachment of fifty enemy soldiers reported by friendly natives.

The operations on Florida had to be suspended when the Japanese counter-offensive to retake Henderson Field got under way late in August and units were shifted from Tulagi to strengthen the Marine lines around the airfield.

HENDERSON FIELD

The objective of the United Nations attacking forces on August 7 and the prize so bitterly fought over during the next six months was the airfield built by the Japanese southwest of Lunga Point.

South of the strip of coconut trees bordering the beach between Lunga Point and the Tenaru River there is a grassy plain and succession of grass-covered coral ridges. These in turn lead into the tree-covered foothills of the mountains. The western end of the field is marked by the Lunga River. Thick underbrush and towering trees line the river. Just east of the river there are several gently sloping coral ridges. Farther east the grassy plain extends broad and flat for two and a half miles, broken now and then by other coral mounds. The Japanese had chosen this grassy plain as the site of their first runway on Guadalcanal. The western end of the runway began near the river, where the tangled underbrush and great trees slope upward to the flat grass-covered tableland. The eastern end lay in a coconut plantation. Many coconut trees had to be cut down to allow for a runway of the length planned by the Japanese.

For a month before our land, sea, and air forces blasted them out, the Japanese had worked night and day to construct the airfield. A landing strip 3778 feet long and 160 feet wide had almost been completed when we landed. Two sections of the runway, one 2400 and the other 1181 feet long, had already been surfaced with coral, clay, gravel, and dry cement. A gap of only 197 feet remained to be surfaced.

Much valuable booty in the form of airport construction equipment and material fell to the Marines. Five power rollers, two tractors, two hundred and thirty tons of first-grade cement, three mobile hoisting power units, three dry cement mixers, two complete electric light units, a complete water system serving the airfield, and an electric light system running the entire length of the runway — all were left behind undamaged by the fleeing Japanese. Power machinery of all kinds, in considerable quantities, was found still crated and in excellent condition. Fifty to sixty tons of steel plates, one-half inch or three-quarters of an inch thick, were also found.

The Japanese had completed three blast pens to accommodate one large bomber each, and were working on others. Five open-sided workshops or hangars, constructed of steel trusses and steel plates, were ready for use. Dispersal areas for aircraft had been cut out of the neighboring coconut groves.

This was the rich prize which fell to our forces. It represented great expenditure of Japanese equipment, material, and man-hours. It is no exaggeration to say that the existence of this airfield in its amost completed state may have saved the Marine force in the Solomons and ensured the success of their mission. If this field had not existed to serve as a base for Army, Navy, and Marine fighters and dive-bombers, enemy warships would have had much more freedom to roam the surrounding waters, shell our positions, land troops, and cut our supply lines. Enemy aircraft could have raided us with relative impunity. If our aircraft had had to await the construction of an air base in the Solomons, started from scratch, the story of the First Marine Division, Reinforced, might have been a very different one.

When we had occupied the airfield area, the job having top priority was to fill the small gap in the runway and prepare it to receive planes. The First Engineer Battalion (Major J. G. Frazer) immediately went to work on it, using what tools the Japanese had left behind, but having to rely mostly on primitive hand labor. The field was ready within two days, but eleven more days passed before the first planes arrived to be based there. At four o'clock the afternoon of August 20th we heard the sound of a large formation of planes approaching. When enemy planes have been bombing you at will and when you have not seen friendly planes in the sky for many days, you grow suspicious of every droning motor in the sky. That day, as the sound grew closer, men reached automatically for their helmets and began edging toward their foxholes. Our planes were expected that day, but we had heard that before. Then, as the planes circled the field, Marines with field glasses picked out the distinctive stubby wings of Grumman fighters and we knew they were our own. A shout of relief and welcome went up from every Marine on the island. George felt much happier.

The flight consisted of a squadron of fighter planes and a squadron of dive-bombers. The fighter squadron (VMF–223), commanded by Captain John L. Smith, consisted of nineteen Grumman Wildcats and the dive-bomber squadron (VMSB–232), commanded by Major Richard C. Mangrum, had twelve Douglas Dauntless dive-bombers. The Marine pilots, most of them green and just out of school, were to see action very soon. All were tested veterans, and some were aces, within a few days of their arrival.

The field from which they were to operate and make aviation history had been named Henderson Field in honor of Major Lofton R. Henderson, United States Marine Corps, who gave his life in the Battle of Midway June 4 by diving his plane into the stack of a Japanese warship. Major Henderson was squadron commander of the Marine Aviation Squadron based on Midway which played an important part in turning back the attempted Japanese invasion of that island in June.

Chapter 4

The Japanese Strike Back

T HE SAME DAY that three companies of the Fifth Marines were attacking at Matanikau and Kokumbona (September 19), a patrol from Company A, First Marines, led by Captain Charles H. Brush, Jr., set out for Taivu Point to destroy a Japanese outpost.

The Marine patrol had passed Beach Red and was approaching Papangu beyond Koli Point in the evening when they suddenly came upon an enemy detachment about thirty-five strong, including four officers, with some light machine guns. The encounter was a mutual surprise, but Captain Brush's men moved quickly to the assault and pinned down the enemy patrol.

Second Lieutenant John J. Jachym led his platoon in an enveloping maneuver which prevented the escape of all but a few Japanese. Private George H. Grazier lost his life in a gallant attempt to knock out an enemy machine gun which had pinned down two Marine squads. Unable to bring fire to bear on the enemy position from concealment in the jungle, Grazier ran out on the exposed beach to fire on the Japanese gunners. He was killed in the attempt. The Japanese, all naval personnel, had just landed in rubber boats, and were equipped with considerable radio equipment. The Marines killed twenty-two of the enemy in this encounter, including all four officers, with losses to themselves of three killed and three wounded.

The enemy unit engaged by the Marine patrol evidently was an advance scouting party for a much larger force. They had the healthy clean appearance of men who had not been long on the island. The equipment they carried and the relatively large number of officers also indicated their party was not an ordinary patrol. There were other signs that the Japanese were growing more active on Guadalcanal. At dawn that morning (the 19th) Japanese destroyers and cruisers had shelled our position for about an hour and had sunk two Higgins boats on anti-submarine patrol. Cruiser-type aircraft had operated over Guadalcanal during the day and twice had strafed Company I of the Fifth Marines near Kokumbona. A Flying Fortress, the first friendly plane we had seen in many days, appeared over the channel at noon and sent a destroyer or light cruiser limping away, smoking from a direct bomb hit. The day-long activities of enemy warships off our shores indicated something was afoot. The activities continued the next day (August 20), when a destroyer shelled Tulagi in the morning and a reconnaissance float-plane was seen between Savo and Florida.

ACTION AT THE TENARU

We learned the meaning of this increased activity on the night of August 20–21. It began much as any other night on Guadalcanal — quietly. The first indication that something might be brewing came about ten-thirty. An outpost near the mouth of the Tenaru saw a white flare rise from the woods east of the river. Then all was quiet on the east side of the Tenaru until midnight, when someone on that side failed to answer a sentry's challenge and was fired upon. Another period of quiet lasted until about two o'clock in the morning, when suddenly the eastern bank became alive with shadowy figures making a dash for the sand bar that separates the river from the sea.

Marine machine guns opened up as the Japanese charged across the sand to engage the defenders with the bayonet. Two platoons of Battery B of the Special Weapons Battalion, attached to the First Marines, bore the brunt of the first assault. About two hundred Japanese tried to overrun the Marines' positions. Some succeeded in crossing the sand bar and reached the beach on the west side of the river, but these were killed and the remainder of the attacking force was driven back. A few strands of barbed wire salvaged from a plantation fence had been strung along the beach at the river's mouth and proved invaluable in helping to check the enemy's assault. On the east bank the Japanese dug in and engaged the Marines in a fire fight. They concentrated mortar fire on the point, trying to knock out the Marine machine guns that had stopped the first assault.

The defending Marine forces on the west bank of the Tenaru were commanded by Lieutenant Colonel E. A. Pollock, whose cool courage and sure leadership in the action won him the Navy Cross. As soon as the battle started, he left his command post and went to the front line where for more than twelve hours he moved among his men under heavy fire, personally directing the units under his command. Private Raymond D. Parker of Lieutenant Colonel Pollock's battalion also won a Navy Cross for his bravery in the action at the Tenaru. The Japanese were using the reverse slope of the beach, inclining toward the sea from the Marine defenses, as cover for approaching the Marine lines. Wriggling on the sand in the shelter of the slope, they tried to outflank strong positions at the river's mouth and infiltrate through the beach defenses farther west. Parker took up an exposed position on the beach to oppose this infiltration tactic and did much to break up the enemy's attempts to cross the sand bar. When his automatic rifle jammed, he got a rifle and continued the fight.

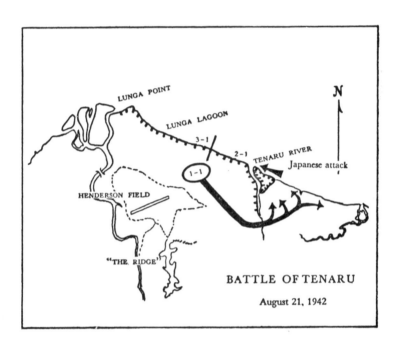

LUNGA POINT

LUNGA LAGOON

3 – 1

2 – 1

TENARU RIVER

Japanese attack

1 – 1

HENDERSON FIELD

"THE RIDGE"

BATTLE OF TENARU

August 21, 1942

TENARU — SURPRISED BY ENEMY ASSAULT

Corporal William H. Wolvington's heroism cost him his life. His platoon was receiving heavy fire from an enemy machine gun. Wolvington went to the front line, picked up an abandoned light machine gun and, firing from the hip, killed enemy soldiers who had filtered across the river and helped knock out the machine guns firing into his platoon on the far bank of the river. He fought on until he was mortally wounded.

Three members of a machine squad of Company H, First Marines, were awarded the Navy Cross for their part in repelling the Japanese charges. Corporal LeRoy Diamond, Private John Rivers, and Private Albert A. Schmid were together in a dugout near the bank of the Tenaru where they were manning a machine gun. Their emplacement was on the river bank directly in the path of the first Japanese charge. Rivers was wounded in the face, then, as the other two kept their gun firing and stopped the enemy charge, Diamond also fell, wounded in the arm. Schmid carried on alone. Japanese had infiltrated the Marines' river line, bullets began hitting into Schmid's dugout, and finally a grenade struck the machine gun, blinding Private Schmid. The wounded men lay helpless in the dugout until Private Whitney W. Jacobs dashed through the intense Japanese fire to give them first aid. It was long after daybreak when other Marines helped them out of the hole.

Platoon Sergeant Nelson Braitmeyer, Private First Class Barney Sterling, and Private First Class Arthur J. Atwood were among those killed while throwing back the Japanese assault. Braitmeyer, second in command of the first platoon of the Special Weapons Battalion, gave his life clearing out enemy positions at the mouth of the Tenaru when the Japanese had penetrated his platoon's gun positions and set up their own machine guns. Sterling, Atwood, and Corporal Joseph G. LeBlanc, all armed only with rifles, were on patrol duty on the opposite side of the river when the Japanese launched their first surprise attack at the sand bar. The three promptly deployed, opened fire, and held off the enemy at first in gallant but hopeless stand. Atwood was killed, and LeBlanc and Sterling fell back, manned a light machine gun and continued to fire on the forces that threatened to overwhelm their forward position. Sterling, too, fell to a Japanese bullet, and LeBlanc continued to resist alone until his ammunition was spent.

Second Lieutenant James F. McClanahan commanded the first platoon of the Special Weapons Battalion. When his line was penetrated in several places, McClanahan organized the defenders and drove the Japanese back, carrying on even after he had been wounded.

With the coming of dawn and the realization that a strong enemy force was attempting to force a crossing of the Tenaru, the Second Battalion, First Marines, under Lieutenant Colonel E. A. Pollock, doggedly clung to its defensive positions along the west side of the Tenaru to hold the Japanese while a plan to encircle them was executed. The First Marines had effective support from the artillery of the Eleventh Marines. which laid down heavy concentrations on the enemy positions in the coconut grove east of the Tenaru. They fired at intervals at the request of the infantry until nine-thirty, when the First Battalion, First Marines, had begun to move into positions to start closing in on the enemy. As the effectiveness of the Marines' small-arms and machine-gun fire and artillery concentrations grew, some Japanese attempted to withdraw to the east in landing boats which had been lying near Beach Red. They were strafed by our planes which had just come in the previous evening.

At the Division Command Post plans were made to envelop the attackers and wipe them out. At eight o'clock the First Battalion, First Marines, under Lieutenant Colonel L. B. Cresswell, was ordered into positions east of the Tenaru, to the right and rear of the enemy, to execute the enveloping movement. The battalion struck out through the jungle from its bivouac area near Lunga Lagoon and crossed the Tenaru between one and two miles above its mouth. At first it had been planned to send tanks with Cresswell's battalion, but the tangle of jungle along the river held them up and the infantry went on alone.

Two companies — A and C — advanced abreast through the jungle on the west side of the Tenaru, going north until they reached the coconut groves, then shifted to the northwest, continuing on the beach. Company A, under Captain Brush, was on the right, and Company C, under First Lieutenant Nikolai S. Stevenson, on the left. As Company C approached the beach about two hundred and fifty yards east of Tenaru village, they encountered an enemy unit of thirty-seven men which opened up with light machine-gun fire on Company C's left. Lieutenant Stevenson quickly maneuvered the remainder of his company to the left, cutting off the enemy unit from the main Japanese body farther east. The Japanese, seeing that they were surrounded, attacked with the bayonet, were driven back by Company C's fire, and were wiped out when Lieutenant Stevenson's men counter-assaulted with the bayonet. One Marine was killed, three were wounded in this encounter.

By twelve-thirty the First Battalion was in position to start its westward movement, drawing a tight line around the Japanese at the mouth of the Tenaru. Company A advanced along the beach, Company C, echeloned to the left rear, moved to the west farther inland. Company B, under First Lieutenant Marshall T. Armstrong, was placed in position at the mouth of the Ilu River, as a rear guard.

As Companies A and C prepared to move in from the west, a possible Japanese escape to the south was cut off by one machine-gun platoon and by one mortar platoon of Company D, led by Sergeant Michael Longazel. This relatively small patrol held off several Japanese attacks while the noose was being drawn. They killed several small groups as they pushed northward toward the beach — first eight, then two, then twelve — securing the left flank of the machine-gun platoon.

When a group of thirty Japanese started to attack, Sergeant Longazel borrowed a Reising gun from one of his men and held off the attackers while his wounded were carried out of range.   Company A was delayed by its engagement with the enemy unit east of Tenaru village, but Company C pushed ahead.   The encirclement was complete when Company A, advancing with its right on the beach, arrived in the vicinity of the Tenaru, and Company C took up positions along the river facing the beach, about four hundred yards inland.

Some of the cornered Japanese tried to escape out to sea, but were picked off by sharpshooters and automatic fire.   For days afterward bodies floated in on the breakers.   Five tanks, under Lieutenant Leo Case, crossed the sand bar about three o'clock in the afternoon and helped mop up the doomed Japanese force.   Ranging the coconut grove east of the Tenaru, they crushed enemy emplacements and blasted them with thirty-seven-millimeter canister and machine-gun fire. On two occasions tanks broke down and the crews were daringly rescued by other tanks.   Once Sergeant Earl Mowery, in the midst of the enemy and under heavy fire, climbed out of his own tank to attach a towline to the disabled tank of his platoon leader, which had become stuck in a ditch, and pulled the tank out.   Lieutenant Case, the platoon leader, had also got out of his disabled tank, helped to attach the towline, and thus saved his tank and crew.   No casualties were suffered by tank personnel.

By five o'clock the action had come to an end with almost complete annihilation of the enemy.   More than seven hundred Japanese were known to have been killed, one surrendered, and fourteen were taken prisoner.   Marine losses were relatively light.   Thirty-four were killed and seventy-five wounded.

The attacking force had been about one thousand strong. Only the rear guard which had stayed near Koli Point escaped annihilation that day.   The enemy troops — some of whom came direct from Japan, others being veterans of actions at

Saipan, Guam, Midway — had landed on Guadalcanal from destroyers on the 18th. They were well equipped with automatic rifles, machine guns, mortars, hand grenades, bangalore torpedoes, smoke bombs, flame-throwers, anti-tank grenades, and camouflage nets. Many carried serviceable spades (an implement badly needed, among many other things, by Marines on Guadalcanal), and more than fifty were recovered from the piles of dead Japanese that covered the beach and lay in the coconut grove at the mouth of the Tenaru.

The carnage on the battlefield was dreadful. Japanese bodies lay piled together in stinking heaps — burned, crushed, and torn. A tide flowed and ebbed before all could be buried, and here an arm, there a head, stuck up through the new-washed sand on the beach. It was a complete and terrible defeat for the enemy. Later we learned that Colonel Ichiki, their commander, had gathered his remaining subordinates about him, burned the unit colors, and shot himself through the head. 'Remember the Ichiki Suicide' became a watchword for later Japanese forces on Guadalcanal. They felt they must wipe out the disgrace of this humiliating defeat.

BATTLE OF THE EASTERN SOLOMONS

As Colonel Ichiki's unit was meeting disaster in the coconuts by the Tenaru, a strong Japanese surface force, including carriers, battleships, cruisers, destroyers, and transports, was beginning to move toward Guadalcanal. The engagement in which this invasion armada was turned back took place far from Guadalcanal. The United States aircraft carriers which had supported the original landing operation turned back toward Guadalcanal to meet the new threat. The Ichiki unit, sent in ahead of the invasion fleet to raid the airfield, had failed in its mission and our aircraft remained intact to attack the approaching transports.

The action began August 23, when eight Japanese ships, one

column of the forces converging on Guadalcanal, were sighted. Carrier planes took off to attack them and Marine pilots in Grumman Wildcats and Douglas dive-bombers went out from Henderson Field to attack the same force. The enemy ships, however, were concealed by heavy cloud formations which prevented our pilots from finding them. At sundown the planes returned to Henderson Field. A striking group from one of the carriers also landed there, spent the night, refueled, rearmed, and returned to its carrier.

The enemy task force was still intact, and getting closer to Guadalcanal, but the night passed much as any other on the island. A supply ship unloading at Kukum was the target of a Japanese torpedo in the evening, but the torpedo missed its mark and skidded up on the beach, where it was the object of much curiosity, exercised at a respectful distance. At two in the morning Oscar the Submarine shelled us for a few minutes. Nothing else indicated that anything out of the ordinary was happening.

On the 24th the action grew livelier. Our carrier planes located one of the enemy carrier groups and attacked, scoring hits on a carrier (the small *Ruyjo*), a cruiser, and a destroyer. The Japanese had found our carriers, too, and a few of their dive-bombers got through the screen of fighter planes to hit the flight deck of one of our carriers. Meanwhile, the Japanese staged a big air raid on Henderson Field — and paid for it heavily. A large flight of bombers, some twin-engined, some single-engined, came over Guadalcanal escorted by Zeros. The Marine Wildcats got into their formations and shot down twenty-one enemy planes — five twin-engined bombers, five single-engined bombers, and eleven Zero fighters. Our losses were three Wildcats and their Marine pilots. That night eleven dive-bombers from the carrier which the Japanese had hit landed on Henderson Field and thereafter flew side by side with the Marine pilots operating from the field.

We spent another tense night, wondering if the Japanese

were closing in. They had several carriers in the vicinity and a heavy dawn air raid seemed likely. At midnight Japanese destroyers made a run past Lunga Point shelling our position. The moon was bright and dive-bombers took off from Henderson Field to attack the destroyers. Three groups went up. The first group found four destroyers near the northwest end of Florida Island, dived to attack, scored a possible hit on one destroyer, and strafed their decks. The second group of dive-bombers failed to make contact, but the third flight found the destroyers again and scored a direct hit on one. At four in the morning, after the moon had set, two Japanese planes swept over the airfield, strafing and dropping bombs, but caused no damage.

The next day, the 25th, was the most active for our planes on Henderson Field and ended with disruption of the enemy transport force which had been hovering off the island. Early in the morning a striking force of Navy and Marine dive-bombers took off from Henderson Field to seek out a force of seven or eight Japanese warships and four transports. As they passed over the northwest end of Florida, they saw below them long oil slicks on the scene of the dive-bombers' moon-light attack earlier in the morning. At eight-thirty-five they found an enemy force of one light cruiser, six or seven destroyers, and four transports, including one transport of fourteen thousand tons. The dive-bombers scored two direct hits on the Jintsu-class cruiser, almost certainly sinking her, and a hit on the big transport. Another bomb fell very close to the fantail of another transport — close enough to do heavy damage. Two cruiser-type planes were foolish enough to attack the dive-bombers and were shot down.

Major Richard C. Mangrum, leading the Marine and Navy bombers in their attack, found that his bomb had failed to release, and as the other bombers turned back to Henderson Field after finishing their run, he returned to drop his own bomb. He found the big transport blazing and floundering helplessly. The stricken cruiser was beginning to settle. He planted his bomb close to a destroyer and rejoined his flight.

In the afternoon the dive-bombers returned to the attack. Three Navy and six Marine planes scouted for seventy miles around the area where the Japanese ships had been found in the morning. They saw large oil patches on the sea below them, but no sign of the ships until they found one lone destroyer, trailing oil and making heavy way off the north coast of Santa Ysabel. They were after bigger game and ignored the destroyer until a thorough search had failed to uncover the rest of the Japanese ships. Then they returned and bombed the destroyer. No direct hits were scored, but all fell close.

Meanwhile, twenty-one Japanese twin-engined bombers made their noontime visit to Henderson Field. In the heaviest raid yet made on Guadalcanal they dropped more than forty bombs, killing four and wounding five Marines.

In the three days of skirmishing the Japanese carriers had lost so many planes that they had to return to base for replenishments. The American and Japanese naval forces withdrew from the area. The first substantial seaborne invasion of Guadalcanal had been turned back.

MORE ACTION AT KOKUMBONA

When the Japanese transports had turned back after the Battle of the Eastern Solomons, the Marines again looked to the west across the Matanikau. The village by that name had already proved a thorn in the flesh. There the Goettge patrol had met disaster. Several patrol skirmishes and the action of August 19 had killed some of the two or three hundred Japanese concentrated there, but the area remained a rendezvous point for enemy forces, and the nucleus of Japanese strength built up on the western end of Guadalcanal in later weeks.

August 27 another effort, again inconclusive, was made to rid the area of Japanese. The First Battalion, Fifth Marines, under Lieutenant Colonel W. E. Maxwell, was to land from Higgins boats east of Kokumbona, sweep through the coastal area between the shore and the mountains from Kokumbona to Matanikau, and join Company I of the Third Battalion, which was to move westward from the Matanikau River.

The First Battalion embarked at Kukum at five-thirty in the morning and began landing on the beach one thousand yards east of Kokumbona about an hour later. They met no resistance and all troops landed safely. Company D then began moving up along the coast, its left on the beach. Company C was in contact on B's right flank and had a patrol on the ridge about three hundred yards inland. Company C, however, had trouble cutting through the jungle along the ridge and was ordered to follow Company B. Headquarters Company followed and Company A formed the rear guard, destroying the village of Kokumbona as they passed through. The village was deserted and the Marines met no resistance until they got about one thousand yards east of the village.

There the leading platoon of Company B was caught in an enemy cross-fire from machine guns and mortars on the beach and on the ridge where the enemy left flank appeared to be. The encounter started about ten o'clock in the morning and for several hours the exchange of rifle, mortar, and automatic arms fire continued.

In the early stages of the fight nine men from the second platoon of Company B had fallen under enemy fire. They lay well forward of the company position, wounded, helpless, and exposed to heavy enemy fire. Four members of Company B won the Navy Cross by their heroism in rescuing the wounded. First Lieutenant Walter S. McIlhenny, in command of the platoon which was caught in the enemy cross-fire, organized the volunteer party that evacuated the wounded from their exposed position in front of the company. McIlhenny covered the rescuers, showing himself to draw enemy fire while they advanced on their voluntary mission. Later, although shocked by the concussion from a mortar shell, he acted as forward observer for Marine mortar fire near the enemy lines. Privates First Class Emmett R. Morris and

Wesley P. Simmonds, two members of the rescue party, were wounded as they tried to reach their stricken comrades. One of the nine wounded men was Private Bernard Fetchko. One of his comrades had already tried to rescue Fetchko, only to fall wounded himself, when Private Robert J. Hilsky made a second attempt. Through heavy mortar, machine-gun, and sniper fire he crawled out toward the wounded men. A mortar shell exploded almost at his side and stunned him, but he continued on toward Fetchko and succeeded in carrying him back to safety.

While Company B was pinned down, Company C tried to work along the beach on the enemy's right flank, and a patrol from Company B, consisting of a rifle platoon and a machine-gun platoon, was put on the ridge to try to turn the left flank. Their advance was slow in the face of heavy mortar fire and little progress had been made by the middle of the afternoon.

The original plans called for a withdrawal from the area before nightfall, and at two-thirty Lieutenant Colonel Maxwell sent a message requesting that boats be sent to pick up his battalion. Instead of withdrawing them, however, Colonel Hunt, Commanding Officer of the Fifth Marines, ordered them to remain overnight to continue the attack and himself assumed command. The troops bivouacked on the rolling grassy ridge about five hundred yards inland, where they spent an uneventful night.

The next morning, at five-forty-five, Company C started moving through the jungle, with Company B in the center on the ridge and Company A on the right flank. The three companies combed the area to the east and met at a point directly in front of the enemy's main prepared positions, now deserted. They found strong emplacements, with a well-cleared field of fire, extending from a fifty-foot cliff on the left to the beach. Behind these positions were secondary lines of defense all the way back to Matanikau. The enemy, taking a lesson from the Marine attack on the 19th, had anticipated an attack from the west.

All buildings, ammunition, and food found in the sweep from Kokumbona to Matanikau were destroyed. Little food or ammunition, however, was found and the enemy had left no weapons behind. The Japanese had withdrawn after the contact on the 27th, taking everything they could with them. The action thus ended inconclusively and Matanikau remained available to the enemy. Later the area became the scene of the most prolonged fighting on Guadalcanal.

JAPANESE REINFORCEMENTS

After the Battle of the Eastern Solomons, the Japanese were reluctant to send down slow, vulnerable transports loaded with supplies and equipment so long as we had planes based on Henderson Field which found such ships easy targets. They developed much less costly plans for sending reinforcements to their forces on Guadalcanal.

They used two methods. One was to send in speedy destroyers with deckloads of men and equipment, unload them about midnight, then dash away in the early morning hours. Destroyers which can twist and turn at high speed under bombing attack are hard targets for bombers. Moreover, their speed enabled them to be so far from Guadalcanal when our morning search planes found them that they sometimes were out of bombing range by the time striking forces could be sent after them. We had only dive-bombers, relatively short-ranged, on Henderson Field. Long-range bombers could have struck at the destroyers speeding for home.

The second method used by the Japanese was to load men and equipment into large ocean-going landing boats and send them down from bases in the northwest Solomons by easy stages. Transports brought the soldiers to Shortland Island, where the men were transferred to the boats. At night the boats crossed from Shortland to the northwest end of Santa Ysabel, from there to the southern end of the island, and finally to Cape Esperance on Guadalcanal. During the day the

Japanese hauled their boats up on the beach out of sight and the men lay in concealment if our planes came over. The next night they pushed on to a point nearer Guadalcanal and finally they arrived at Cape Esperance.

The first known venture of enemy surface craft into the channel between Guadalcanal and Florida occurred August 19, the day of the Marine attack against Matanikau and Kokumbona. Just before dawn destroyers (large ones, possibly cruisers) shelled Higgins boats on anti-submarine patrol and sank two of them. After Company I had landed at Kokumbona, one of the Japanese ships shelled the landing boats engaged in that operation and in the ensuing confusion four of them were abandoned. Two planes, apparently cruiser-borne, twice strafed Company I during the day. The enemy ships had the freedom of the waters off our position until a Flying Fortress, summoned from Espiritu Santo when the destroyers were sighted, attacked them, scored a direct hit on one and sent it limping away. In the light of later developments, particularly the action at the Tenaru, it appeared likely that these ships had earlier landed troops east of the Marines' position.

After midnight of the 23d, destroyers shelled the Lunga Point area. Those were the destroyers that were pursued by dive-bombers from Henderson Field in a moonlight chase off the northwest coast of Florida.

After the Battle of the Eastern Solomons, visits by enemy destroyers to the shores of Guadalcanal became more and more frequent. The evening of the 28th our evening patrol of dive-bombers sighted four ships — three large destroyers and one small one — only seventy miles north of Guadalcanal and headed south. The patrol planes that found them (two Douglas dive-bombers) attacked and hit the small destroyer. Immediately eleven more dive-bombers took off from Henderson Field and attacked the enemy ships. After a direct hit, one destroyer blew up and sank. Another was hit amidships behind the stack and began to blaze. The small destroyer, when last seen by the pilots, was low in the water, trailing oil, and smoking. The fourth escaped into a rain squall, apparently undamaged. Our pilots saw considerable gear piled on the decks of the ships, indicating that they carried supplies or reinforcements for the Japanese detachments on Guadalcanal.

We kept planes in the air at night during the moonlit nights late in August, trying to locate Japanese ships that slipped in to unload east or west of our position. Just after midnight on the 30th, a patrol spotted an enemy force of at least two cruisers and two destroyers lying close to the shore off Taivu Point, about twenty miles east of us, and apparently landing troops. Our planes attacked, but could not observe the results, and ten more dive-bombers which immediately went out to resume the attack could not find the ships in the darkness. Probably they had dispersed after the first attack. Again, the night of September 1–2, an aerial patrol found enemy warships — three destroyers this time — unloading troops and supplies near Taivu Point, and again the enemy force dispersed after the bombers attacked them.

Although some attempted landings were thus discovered and broken up, the enemy was steadily building up a considerable force near Taivu Point. Early in September we learned that the Japanese were also building up a force west of us, by landings near Cape Esperance.

September 3 patrol planes discovered that the Japanese were landing in near-by islands — staging points on their journey to Guadalcanal. They found two small boats and several larger landing craft landing troops near Mufu Point, on the southern shore of Santa Ysabel Island near its southern end. The patrol planes dropped their bombs and strafed the enemy craft, and twelve more dive-bombers immediately took off to continue the attack. They found thirteen boats, about forty feet long and well camouflaged, between Mufu Point and San Jorge Island. The planes bombed the boats and left them sunk or burning, and also found about thirty more landing craft, some of them seventy feet long, in a cove on the southwest side of San Jorge. Three groups of planes bombed and strafed these boats, destroying many. In all these attacks the pilots saw no Japanese soldiers on the beaches near the boats.

Early the next morning our patrol planes intercepted fifteen large landing boats, each carrying about seventy-five men, approaching Cape Esperance on the northwestern tip of Guadalcanal. The patrol planes sank three of the boats by strafing, and other planes joined the attack, bombing and strafing the boats as they approached Esperance and after they were drawn up on the beach.

Again on the 6th and 7th our planes spotted landing boats on the southeastern end of Santa Ysabel — ten or twelve one day and eighteen landing barges the next.

MARINE RAID ON TASIMBOKO

The first blow against the Japanese force which was being built up near Taivu Point was struck September 8, when the First Raider Battalion under Colonel Edson raided the enemy position and destroyed large quantities of supplies and equipment.

The Raiders, with the First Parachute Battalion in reserve, embarked at Kukum on two destroyers converted to serve as transports and two smaller patrol boats. Before dawn the ships began bombarding the enemy shore positions and the Raiders began landing just east of Taivu Point. Companies B and C of the Raiders went in the first wave, landing at five-twenty. Company C secured the left flank on the beachhead while B began advancing to the west, toward the Kema River. The second wave — Companies A and D — landed from the patrol boats and started ashore at six-fifteen. Airacobras and dive-bombers from Henderson Field attacked enemy positions throughout the day, helping to break their resistance at Tasimboko and harassing them farther west.

The Marines didn't meet any opposition on the beach. It

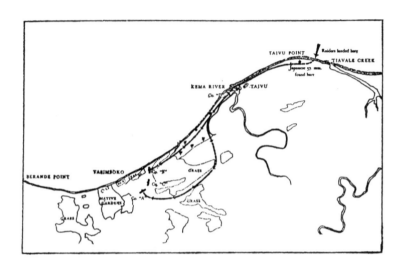

TASKIMBOKO — EDSON'S RAIDERS STRUCK HERE

was not until about eight o'clock that the Raiders ran into slight Japanese opposition about half a mile west of the Kema River. The Raiders had landed behind the enemy position and the main body had pulled out. As Colonel Edson said, the Raiders 'came in the back door.' The enemy, as we learned, were ready to oppose an attack from the west, from the direction of our position, but hadn't prepared for an assault from the rear.

About five hundred yards west of the landing point a thirty-seven-millimeter gun was found, pointing northward to the sea. Around the position the Raiders found about fifty brand-new packs belonging to Japanese soldiers, with new shoes, new shelter-halves, and other kinds of personal gear — all apparently unused.

The plan of attack called for an enveloping movement on Tasimboko by two companies, to cross the stream tributary to the Kema which runs parallel to the shoreline west of the Kema, then to recross the stream south of the village, encircling any enemy force that might be in the village.

The Kema tributary, however, turned out to be deep and marshy — almost impossible to cross without a bridge. The Raiders found themselves, after crossing the Kema, confined in the narrow space between the tributary and the beach, in such a position that no more than one company could deploy in attack formation. Company B was farthest west, toward Tasimboko. Company A was to its left and rear and Company C was behind the other two. At about eight-thirty Company A, Reinforced, started along the bank of the tributary to get south of Tasimboko. The going, through the thick jungle, was so hard that it took them three hours to get into position behind the village.

About halfway between the Kema and the village the Raiders ran into some opposition. The Japanese opened up with seventy-five-millimeter field pieces, but the fire had little effect. Two Marines, however, were killed when a seventy-five shell, fired from only one hundred yards, burst in the trees over their heads. One seventy-five-millimeter piece was firing from the coastal path just west of the Kema. A runner from Company B shot the gunners after they had fired about twenty rounds. Scattered artillery, machine-gun, and rifle fire continued to harass the Marines advancing on Tasimboko, but did not pin them down.

About one-thirty in the afternoon the three companies which had been advancing westward — A, B, and C — closed in on the village of Tasimboko and found it deserted. Meanwhile, Company D, given the job of demolishing Japanese stores, weapons, and dumps found by the Raiders in their advance, followed the other companies, performing their mission of destruction.

Earlier in the day Colonel Edson had hoped to bring back some or all of the captured field pieces. In all four seventy-five-millimeter guns and two thirty-seven-millimeters were found. When the enemy withdrew before the Raiders, however, giving them freedom to sweep farther westward than they had thought possible, it appeared that there would not be time to load captured equipment. Most of it, including the six field guns, was destroyed. Large dumps of ammunition, medical supplies, and food were found all the way from Taivu Point to Tasimboko. Combat equipment in great variety was found — machine guns, rifles, flame-throwers, land mines, and hand grenades. A large radio was captured and brought back to Kukum after the generator was destroyed.

There was no contact with the enemy after twelve-thirty, and when the Raiders had completed as much demolition work as time permitted, they re-embarked from the beach near Tasimboko, starting about three-thirty. The Parachutists, who had landed west of the Kema as reserve for the Raiders, were never committed to action.

By five o'clock the raiding party was on its way back to Kukum. They had caused twenty-seven known casualties by rifle fire, had lost two killed and a few wounded. The most important result of the raid was the destruction of large quantities of supplies and equipment which the Japanese had slowly accumulated in the Tasimboko area. Their beachhead to the east of us had been wiped out.

As we learned later, the main body of Japanese whch had landed near Taivu Point had already begun to move west along the beach at the time of the raid. They had left only a small, inexperienced rear guard to protect the beachhead and they had fled, after putting up a weak show of resistance, as the Raiders attacked.

For a long time the Japanese thought that we had not only raided Tasimboko, but occupied it. They never again tried to use it as a landing point.

PART TWO

Chapter 5

~~~~~~

Battle of the Ridge

R EPORTS FROM MARINE PATROLS indicated
that the enemy forces that had landed in the Taivu
Point area were quickly moving up to attack the Marines'
position around the airport. As the week wore on, after the
raid on Tasimboko, patrol contacts became more frequent.
At the same time the enemy sent more and more planes over
Guadalcanal. The new enemy drive culminated in the nights
of September 12 and 13, when the Japanese launched their
main effort on land from the south of our position, supported
by naval gunfire at night and air raids by day.

Beginning September 9, after a lull in aerial activity, the
enemy sent over formations of twenty-six or twenty-seven
bombers each day, escorted by Zero fighters. On the 9th
their targets were two supply ships and their escort returning
to the area to continue unloading after withdrawing during
the night. The bombers scored no hits and five of them
were shot down. The Japanese also lost four Zeros in this
encounter. Two of our fighter planes were badly damaged
and two were missing. The pilot of one, Captain Marion
E. Carl, an ace who already had eleven planes to his credit,
later made his way back to our lines with the help of friendly
natives.

The next day twenty-seven twin-engined bombers covered by thirty Zeros bombed our position, killing eleven and wounding fourteen. Again, on the 11th and 12th, formations of twenty-six twin-engined bombers came over.

Our planes shot down six bombers and one Zero on the 11th, while we lost one Grumman Wildcat, but recovered the pilot. That evening twenty-four more Grummans and three Douglas dive-bombers arrived to reinforce the steadily dwindling number of aircraft on Henderson Field. The raid of the 12th cost the enemy three bombers shot down by anti-aircraft fire and seven bombers and four Zeros shot down by fighters. One of our fighters crashed and the pilot was killed. In this raid the base radio station was demolished, some gasoline was destroyed, and three dive-bombers were burned on the ground.

Meanwhile, Marine patrols learned that the enemy was moving in from the east. By the 10th an enemy force was less then five miles east of our lines, cutting a road to the south. The same day a Japanese patrol was seen moving into Matanikau village to the west. The next day we learned that natives were evacuating their villages on the Malimbiu River before a large enemy force and that the enemy had advanced in force to the area between the Malimbiu River and Tenavatu, building a road through the bush capable of taking field guns.

The persistent air attacks and enemy land movements presaged an early attack, which started the night of September 12 with intermittent naval shelling throughout the night and spirited patrol action to the rear of our position. When the enemy activity was first observed, the eastern sector, where the apparent threat lay, had been manned by moving the Third Battalion, First Marines, commanded by Lieutenant Colonel William M. McKelvy, into position along the Tenaru River south of the area attacked by the enemy on August 21, which was already strongly defended by the First Battalion, First Marines. The First Raider and First Parachute Battalions, which had been very active throughout the first month of the Solomons campaign, were moved to the

sector south of the airfield.   In the little area we held on
Guadalcanal there was no such thing as a quiet spot where
men's nerves and bodies could rest, but the southern sector
was relatively quiet — at that time.   Their position on the
ridge south of the airfield, however, turned out to be the point
of the enemy's strongest attack.   They discovered the enemy
activity in front of their lines and put a strong outpost well
south on the ridge.

The ridge in question extends from a point about a mile
south of the main runway of Henderson Field for about one
thousand yards southward toward the mountains.   Its upper
slopes are grassy, with thick jungle in the ravines below.
Several spurs extend east and west of the main ridge line and
three distinct summits or knobs rise from the backbone.   The
ridge is nameless, a place of no interest to map-makers and
place-namers before the battle.   Now, whenever a Marine
then on Guadalcanal hears of 'The Ridge,' he thinks of the
winding chain of coral hills where the Japanese tried to break
through to the airfield in September.

Along one of the spurs the Division Command Post had
been set up.   (See sketch.)   In the first month of the campaign
the Command Post had been located on the inland side of a
low coral ridge northwest of the main runway at the edge of
Henderson Field.   It was a convenient location, roughly in
the center of the Marine position, but we soon began to call it
'Impact Center.'   The area always caught a few bombs as the
Japanese planes made their runs over Henderson Field and
several times bombs straddled the Command Post, showering
us with coral rock and bomb fragments.   It was decided to
move the nerve-center of Marine activities to a spot less favored as a target by enemy bombers.   September 9 we began
moving to an L-shaped spur of the Ridge south of the airfield.
A road winds up from the airfield, turns off along the bare
crest of the spur, and leads to a heavily wooded spot farther
along the crest where towering trees conceal the ground.   The
sides of the spur drop away steeply and in the ravines below

there is a tangle of jungle plants and creepers. Our tents were pitched along the crest of the Ridge and on the slopes on the seaward side. Some of us — unfortunately, as it turned out — set up our tents on the landward side at the foot of a steep slope. Incidentally, few officers and men had yet enjoyed the luxury of a tent since our arrival on Guadalcanal.

The Raiders and Parachutists had taken up their new positions and had just enough time to dig some foxholes and put in a little barbed wire. The right (west) flank of their line was fifty yards west of the Lunga River and extended across the Ridge and down to the east into the tall grass and heavy scrub.

At nine o'clock the night of the 12th came the signal of the enemy's approaching attack. An enemy plane dropped a flare over the airfield, the usual forerunner of a naval bombardment. As the eerie light filled the sky we rushed from our sleeping places. Those who had them went to dugouts, but in the new Command Post few had such shelters. We could only drop to the ground and hope for the best in what was coming.

The Raiders and Parachutists had planned to move out in force the next morning and make contact with the enemy force known to be south and east of their lines. Company commanders, after getting their instructions, had just left Colonel Edson's Command Post, in a ravine a quarter of a mile down the Ridge from the Division Command Post, when the bombardment started. At nine-thirty cruisers and destroyers which had entered the strait between Guadalcanal and Florida opened fire and for twenty minutes bombarded the shore east of our position. The sound of boats operating to the east and northeast, out toward Koli Point, could be heard, indicating that the Japanese were landing troops under cover of the bombardment. In the Command Post we hugged the earth on the landward side of the Ridge while some salvos screamed overhead to crash in the jungle behind.

Then a rocket flare fired by Japanese troops south of us signaled the end of the bombardment and their readiness to

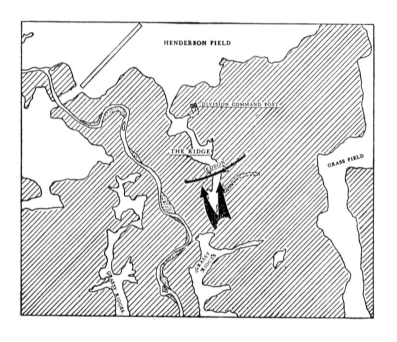

BATTLE OF THE RIDGE — GUADALCANAL

attack. Long dripping fingers of phosphorescent light stretched over our heads, hung there for a few minutes illuminating the ground below, and faded out in smoky streamers. The enemy facing Colonel Edson's lines went into action.

Strong groups of Japanese pushed through between Company C on the right flank and Company B on the Ridge in the middle. To confuse the Marines and draw fire while detachments infiltrated our lines, the Japanese talked loudly and made noise on the flanks. Then, after groups had infiltrated, they began to fire on the Marines from the rear. While the Raiders were occupied with this threat, another enemy group slipped in and cut the barbed wire along the advanced position.

The enemy then launched a frontal attack and the right flank platoon of Company C was forced out of position. Platoon Sergeant Lawren A. Harrison was in a group overrun and isolated by the Japanese. He took charge of the men cut off from the main body, directed machine-gun fire with such effect that the enemy was stopped, and at dawn he led the Marines back through a ring of Japanese. Strong parties of Japanese swam the Lunga River and sought to envelop C Company, attacking from both flanks and forcing the company to drop back in order to maintain its line. When Company C moved back, Company B also retired in order to keep contact. The new position was held and toward morning the enemy moved back from the immediate front.

Private John W. Mielke helped largely to hold the Japanese attack. He stuck by his machine gun under heavy enemy fire from three directions, driving off Japanese trying to capture his gun. He killed six of the attackers and kept the machine gun, covering the withdrawal to the reserve line.

There was little enemy activity on the Tenaru River front that night and none at all to the west. Apparently the main Japanese forces had not yet moved into position.

At midnight the Japanese warships had again begun to shell our position and for forty-five minutes their fire swept

the airfield and our lines. Then, as flares announced the end
of the bombardment, the Japanese patrols to the south again
hit Edson's lines. From one o'clock in the morning until
dawn Louie the Louse, the Japanese spotter plane, droned
back and forth over our position. All was dark below him,
except for the flashes of small-arms fire, mortars, and hand
grenades where the Raiders and Parachutists were mixing it
up with the Japanese along the Ridge. One impatient anti-
aircraft gunner on the airfield sent a stream of tracers toward
Louie's approximate position, but his only reward was the
sound of the plane's engine speeding up a bit. The pest continued to cruise over the field. At three o'clock in the morning the Japanese ships bombarded Tulagi for a few minutes,
then withdrew. They had stayed uncommonly late, for usually they wanted to be far out to sea before our planes took off
at dawn. They would be back the next night.

On the morning of the 13th, Colonel Edson sent Company
A and Company D, which had been held in reserve, up a
branch of the Lunga River in an attempt to regain his original
position and strengthen the right of Company B. The Japanese, however, had dug in at their farthermost point of advance and Company A could not dislodge them during the
day. At three o'clock in the afternoon, when Company A
reported back, Colonel Edson decided to shorten his line. He
moved his forces back to a high, rugged knoll some two hundred yards behind the previous position. At the same time
Company B of the First Engineers was attached to Company
B of the Raiders to strengthen the center of the line.

The front covered about eighteen hundred yards. From
left to right there were two eighty-man companies of Parachutists, Company B of the Raiders on the Ridge itself and
Company A on the right flank. Company C had taken the
brunt of the attack the night before and was pulled to the rear
as battalion reserve. They were situated on a knoll about one
hundred and fifty yards back of the front lines.

Rugged terrain on the right was a source of worry. There

were intervals of about one hundred yards between platoon strong-points. It was a thin, tenuous line of only four hundred men. They dug in, however, and prepared to meet the attack which night would bring. Telephonic communications were established with the rear.

There were four air alerts on the 13th. At five-ten in the morning, as Louie the Louse finally left us, a formation of unidentified aircraft approached from the northwest, but turned back before it reached Guadalcanal. At ten-twenty twenty-six Zeros came over Henderson Field and were engaged by twenty-eight Grummans. Three hours later twenty-eight twin-engined bombers covered by Zeros were intercepted by twenty Grummans and jettisoned their bombs fifteen miles away. In these encounters four enemy bombers and four Zeros were shot down, while we lost two Grummans and two pilots. At five-fifty two single float-seaplanes sneaked in at low altitude, shot down a Dauntless dive-bomber approaching to land, flew over the field, and escaped out to sea.

The enemy's main effort against the Ridge was launched at six-thirty that night. The Japanese struck at the center of Colonel Edson's line and at the same time a strong enemy force moved down the lagoon to hit the right platoon of B Company. The platoon fell back under the assault, was forced out of line, and almost completely surrounded. The platoon, however, fought its way out of the pocket and joined Company C in the rear. Their withdrawal left a gap of almost two hundred and fifty yards in the line, which the enemy was quick to exploit. Strong enemy parties moved through the opening, cutting all telephonic communications. Contact between units was re-established, however, by the use of portable radio equipment.

Then the pressure began in earnest down the Ridge in the center of the line. Colonel Edson learned of the gap and pulled in Company B to connect the flanks. The main enemy thrust, which reached full strength about ten-thirty, was down the Ridge against Company B and the Parachutists. Colonel

Edson estimated there were fifteen hundred to two thousand enemy troops in front of him. He then had only about three hundred men holding the Ridge.

At the height of the fighting, about eleven, a Japanese cruiser and two destroyers shelled the Kukum area. The enemy surface force was still hanging about, waiting for their ground forces to signal that they had swept out on the airfield.

The Japanese used a smoke-screen to cover their advance and shouted, 'Gas attack! Gas attack!' in English in an attempt to demoralize the defenders. The Japanese finally got their mortar fire to bear on the Parachutists and drove them back on the left. Company B of the Raiders, less the platoon that had been knocked out earlier, was holding the Ridge all by itself. Just sixty men held the enemy advance at this point.

By walkie-talkie radio Captain John B. Sweeney, commanding Company B, called Colonel Edson and asked for instructions. They identified each other, then Colonel Edson asked the Captain what his situation was at the moment. It was obvious that the enemy had learned the Raiders' wave length when a cultured voice, using a kind of academic English hardly expected from a Marine in the heat of battle, broke in and said, 'My position is excellent, thank you.'

Captain Sweeney's position was far from excellent and Colonel Edson knew it. The company was ringed in by Japanese and was receiving rifle, mortar, and machine-gun fire from all directions. Colonel Edson instructed Company B to pull back to the reserve line. Just as the company began to withdraw, the enemy launched another attack.

Our artillery had been firing steadily all night and now their heavy pounding was decisive in breaking up the Japanese attack. Batteries of seventy-five-millimeter pack howitzers and 105-millimeter howitzers had been brought into positions just north of the Ridge, and all night long round after round whistled over the Division Command Post toward the enemy lines. At first friend and foe were so mixed up, the range could not be brought down enough to stop the enemy. Twice artillery officers acting as forward observers were out of communications with their batteries as the enemy swarmed around them and cut the wires. As Company B started to pull back to the last hump of the Ridge, however, the artillery concentrated on the intervening gap and laid down deadly concentrations at Colonel Edson's urgent request. 'Perfect,' came the report from the front lines, 'now march it back and forth.' The artillery 'marched it' and the effect was deadly to the enemy. Two prisoners captured after the battle used the same word to describe its effect, saying that their units caught in the barrage were 'zemetsu' — annihilated. One estimated that perhaps ten per cent of his company got away through the barrage. .

Under cover of the artillery Colonel Edson re-formed his lines. Everyone in the fight gave high praise to Major Kenneth D. Bailey, Commanding Officer of Company C, for the successful resistance during this critical period. At a time when our line was badly shattered, when the morale of individuals was beginning to give under the strain of hours of steady fighting and sleeplessness, and when great confusion existed, Major Bailey, by his coolness, efficiency, and personal bravery in walking calmly about under heavy fire shouting encouragement to the men, did much to straighten out the situation and create a solid front. He was awarded the Medal of Honor for his extraordinary performance that night.

There was an apparent lull about two-thirty, when the artillery seemed to have checked any further Japanese advance. By four-thirty, however, the enemy had quietly pushed patrols around to the left rear of Colonel Edson's lines, near the Division Command Post and started to lay mortar and machine-gun fire against them from the rear, but it was ineffective to dislodge them.

Of the Marines who gave their lives in that night of bitter fighting, some had particularly distinguished themselves. Major Robert S. Brown, Colonel Edson's Operations Officer, had reorganized the defenders when they began to fall back under enemy pressure and put them into action again. He took up a position in a part of the line threatened by a break-through and there fell wounded by a hand grenade. He was taken to an ambulance, but as it was leaving, a Japanese machine-gunner riddled the car and killed Major Brown.

Private First Class Herman F. Arnold, a radio operator with the Raiders, was separated from his own platoon and unable to find them again in the mêlée. On his own initiative he made his way to the very front line, joined in the fight, and gave his life.

Private First Class Jimmy W. Corzine worked his way forward along the Ridge and found four Japanese setting up a machine gun in a commanding position. He rushed the enemy group, bayoneted their leader, chased the other three away, captured the machine gun, and turned it against the enemy. He fired the gun until the ammunition was gone, then disabled it and continued to hold his position stubbornly until he fell mortally wounded. Sergeant Daniel W. Hudspeth was killed in one of the attacks he repeatedly led against Japanese positions.

Others showed a volunteer spirit, a willingness to join in the fight when duty did not require it, that won them the high honor of the Navy Cross. In fighting of the type that took place that night on the Ridge, men who must move about with loads of ammunition or who carry wounded comrades from the battlefield are fully exposed to enemy fire and almost helpless to fight back. Theirs are particularly hazardous jobs, yet many performed them voluntarily. Private Robert G. Schneider, on his own initiative and without orders, helped move up machine and mortar ammunition badly needed in the battle. Sergeant Francis C. Pettus, attached to the Intelligence Section, performed reconnaissance missions for Colonel Edson during the battle, carried up ammunition to forward positions, and helped to evacuate the wounded. Private First Class William Barnes, gunner in a mortar section, kept up a steady fire as long as he could, helped evacuate the wounded from the battlefield, carried up ammunition, and finally, of his own accord, joined the front-line units in their close-quarters fight against the Japanese. Private Nicholas A. Willox, assistant gunner in a mortar section, kept up a steady and accurate fire as long as he had ammunition. Then he helped move up ammunition and evacuate the wounded and in the final hours of the battle he joined the front-line units where he was wounded by a grenade.

Lieutenant Commander E. P. McLarney (M.C., U.S.N.) and eight of the Medical Corpsmen who worked with him were awarded Navy Crosses for their bravery under fire in carrying wounded men from the battlefield and tending their wounds. The Japanese advance threatened Doctor McLarney's first-aid station, but even when heavy fire was coming from the front and flank of the station, he continued to work and aided two hundred casualties. The corpsmen who won Navy Crosses in the Battle of the Ridge were Pharmacist's Mates First Class Delbert D. Eilers and Albern M. Potter, Jr., Pharmacist's Mates Second Class Wilber L. Marsh, Karl B. Coleman, and William Bruce Kincannon, and Pharmacist's Mates Third Class Lloyd T. Mathis, Gerald E. Roebuck, and Thaddeus Parker.

Corporal Walter J. Burak served as messenger for Colonel Edson. He was constantly under fire trying to keep the Colonel in touch with his subordinate commanders. When the telephone lines to the Division Command Post were broken by the enemy and the Raiders' communications were cut off except for radio, Burak repaired a break in the wire under heavy fire and later laid a direct wire from an observation post to the Division Command Post.

Platoon Sergeant Stanley D. Kops commanded a platoon in Company C which had been hard hit in the center of the Ridge. He held his position at first against great odds, and when he was ordered to fall back he organized another platoon of men who had been separated from their own units in the chaos of battle and led his impromptu command in a successful hand-to-hand attack.

By five-fifteen the morning of the 14th there was every indication that the enemy pressure had ceased. Colonel Whaling had come across the airfield early in the morning with the Second Battalion, Fifth Marines, to back up the Raiders and Parachutists as they fell back toward the airfield. These Marines helped strengthen the line and push the enemy back along the Ridge. At dawn airplanes joined the fight and time after time the Airacobras swooped low to strafe concentrations of Japanese withdrawing to the west and south.

The attack along the Ridge was the enemy's main effort. However, the same night he launched attacks against our lines on the eastern and western flanks. The Third Battalion, First Marines, commanded by Lieutenant Colonel W. N. McKelvy, Jr., occupied a sector of the defense perimeter east of the airfield, running from the Tenaru southwestward toward the Ridge. The attack was concentrated against K Company, commanded by Captain Robert J. Putnam. The company protected the east end of a trail cut through the coconut grove from the airfield to a grassy field on the east. The Marine line stretched along the western edge of the field and barbed wire had been put in there. On the far side of the plain, however, four listening posts were established to check on enemy movements. In the one on the right flank was Lieutenant Joseph A. Terzi.

At about nine o'clock the night of the 13th, outposts of the Second Battalion, First Marines, near the mouth of the Tenaru, observed small enemy patrols moving southward through the coconut grove. At nine-fifteen the Japanese began firing into the center of Company K and at eleven-thirty the listening post where Lieutenant Terzi was stationed was overrun by the Japanese and only one man made his way back to our lines.

Captain Putnam then withdrew the three other listening posts and called for artillery fire into the area where the enemy seemed to be concentrated. Suddenly the Japanese attacked toward the center of Company K in considerable numbers. They got as far as the wire and tried to break through, but there they were bayoneted by Marines. At intervals throughout the night they charged the wire and the mortar and artillery fire was almost constant. At five-thirty, just before daybreak, the enemy's pushes ceased, leaving the Third Battalion's lines intact. Estimated enemy casualties were about one hundred, and twenty-seven bodies were found in the wire in front of K Company. Marine losses were limited to four dead and three wounded.

During the morning of the 14th, all was quiet on the enemy side of the Tenaru sector. Thinking that the Japanese might be lying quietly in the tall grass awaiting nightfall, Lieutenant Colonel McKelvy ordered six tanks to sweep the entire grassy field. At nine-forty-five the tanks moved up to the area over the trail from the airfield and searched the tall grass thoroughly without incident. Lieutenant Terzi and one of his men who had been in the listening post out in the field made their way back through the grass to Company K lines with the information that enemy machine guns were located in a native hut on the eastern side of the plain. The tanks were again moved up, at eleven o'clock, to destroy the machine guns. They got within fifty yards of the shack where the machine guns were reported to be concealed when anti-tank guns opened up on them. Three tanks were put out of commission and four in the crews were killed. The crews of two tanks were rescued, but the third tank had toppled over into a stream, imprisoning the crew and making escape impossible for them. This tank was later salvaged, but the others were too badly smashed by armor-piercing bullets to be recommissioned.

At eleven o'clock that night the enemy's attack resumed, but it was weak and ineffective. Five Japanese were killed at the wire. The Japanese used light mortars in an attempt to blast an opening in the wire, but it was an ineffective effort.

At daybreak of the 15th a concentration of three hundred Japanese was seen well to the right flank of the First Battalion position and an artillery barrage was called for and laid directly on them. There was another light attack the night of the 15th, but it was small in scope and was held down by artillery fire.

Action on the west flank, held by the Fifth Marines at a point about halfway between Kukum and Matanikau, did not develop until about eight-thirty the morning of the 14th, when the main attack along the Ridge had already been broken up. Probably this attack was originally planned to coincide with the other two thrusts, but the enemy force in the west had been greatly weakened and delayed by the repeated bombing and strafing attacks delivered by our aircraft against landing boats and landing points in the Cape Esperance–Kokumbona area.

At eight-thirty there was a light attack on the wire in front of Company L, holding the left flank of the Marines' position in the coconut grove two hundred yards from the beach. It was a bayonet charge and was driven off with heavy losses to the enemy. Under the command of Lieutenant Colonel Frederick C. Biebush the Third Battalion, Fifth Marines, held the line throughout the day against several light attacks. Company K was to the right of L with a low ridge separating them. At one-thirty in the afternoon the Japanese made a light attack down the Ridge to feel out the position, but were driven off. I Company then moved out on the Ridge to the west as a patrol, with instructions to engage if necessary. They moved forward along the Ridge, encountered an enemy machine gun, put it out of commission, and moved back to their lines.

There was no further action in this area. The Japanese attack was notable by virtue of being the only occasion on which they undertook offensive operations against the Marines throughout the Guadalcanal campaign. The First Battalion, Fifth Marines (Major W. K. Enright), reinforced by the

Amphibious Tractor Battalion (Lieutenant Colonel W. W. Barr), was moved into position on the extreme left of the Marine line to strengthen the line in case the Japanese should resume the attack in greater force.

The Japanese attack, intended as a triple drive against our lines, had failed. The main effort, launched along the Ridge, had come close to success, but the two supporting attacks, west of Kukum and east of the airfield, were weak and ineffectual. The three attacks were poorly co-ordinated and the feint against the Fifth Marines in the west was not even begun until after the issue on the Ridge had been decided.

The Japanese had lost about five hundred in dead and unknown numbers in wounded. Our own losses in the Battle of the Ridge were eighty-three killed, two hundred and eighty-three wounded, and twenty-eight missing.

THE MOBILE COMMAND POST

It has been mentioned that the Division Command Post had been moved to a spur of the Ridge shortly before the battle — out of the frying-pan into the fire, as it turned out. The tents had scarcely been put up before the battle started.

Rear Admirals R. K. Turner, Commander of the South Pacific Amphibious Force, and J. S. McCain, Commander of Air for the South Pacific, had arrived at Guadalcanal September 12 and spent that night with Major General Vandegrift at the Command Post. As the Japanese ships shelled our position and their ground patrols began the drive against the Raiders' lines farther south on the Ridge, Headquarters personnel threw up a hasty skirmish line at the top of the spur running through the Command Post, wondering if a major attack would engulf the Ridge.

The enemy's main effort, as had been expected, was launched the next night. The first night's experience had demonstrated how vulnerable the new site would be to infiltration by Japanese soldiers through the thick underbrush under cover of darkness and precautions were taken to ensure that the Commanding General and his Staff were not caught in the net the enemy might throw about the spur. Secret files had already been removed to a place of greater safety during the clash of September 12. A defile to the north, toward the airfield, offered the safest line of withdrawal in case the Japanese should swarm about the hill. (See sketch, facing p. 94.)

Our worst fears were almost realized the night of the 13th. The battle line drew closer and closer to the Command Post as the Raiders were pushed back along the Ridge. Our artillery, firing from positions so close behind us that the firing orders could be clearly heard above the sound of battle, kept a steady stream of shells whistling over the Command Post at the advancing line of the Japanese. Two short bursts wounded several men near the Commanding General's shack. One gun, it turned out, had developed a defect and it was secured for the night to avoid any more such accidents. The next morning Major General Vandegrift called Colonel del Valle, commanding the Eleventh Marines, and the Colonel reported he thought the General was going to 'read him off' for firing into his Headquarters. The General, however, was calling to congratulate him on the splendid work done by the artillery in breaking up the Japanese attack.

After a lull about two o'clock in the morning, the fire fight rose to a new pitch of intensity very close to the Command Post. Japanese riflemen and machine-gunners had infiltrated our lines all around the spur we occupied. A light machine gun or automatic rifle kept up a constant chatter near-by, sending a stream of bullets over the crest of the Ridge. Officers in the Operations Section, exposed in an open tent on the crest of the Ridge, had to spend most of the time on the ground. Enemy fire was now coming from all directions. The previous day I had told one of the war correspondents then staying at Headquarters that, in a pinch, we could withdraw through the defile leading northward to the airfield. Next morning he commented, rather reproachfully, that the

defile had been covered by Japanese snipers and escape would
have been almost impossible.

Even after day broke and the Japanese withdrew to the
south, the sniper fire continued. For three days the Command
Post was under intermittent fire from Japanese concealed in
the tall trees surrounding the spur of the Ridge. Most of the
snipers were concentrated in the deep ravine south of the spur
and no one was permitted to go to the tents on that side of the
Ridge until patrols had cleaned the pests out. The morning
of the 14th a Japanese officer and two of his men emerged
from the underbrush at the top of the spur, at the edge of the
Command Post, and with a war-cry set upon a group of Marines sitting on the ground. One Marine was killed by a bayonet thrust before the others were able to cut down the Japanese. The officer and one man were killed, but the third escaped into the jungle.

In such difficult circumstances the Command Post continued to function. Since the communications center was located there, the Headquarters group could not quickly be
transferred to a spot less exposed to enemy fire. So operations continued on the spur during the daytime, then at dusk
the Headquarters personnel packed into jeeps and trucks and
moved down to the airfield to get a little sleep.

For two days and nights the ambulatory Command Post
functioned in this fashion, then on the third night it was decided that we would stay on the spur again. Night had
scarcely fallen when the shooting started again as Japanese
snipers and Marines exchanged shots. By this time it was beginning to seem normal for the Command Post to be under
rifle fire and no one seemed to mind very much. The purple
nights on the Ridge, however, led to a decision to move the
Command Post back to the edge of the airfield, and on the
18th the trek back across the airfield began. The night of the
19th, for the last time, we slept at 'Snipers' Roost' ('Bloody
Gulch' was the name more favored by some), and the firing
still continued. The next few days were taken up with con-

struction of the new, and we all hoped final, Command Post
on Guadalcanal.

The new establishment bore signs of permanence disturbing
to those who thought it high time that the First Marine Division be removed from Guadalcanal to some place where it
could organize for future offensive operations. George began
to think that he was destined to be part of the permanent garrison Guadalcanal. One veteran officer summed up many
men's thoughts on the subject. 'You can't put assault troops
behind barbed wire and expect them to keep the offensive
spirit. They get dugout-minded. I saw it happen in the last
war and it will happen here if this outfit isn't taken off soon.'

Tents were put up for all personnel. Walks of dry cement
and gravel were built at the Command Post. New dugouts,
bigger and sturdier than earlier ones and covered with heavy
palm logs, were made by the Engineers. The new tents had
wooden decks, almost unknown in earlier Guadalcanal quarters. Canvas cots and mosquito bars arrived for officers and
men. The Commanding General got a shower bath, fed by a
pipeline from the Lunga.

Another Marine regiment arrived to reinforce our defenses. A long respite from air raids, lasting two weeks, gave a
false feeling that all was quiet in the Solomons. But the campaign had scarcely begun. Soon the moon, now bright over
Guadalcanal, would wane and the Japanese would be ready
for another night attack. Their shuttle service between
Guadalcanal and island bases to the northwest continued.
The betting was that the lull would end about October 1.

SEVENTH MARINES ARRIVE

Sunday evening, September 6, Colonel James W. Webb,
then commanding the Seventh Marines, had arrived at Guadalcanal with some of his Staff. Soon after our initial landing
on Guadalcanal, Major General Vandegrift had urged that
the Seventh Marines be sent to the island to reinforce our

insecure toehold. Colonel Webb's appearance, of course, started a round of scuttlebutt to the effect that the regiment would soon arrive.

The Seventh Marines, one of the three infantry regiments of the First Marine Division, had preceded the rest of the Division overseas. In the spring of 1942 they had gone to Samoa as part of the garrison of those islands. Now it appeared they were about to rejoin the Division.

Colonel Webb remained several days and plans were developed for the Seventh Marines to land east of the Tenaru River, then our easternmost defense line, and extend our defense perimeter toward the Ilu River. They expected to arrive September 16, unfortunately for the security of the airfield just too late to help repulse the Japanese attack of the 12th and 13th. But the 16th passed and they did not come, nor yet the next day. Finally on September 18 they arrived and George was thrilled to see many ships — warships and transports — standing in Lunga Roads off Kukum. The tactical situation prevented their landing east of Tenaru according to the original plan. They unloaded in record time, unchallenged by Japanese sky raiders, and by nightfall all personnel and gear were ashore.

The new arrivals took over the defensive sector south of the airfield where the slender line of Raiders had been punctured by the Japanese in the Battle of the Ridge, and there they set up a strong defensive line which at last gave the airfield a solid all-around defensive cordon. With such reinforcements the Marine Command was able to plan more extensive and aggressive patrol actions against the Japanese south and west of us and soon whole battalions were scouring the jungle outside the defense perimeter.

Our strength had increased in other ways during September. On the 9th a new fighter strip east of the Japanese-built main runway was used for the first time. It had no surfacing other than its native grass and was useless after heavy rains, but it provided one of the dispersal strips so urgently needed for scattering our aircraft to make them less attractive targets for Japanese bombs and shells.

On the 10th two five-inch coastal guns were emplaced east of Lunga. Another battery was set up at Tulagi and a third was ready near Kukum a few days later. More than a month after the original landing we at last had some coast defenses able to deal with Japanese surface craft approaching close to the shores of our position.

AIR OPERATIONS

The aviation units based on Henderson Field built up a brilliant record from the outset. Almost without rest they had operated under the most adverse conditions imaginable, against great odds, and had taken an impressive toll of Japanese aircraft and shipping.

In the early weeks the Marine ground forces had slept in the dirt and mud, living on short rations, harassed night and day by enemy bombings and shellings. The pilots shared these discomforts with the rest of us, yet managed to keep the alertness and efficiency so necessary in the handling of their planes in combat. Henderson Field at that time, and for weeks to follow, was only a grassy plain with a runway down the center, with a surface fairly satisfactory in dry weather but turned into a bog by rain. There were no hangars, no repair shops, few shelter-pens to protect grounded planes from flying shrapnel and bomb fragments, and none of the amenities of a smoothly operated air base in a rear area. Facilities in all categories were primitive. Fuel for the planes had to be poured from drums. No bomb trucks or hoists were available for arming the bombers. The ground crews would have envied a corner garage on Main Street its tools and equipment; they had to carry on repair and maintenance work with few tools, working in the sun and rain.

There were no lights for the runway, increasing the hazards of night operations. On occasions a general call was sent out for jeeps inside the defense perimeter, to come to the runway and throw the light from their headlamps on the runway to guide in planes coming from patrols or from a late bombing mission.

The pilots had little rest. Air alerts were frequent, and invariably small groups of Wildcat fighters and Airacobras had to meet far greater numbers of Japanese bombers and Zero fighters. The activities of enemy combatant ships in the waters near Guadalcanal gave the scout bombers equally tiring and frequent missions.

The two Marine squadrons of Wildcat fighters and Dauntless scout bombers which arrived August 20 were soon reinforced by a naval squadron of scout bombers from a carrier, commanded by Lieutenant Turner Caldwel, U.S.N., and a fighter squadron of Airacobras of the Army Air Corps commanded by Captain D. D. Brannon. In the first ten days of operations from Henderson Field the planes of those four squadrons shot down sixteen twin-engined Mitsubishi bombers, five single-engined bombers, and thirty-nine Zero fighters, and sank three destroyers in addition to inflicting probably fatal damage on one Japanese cruiser, two more destroyers, and two transports. In that period they were under the command of Lieutenant Colonel C. L. Fike, with whom Lieutenant Colonel Charles H. Hayes was temporarily serving as Field Operations Officer.

Every member of the Marine ground forces joined heartily in the message of congratulation which Major General Vandegrift sent to the aviation units which had achieved such results in ten days of operations. 'The Commanding General,' he said, 'takes pleasure in conveying to the officers and men of the above-named units in behalf of the officers and men of the 1st Division appreciation and felicitations for their outstanding performance of duty.'

August 30 welcome reinforcements arrived. Nineteen Wildcats commanded by Major Robert E. Galer and a squadron of twelve Dauntless dive-bombers commanded by Major

Leo R. Smith arrived at Henderson Field. At the same time Colonel William J. Wallace, Commanding Officer of Marine Air Group 23, whose Executive Officer was Lieutenant Colonel Fike, arrived and assumed command of air operations from Henderson Field.

Three days later Brigadier General Roy S. Geiger, a pioneer officer in Marine Aviation and Commanding Officer of Marine Air Wing One came to Guadalcanal. His Chief of Staff, Colonel Louis E. Woods (soon thereafter promoted to Brigadier General), and Intelligence Officer, Lieutenant Colonel J. C. Munn, accompanied him. They flew up to Guadalcanal by transport plane the afternoon of September 3 and at the Division Command Post we went through an anxious period as darkness fell and their plane had not yet arrived. We had no searchlights to mark the field and lead them in. As an expedient, the ninety-millimeter anti-aircraft battery then emplaced on Henderson Field was ordered to open fire, with the hope that the bursts high in the sky would serve as a beacon. Still there was no report from the missing plane. Colonel Cates, of the First Marines, occupying the west bank of the Tenaru River, ordered flares to be sent up, and finally we were relieved to hear the hum of a plane's motor out toward the east.

Brigadier General Geiger, who soon thereafter was promoted to Major General, remained in command of aviation units on Guadalcanal until November 5, when he set up his headquarters at another base and was succeeded by Brigadier General Woods. Lieutenant Colonel Raymond C. Scollin served as Operations Officer, Lieutenant Colonel Frank G. Daily as Ordnance and Assistant Operations Officer, and Lieutenant Colonels Walter L. Bayler and Robert G. Black as Communications Officers.

Although the fighters operating from Henderson Field consistently shot down five or six times as many enemy planes as we lost, even minor combat losses and operational losses on the crude airfield steadily cut down their numbers. At the end of August, just before the two Marine squadrons of fighters and scout bombers arrived as reinforcements, only eight Wildcats and seven Airacobras were in condition to take the air and meet a large flight of Zeros, numbering about thirty. The fighters shot down eighteen of the Japanese planes, Major John Smith getting four by himself. We lost no Wildcats, but the Airacobra squadron, consisting of export models not equipped for high-altitude work, lost four planes. Two of the pilots parachuted and walked in.

From time to time other reinforcements and replacements arrived. As the Japanese were closing in for the Battle of the Ridge in the middle of September, Naval squadrons of Wildcats, Dauntless dive-bombers, and Avenger torpedo bombers came to Henderson Field to help meet the enemy's aerial onslaught. Twenty-four Wildcats arrived on the 11th, led by Lieutenant Commander L. C. Simpler, to be based temporarily on Henderson Field, and two days later a squadron of twelve dive-bombers (Lieutenant Commander L. J. Kirn) and six torpedo planes (Lieutenant H. H. Larsen), and the same day eighteen more Marine Wildcats arrived.

These reinforcements had come in at a crucial moment. In the aerial fighting preliminary to the Battle of the Ridge our fighting strength had been dangerously low. On the 11th of September, when twenty-six bombers escorted by twenty Zero fighters had come over Guadalcanal, only four Marine Wildcat fighters, led by Major John L. Smith, had made contact with the enemy formations. The four Marine pilots shot down five bombers without any losses to themselves, and again, the next day, the same four pilots rose from Henderson Field to engage another large Japanese force of twenty-six bombers and sixteen Zeros. Again Major Smith and his pilots returned without loss after shooting down six bombers and one Zero.

In little over a month of aerial combat over Guadalcanal, three Marine pilots had become aces with records unequaled by American fliers on any other war front. Two squadron leaders won Congressional Medals of Honor for the fearless way they had led their squadrons into combat against heavy odds and for their own remarkable records in shooting down enemy planes. Major Smith was credited with shooting down twenty planes and Major Robert E. Galer was credited with thirteen. Another great ace emerged from the early critical days of aerial fighting over Guadalcanal. Captain Marion E. Carl, who shot down sixteen Japanese planes, was twice awarded a Navy Cross.

The records of these fliers were not surpassed until Captain Joseph J. Foss came to Henderson Field in October and in six weeks of fighting shot down twenty-three Japanese planes, later adding another three to his score. He, too, was awarded the Congressional Medal of Honor.

September 22 all fighters — Army, Navy, and Marine — were grouped under the command of Colonel Wallace, and the bomber squadrons were formed in a group under Lieutenant Colonel Cooley.

By the end of the month, 171 Japanese planes had been shot down by planes based on Henderson Field. Marine Fighter Squadron 223 accounted for 41 Zeros, $50\frac{1}{2}$ twin-engined bombers (half the credit for one going to a pilot from another squadron), 1 four-engined Kawanishi flying boat, and 1 twin-tailed, twin-engined bomber. Marine Fighter Squadron 224 had shot down 9 Zeros, $21\frac{1}{2}$ twin-engined bombers, and 6 float-biplanes. Naval Fighter Squadron 5 had shot down 12 Zeros, 4 float-plane Zeros, 15 twin-engined bombers, and 3 float-biplanes, and the Airacobras of the United States Army Fighting Squadron 67, used primarily as attack planes in bombing and strafing enemy troops and installations, had accounted for 4 Zeros. In addition a scout bomber had shot down a float-biplane which attacked it on a mission.

Chapter 6

Matanikau Seesaw

THE ENEMY'S SECOND ATTEMPT to storm the fort had failed. His first effort to recapture Henderson Field had been frustrated at the Tenaru and in the Battle of the Eastern Solomons. His September attack had ended in defeat on the Ridge.

The citadel stood, but its position was precarious, and its ultimate fate depended not only on the strength and tenacity of the defenders who had thrown a cordon around the airfield and of the airmen who flew from that field, but on the maintenance of a supply line leading to bases south and east of us. Our contact with the outside world lay along the sea lanes extending southeastward from the six miles of beach we held north of the airfield and, to a lesser extent, through the air. Upon a steady flow of supplies into the beachhead at the Lunga depended our ability to hold the air base and push the enemy off the island.

By day our supply ships came. By night the Japanese came. Almost as if by agreement, the ships of the two enemies did not interfere with each other's movements. The arrival of an American supply ship was always a great occasion for George, who had come to realize the significance of supply. 'There's a ship in today,' he would say excitedly, and his buddies would joke, 'Ours or the Japs'?' But they knew if it arrived by daylight it was probably ours, and if it slipped furtively through the straits at night it was Japanese.

Ground activity shifted more and more to the west, toward the Matanikau River, beyond which Japanese reinforcements were now pouring in. On either side of the river lay a No Man's Land, between the main concentrations of the Marines and the Japanese. Shortly began the surge back and forth across the river which made the coconut groves, jungle thickets, and steep ridges near the river's mouth the bloodiest battlefield of the Guadalcanal campaign.

When the Japanese withdrew to the south and west after the Battle of the Ridge, Marine patrol activity grew more intense as the defenders of Henderson Field sought to run down isolated groups bivouacked deep in the jungle up the Lunga and to feel out the enemy's strength beyond the Matanikau. That strength increased steadily as the Japanese continued to ferry in reinforcements by destroyers and landing barges. Our strength, too, had increased with the arrival of the Seventh Marines and now whole battalions could be detached from the defense perimeter to hunt down the enemy.

Within a week of the exhausting battle they had fought on the Ridge, Edson's Raiders were taking part in such patrol activities. The evening of September 20 they marched across the airfield to bivouac near the main line of resistance south of the airfield, ready to go through the wire on the morrow and scour the jungle. Their numbers had been cut in half. They now looked more like a company than a battalion. Their faces were tired, too, but at the same time they had a look of self-assurance and determination, and of refusal to leave the fighting to others, even though they had suffered so heavily in their gallant stand on the Ridge.

Another patrol, which went out September 17, is remarkable for the heroism of one of their members who was lost in the action which ensued. The patrol consisted of Companies A and B of the First Marines and the story concerns Private

Harry Dunn, Jr., of the light machine-gun section of Company B. The patrol was making its way up the right bank of the Lunga River when it ran into a Japanese ambush. Suddenly six machine guns, in position on both banks of the river, opened up on the leading elements of the patrol and killed or wounded five Marines before they could deploy. The leading elements and the light machine-gun section of the company were cut off from the main body, surrounded by the hostile detachment. Three times the isolated group tried to fight its way back to the main body, but each time it was thrown back. Fourteen more men were killed or wounded in these encounters. Night was approaching and the company was ordered to withdraw and return within the defense perimeter, having to leave some of the wounded and the isolated detachment in the darkness, surrounded by the enemy. Private Dunn was among these.

He spent the night in an abandoned Japanese foxhole. Twice he fought off enemy detachments trying to mop up the field and he killed or wounded at least three of them. As day broke, more Japanese came up and Dunn 'played dead,' even when the Japanese stripped some of the equipment from his body. He was getting ready to try to make his way back to our lines when he heard a groan and found Private Jack Morrison lying wounded near-by. He, too, had spent the night in the midst of the enemy. Dunn gave first aid to Morrison and started carrying him back down the river. A Japanese patrol, however, saw them and opened fire, and the two Marines hid in the brush. When night fell, Dunn again started down the river, carrying Morrison. Part of the time he had to crawl across open spaces with Morrison clinging to his back. Several times he saw Japanese patrols, one of which sighted and searched for them. The two Marines eluded the searchers by hiding in the jungle growth at the river bank, Dunn holding his hand over Morrison's mouth to stifle his groans. Just before dawn on the 19th, they finally reached our lines. Morrison was evacuated and Dunn was sent to the Field Hospital

suffering from complete exhaustion. He had carried his com
rade about two and a half miles.

Every day the patrols went out. At first the contacts were
few and unimportant, indicating the area from Koli Point to
the Matanikau was pretty well cleared of Japanese except for
the upper reaches of the Lunga, where small detachments and
stragglers were found. We also learned that small groups of
Japanese were moving about farther east, between Taivu
Point and Aola. Their principal concentration seemed to be
at Koilotumaria, thirty miles away. Now and then patrols
came across caches of ammunition and supplies which they
destroyed.

Then, September 26, the area south and west of the Matanikau became the scene of spirited patrol clashes between
considerable groups of Marines and Japanese. The First and
Second Battalions, Seventh Marines, had pushed far inland,
along Grassy Knoll toward the Matanikau and began to run
into stiff opposition, showing that the Guadalcanal Express
had continued. It had been harassed by planes from Henderson Field which attacked the shuttle service of destroyers coming down from the northwest and returning to bases in the
northern Solomons, but it went relentlessly on. Thousands of
fresh Japanese soldiers came ashore at the northwestern end
of the island to reinforce their jungle-weary and battle-tired
comrades and the new forces met by our patrols showed a
more aggressive spirit. It was apparent that soon the Japanese would feel strong enough to attack again.

The opponents felt each other out late in September. The
First Battalion, Seventh Marines (Lieutenant Colonel Hul-
ler), had cut inland through the jungles and across the coral
ridges lying between the Lunga and Matanikau. The Second
Battalion, Fifth Marines (Major D. S. McDougal), moved out
along the coast road toward the Matanikau, expecting to cross
the river, advance toward Kokumbona, and return late in the
afternoon or evening. They met the Japanese near the
Matanikau. At first it was supposed that few enemy forces

were in the neighborhood, but the First Raider Battalion was
sent out to reinforce the Second Battalion, Fifth Marines.
The First Raiders were then commanded by Lieutenant Colonel Samuel B. Griffith, II, who had succeeded to the command when Colonel Edson became Commanding Officer of
the Fifth Marines late in September.

When the Second Battalion reached the Matanikau, they
found their crossing denied by strong machine-gun and mortar
opposition. The Japanese had moved into Matanikau village
in some strength. Late in the afternoon the Second Battalion
informed the Commanding General they were unable to
cross and it was seen that a major encounter was in the offing.
Colonel Edson was placed in command of all forces involved
and ordered to continue the attack.

The First Raiders had followed the Second Battalion, Fifth
Marines, to the Matanikau. As they approached the river
late in the afternoon, they heard firing ahead of them and
soon came into contact with the other Marine units — First
Battalion, Seventh Marines, and Second Battalion, Fifth
Marines — pinned down on the east bank of the river. The
Marines stopped for the night, bivouacking on the right bank
of the river.

At daylight on the 27th the Raiders moved south along the
east bank of the Matanikau through thick jungle to a point
two thousand yards from the beach, where they were to try to
cross the river. Their orders were to cross, advance in the
rear of the enemy, wipe out his force, and continue on toward
Kokumbona. Company C of the First Battalion, Seventh
Marines, was attached to the Raiders for this operation.

As Company A, reinforced, making up the advanced guard,
reached the designated crossing point, it came under heavy
machine-gun fire from well-prepared emplacements on the
west bank of the river and also received small-arms fire from
the high ground on their left, on the east side of the river. It
was at this point that a very gallant marine was killed. Major
Kenneth D. Bailey, who had fought with such distinction on

Tulagi and on the Ridge as commander of Company C, wa now Battalion Executive Officer. Now, as he led the advanced guard into the fight with all the dash and aggressiveness that marked his earlier actions, he was cut down by a Japanese bullet. Lieutenant Colonel Griffith remained as the only officer above the rank of Captain in the entire battalion.

Lieutenant Colonel Griffith directed Company C of the Raiders to seize the high ground to the east overlooking the river in order to flank enemy resistance encountered by the advance guard. Company C of the Seventh Marines was to move even farther left and thus assist in the flanking maneuver. Both companies received enemy machine-gun and rifle fire as they moved against the high ground and came under mortar fire delivered from the other side of the river. Trying to advance against the commanding heights held by the enemy, the two C Companies suffered many casualties and, as they inched forward, trying to work machine guns and riflemen into position, Lieutenant Colonel Griffith was wounded by a sniper's bullet. He refused to relinquish his command, however, returned to his command post, and personally directed his battalion throughout the remainder of that afternoon of discouraging fighting. The Raiders found themselves in a pocket almost surrounded by Japanese, and at three in the afternoon received orders from Colonel Edson to disengage an hour later and make their way back to the beach near the mouth of the river. They withdrew as ordered, helped to cover the withdrawal of the other units who had made no progress in forcing a crossing of the river, and returned to bivouac inside the defense perimeter that evening.

Meanwhile, other units of the First Battalion, Seventh Marines, had tried to get to the rear of the enemy forces at the mouth of the river by landing near Point Cruz and pushing inland behind the Japanese. Their landing was covered by fire from a destroyer, and the main body pushed inland to the coral ridges early in the afternoon, leaving a rear guard on the beach. Soon the rear guard found that the Japanese were closing in on them, and as the fighting grew heavier the few Marines on the beach fought their way inland to rejoin the main body.

For two hours the Marine detachment was isolated on a ridge, cut off from the beach and from every other way back to their own lines by Japanese in numbers far greater than those estimated when the combat patrol had started across the Matanikau the day before. Then the destroyer, which had covered their landing by firing on the beach area, again approached the shore and began to signal to the trapped Marines. Sergeant Robert D. Raysbrook volunteered to return the signal. The destroyer had signaled them to return to the beach, but when Raysbrook sent a message that the Japanese had cut them off the destroyer asked where it should shell. Raysbrook then signaled his captain's request to fire along the beach before them, then later asked the destroyer to shift her fire a bit. Each time he rose to signal the destroyer with his flags, Raysbrook became the target of heavy fire from Japanese snipers, machine guns, and mortars. Marines all about him were killed and wounded, but he continued with his signaling, and finally, under protective fire from the destroyer, the Marine detachment made its way to the beach and waded out to the Higgins boats which had come to take them back to camp.

In this desperate withdrawing action, Platoon Sergeant Anthony P. Malanowski of Company A was killed as he covered the withdrawal of his comrades, exacting a heavy toll from the enemy until he was overrun and killed.

Signalman First Class Douglas A. Munro, U.S.C.G., commanded the group of five boats which came from Kukum to take off the beleaguered Marines. Although the Japanese were firing on the boats as they approached, Munro led his landing craft inshore and evacuated the men on the beach. When the last men were being taken aboard, under no covering fire except that provided by the boats themselves, Munro maneuvered his Higgins boat close to the beach, placing it as a shield between the Japanese gunners and the heavily loaded boats. He had only two light machine guns in the bow to cover the withdrawal. The maneuver succeeded and all boats cleared the beach, but Munro's gallantry in exposing himself to fire while the other boats made off to safety cost him his life. As the last men were being taken aboard, he was mortally wounded. The Congressional Medal of Honor was awarded to him posthumously for his heroic sacrifice. His commanding officer, Lieutenant Commander D. H. Dexter, U.S.C.G., reported that Munro recovered consciousness for a moment after he was hit and his last words were, 'Did they get off?'

The skirmish at the Matanikau had not ended happily. At a cost of forty-two killed and one hundred and twenty-nine wounded in two days (September 26 and 27), with unknown losses to the enemy, we had learned that the Japanese had occupied the area in greater numbers than had been earlier supposed. The thousands that had come ashore on the north-western end of Guadalcanal had moved eastward, undoubt-edly preparing for a general attack. They were trying to occupy the right (east) bank of the Matanikau River and secure positions for light artillery within range of the airfield. Probably a thousand enemy soldiers were near the river's mouth, with strong reserves close behind.

The defense perimeter around Henderson Field, based on a cordon of automatic fire and barbed wire, had proved itself adequate to resist assaults by Japanese infantry. Now a new factor had entered into the calculations of the Marine Com-mand. The Marines' primary mission at that time was to ensure the security of the airfield. Air operations must con-tinue at all costs. Even though Japanese infantry could not puncture the defense perimeter and pour out on the airfield, the Japanese might bring the field under artillery fire and deny us its use as an air base. The new factor was artillery. If the Japanese on the east side of Matanikau could hold posi-tions within light artillery range of the airfield, the situation would be extremely embarrassing. So it was decided to push the Japanese back, beyond the Matanikau to a point where their light field pieces — seventy-five-millimeter or seventy-seven-millimeter mountain guns and howitzers — could not lay a harassing barrage upon Henderson Field.

The Marine Command immediately began to develop plans for such a limited offensive. They had to reckon with an obvious Japanese plan soon to move to the offensive themselves. The 'lull' that followed the Battle of the Ridge was about to end.

Since that battle, on September 14, until October 1, Japanese warships had come close enough to land reinforcements at least seven and possibly many more times. Almost every night a force of destroyers, or of cruisers and destroyers, was found within striking range of Guadalcanal. Often new landing barges were found on beaches between Kokumbona and Cape Esperance. Obviously the Japanese were building up forces preparatory to making another attempt to take Henderson Field.

Japanese aircraft showed renewed aggressiveness late in September. The day when the Battle of the Ridge had ended in the withdrawal of enemy ground forces from the immediate vicinity of our defense lines, more than a dozen Japanese float-planes had swooped over the airfield in the early evening to drop light bombs and strafe the edges of the field. They had paid for their venture with nine planes lost, with no losses to ourselves. After that abortive raid the Japanese did not again attempt to bomb Henderson Field for a fortnight. Several times in that period flights of enemy planes had approached the island, but each time they had withdrawn before they came into contact with our fighters. On September 27, as the Marines were disengaging themselves on the Matanikau front, the Japanese again felt ready to risk sending bombers over Henderson Field. That day eighteen twin-engined bombers escorted by thirteen Zeros came over. Our fighters shot down six of the bombers and five Zeros with no losses to themselves except for slight damage to six Wildcats. The next day Japanese losses were even more shattering. Of the twenty-five bombers that reached Guadalcanal only two began the long return trip to Rabaul. Our fighters shot down a Zero for good measure, one of thirty escorting the bombers, and we did not lose a single plane. That was the day when Lieutenant Colonel Harold W. Bauer, visiting Henderson Field to make preparations for bringing up his Marine Fighter Squadron, volunteered to take up a plane when the warning was sounded, took off, and shot down a Zero. The next day the bombers never reached Guadalcanal. Their fighter escort was engaged, and at least four, possibly six, of the Zeros were shot down, but the bombers turned back without trying to drop their loads on Henderson Field.

Renewed air raids, continued night landings of enemy troops, the enemy's occupation of both banks of the Matanikau, the threat of artillery fire against the airfield — these factors made up the situation facing the Marine Command as they planned to hit at the Japanese in the west.

At the first of October it looked as though a raid against the enemy beachhead at Visale, like the raid against Tasimboko a month earlier, would be helpful in disorganizing the Japanese then moving eastward toward our position. Raiders landing at the northwest end of the island could engage the enemy's rear while the main Marine attack was launched across the Matanikau. Accordingly plans were made for the Second Raider Battalion, under Lieutenant Colonel Evans F. Carlson, to land at Visale October 8, while the main Marine force drove across the Matanikau.

The plan was never executed. The pace of Japanese landings on the northwest end of Guadalcanal increased to such an extent after the first of October that the Raiders would have been met by overwhelming numbers if they had attempted the proposed landing.

The Marine Command decided upon an envelopment coordinated with a frontal holding attack against the Matanikau

to push the Japanese beyond light artillery range of the airfield. The decision was not reached without misgivings, for a
large force had to be used in the operation and the detachment of such a force from the defense perimeter meant that
yawning gaps must be left in that protective line.

Two regiments (less one battalion in each case) and another battalion constituted the infantry force used in the
operation. The Fifth Marines (less one battalion) (Colonel
Merritt A. Edson) were to occupy the right bank of the
Matanikau River October 7, wiping up any enemy troops
found on the east side of the river and occupying a front of
eighteen hundred yards along the river to hold the river
mouth and cover the movements of other units. On the same
day the Third Battalion, Second Marines (Lieutenant Colonel
R. G. Hunt), and 'Whaling's Snipers,' [1] operating together as
the 'Whaling Group' under Colonel William Whaling, were
to move up toward the Matanikau along inland trails to
bivouac on the left flank of the Fifth Marines. October 8
they were to secure a crossing of the Matanikau at daylight,
cover the crossing of the Seventh Marines, then attack to the
northeast, turning the southern flank of the Japanese outpost
line of resistance on the west bank of the river. The Seventh
Marines (less one battalion) (Colonel Amor Sims) was to
follow the Whaling Group on the 7th, bivouac near them that
night, cross the river to the left and rear of the Whaling Group
on the 8th, and attack toward Point Cruz to cut off and
destroy Japanese units that might withdraw toward the
west.

The Eleventh Marines were to cover the movements of the

---

[1] 'Whaling's Snipers' were a group of picked men chosen for their expert
marksmanship with the rifle and skill in woodsmanship. They operated in small
groups as scouts in the jungle under the command of Colonel Whaling, then
attached to Division Headquarters as special adviser on strengthening the defense perimeter. The Colonel, himself a very skilled woodsman and marksman,
trained his group of scouts and often personally led them. Men were picked
from each battalion and learned the jungle trails around Henderson Field so
thoroughly that they could quickly lead their own battalions to any spot where
they might be needed.

infantry units in their approach to the Matanikau on the 7th with artillery concentrations and to support the attack the next day. Aircraft of the First Marine Air Wing (Major General Roy S. Geiger) were to support the attack by bombing and strafing missions in the area Matanikau–Kokumbona during the days prior to the attack and while the attack was in progress. The Third Battalion, First Marines (Lieutenant Colonel W. N. McKelvy), constituted the Division reserve for the operation and a boat group under Lieutenant Commander Dexter, U.S.C.G., was maintained in readiness to carry reinforcements or withdraw elements as the situation might require.

The morning of October 7 the two infantry regiments and the Whaling Group cleared their areas inside the defense perimeter and started moving up to the Matanikau as planned. The Whaling Group and the Seventh Marines crossed the Pioneers Bridge and moved by covered trails, as much as possible, along the ridges and draws inland from the coast, while the Fifth Marines moved up the coast road.

The inland units ran into opposition as they approached the Matanikau. As they tried to cross a gorge leading into the Matanikau to gain the opposite ridge, they were met by well-concealed sniper fire and in the middle of the afternoon Colonel Whaling decided it was best to by-pass the pocket of resistance and move along the ridge to the designated bivouac area. There the Seventh Marines and Whaling Groups bivouacked for the night, on the high ground south of the river forks. (See map.)

Meanwhile, the Fifth Marines were running into trouble. In the middle of the morning, when they were still three hundred yards east of the Matanikau, they ran into a Japanese detachment with machine guns which held up the advance. The Second Battalion (Major D. S. McDougal), moving up on the left flank, encountered less opposition and by noon was able to reach the river, with its left flank about twelve hundred and fifty yards and the right flank seven hundred and fifty

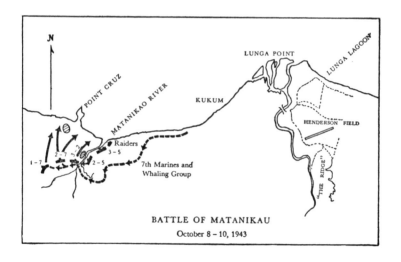

N

POINT CRUZ

MATANIKAO RIVER

KUKUM

LUNGA POINT

LUNGA LAGOON

HENDERSON FIELD

"THE RIDGE"

Raiders
3 – 5

1 – 7

2 – 7

2 – 5

7th Marines and
Whaling Group

BATTLE OF MATANIKAU
October 8 – 10, 1943

BATTLE FOR THE MATANIKAU RIVER

yards from the river mouth. They surprised and killed four Japanese washing clothes in the river.

The Third Battalion, Fifth Marines (Major R. O. Bowen), however, ran into determined opposition. Machine guns and snipers held up their advance to the river line, and even though half-tracks were brought up to fire upon Japanese machine-gun emplacements at point-blank range, the enemy was still in considerable strength on the east bank of the river as night fell.

The Whaling Group and Seventh Marines on the ridges south of the Fifth Marines had a quieter night, although there was scattered sniper fire in the Whaling Group bivouac area. At eight o'clock the next morning, October 8, the Whaling Group started to secure a crossing of the Matanikau after a preliminary artillery preparation. First they attempted to cross below the second fork of the river. The Japanese were waiting for them, but the Marines by-passed most of the opposition. It had rained during the night and continued to rain as the Third Battalion, Second Marines, fought their way through the jungle-choked draw leading down to the river. The jungle trail and ridge slopes had become slippery and added to the Marines' difficulties. By ten-thirty they had crossed the river and gained the high ground to the west and the Seventh Marines began to follow them.

It was mid-afternoon, however, before the leading companies of the three battalions (1–7, 2–7, and 3–2) reached the ridge-top a mile south of Point Cruz, which was their first objective. One of Lieutenant Colonel Hunt's companies was assigned to sweep the lowland along the left bank of the river and ran into strong Japanese positions which held them up — the same pocket of resistance which held up the attempted crossing of Company H of the Fifth Marines at the first fork of the river.

By four-thirty Lieutenant Colonel Hanneken's battalion (2–7) had arrived on the ridge, to the left of Lieutenant Colonel Hunt, and one company of Lieutenant Colonel Puller's battalion (1–7) was coming up still farther to the left. At this time scouts reconnoitering in front of Hanneken's position found five Japanese carrying a field piece into the ravine in front of his line. They killed three of the Japanese and captured the gun, but two got away. Then a large body of Japanese began advancing from the northwest toward the ridgeline held by the Marines. By now the remaining elements of the three battalions were arriving in almost steady columns and taking up positions extending the line well to the left. It looked as though the Japanese were about to attack in force, and Colonel Whaling called for an artillery barrage in front of the Marine line. Shortly after dark the artillery opened up, pounded the area steadily throughout the night, and effectively prevented the Japanese from organizing an assault.

The Marine line west of the river now extended from the river along the top of a steep coral ridge into a very deep gorge almost impossible to negotiate at dark. The Japanese did not succeed in getting through the line or around the flank, and although there was intermittent machine-gun and mortar fire throughout the night, no major clash developed.

Meanwhile, the Fifth Marines had succeeded in closing up to the river at intervals, with isolated pockets of Japanese still among them. The Second and Third Battalions (on left and right respectively) were not in contact. The Second Battalion was to cross the river at the first fork and attack along the west bank toward the mouth when Lieutenant Colonel Hunt's battalion was entirely across the river, but they found themselves pinned down in the steep ravine leading to the first fork by the same pocket of resistance that was holding up Hunt's right company on the opposite side of the river.[1]

When darkness came, the Second Battalion, Fifth Marines, was still at the stream junction. To their right, and not in contact with them, were the Third Battalion, Fifth Marines,

---

[1] In his book entitled *Into the Valley* John Hersey has given a vivid account of the vicissitudes of one company (Company H, commanded by Captain Charles A. Rigaud) in attempting to cross the Matanikau.

and two companies of the First Raiders which had been committed by Colonel Edson as regimental reserve. Those two companies — A and C — were at the river mouth and wired themselves in along the river and beach. There was still a considerable number of Japanese with machine guns and rifles on the east side of the river.

It turned out to be a wild night. The Japanese on the east side of the river made a break for the sand spit at the river's mouth, to get back to the main body on the other side. As night fell, the Japanese set off smoke bombs. Coming out of their hiding-places under cover of the smoke and gathering dusk, the enemy soldiers organized to attack, and in a succession of charges some succeeded in gaining the other side. It was a night of bitter hand-to-hand fighting, when a man could not tell friend from foe in the jungle darkness, or know who shared the foxhole next to him.

The platoon commanded by Second Lieutenant Richard E. Sullivan of the Raiders was hit by the spearhead of the Japanese attack. His men had hastily thrown up barbed-wire defenses as darkness approached and it was through this barrier that the Japanese sought to break. In the desperate close-quarters combat Lieutenant Sullivan was three times wounded but kept his position throughout the night.

Private First Class Michael P. Fedorak, of Company A of the Raiders, manned a light machine gun. As the first enemy charge came, he maintained a steady fire, killing fifteen of the attackers. When his gun jammed, he coolly removed the base plate to make the gun useless to the enemy, and withdrew.

The next morning (October 9) at six-forty-five the Marines then west of the river again moved forward after an artillery preparation. Lieutenant Colonel Hunt's battalion advanced toward the coast between the west bank of the Matanikau and Point Cruz, Lieutenant Colonel Hanneken's battalion (Second, Seventh Marines) moved to the shore line the other side of Point Cruz, while Lieutenant Colonel Puller's battalion (First, Seventh Marines), echeloned to the left rear, supported Hanneken's advance. In the morning they swept the area clean of what few Japanese remained. The enemy's break for the river mouth from the east side had been part of a general withdrawal and the main force west of the river had pulled back farther west during the night as the Marines' enveloping maneuver threatened to trap them near the mouth of the Matanikau. Remaining Japanese resistance was stiffest along the front attacked by Hanneken, with machine guns firing from the ridge southwest of Point Cruz. Company E was sent to outflank the Japanese position and by ten o'clock Company F had succeeded in reaching the beach.

At noon the Whaling Group and Seventh Marines began to withdraw from the western side of the river. In the three days of fighting at least two hundred and fifty-three Japanese had been killed, with additional unknown casualties as a result of the steady artillery pounding and attacks by aircraft in the area west of the Marines' zone of advance. Our own losses were sixty-five killed and one hundred and twenty-five wounded.

Fewer Japanese had been caught in the trap than had been hoped, but the important accomplishment had been to deny the enemy artillery positions on the east side of the river within light artillery range of Henderson Field. The Marines' attack of October 8–10 had wiped out the Japanese bridgehead on the eastern bank of the Matanikau. The timeliness and importance of the attack quickly became apparent as the Japanese launched a powerful offensive from the air and sea, intended to knock out our air power on Henderson Field long enough to clear the way for a large landing party aboard transports.

If the Japanese had been able to add the fire of a multitude of light field pieces to the weight of steel and high explosive that was hurled at Henderson Field in the ensuing week, they might well have completely succeeded in making the field temporarily useless as a base for air operations. Naval and aerial bombardments may be intense and damaging, but once

the ships or planes have departed the bombardment must end.
Field artillery, on the other hand, might open up at any hour
of the day or night, maintaining a harassing fire that would
deny us use of the airfield.

GURABUSU–KOILOTUMARIA PATROL

While the Marines were engaged in driving the Japanese
back across the Matanikau, another group of Marines was
moving against small enemy detachments far to the east of us
on Guadalcanal.

For some time small groups of Japanese had roamed the
island east of the airfield. They were the remnants of lookout
stations which the Japanese had posted at favorable spots east
of Lunga Point before the United Nations attack of August 7
and survivors of the Ichiki unit and Kawaguchi unit involved
in the action at the Tenaru and in the eastern phases of the
Battle of the Ridge.

One group had come from Marau Sound, at the southeastern end of Guadalcanal, and had set up camp at Gurabusu, a
village about thirty miles from us near Aola. Equipped with
radio and supplied from submarines which visited them at
night, this group of naval personnel undoubtedly supplied the
Japanese with information concerning movements of our shipping off Guadalcanal and helped arrange landings of enemy
troops.

The Koilotumaria detachment, a few miles west of the
other, numbered between one and two hundred, probably
survivors of actions on our defense perimeter.

The mission of destroying the enemy outposts was given to
the First Battalion, Second Marines (Lieutenant Colonel
R. E. Hill), then stationed on Tulagi. They were to cross to
Aola by 'Yippee' boats and Higgins boats, move inland in
rear of the enemy camps, split into two groups, and simul-
taneously attack the Gurabusu and Koilotumaria detachments.

Captain Martin Clemens, the British District Officer, went to Aola ahead of the others to reconnoiter and prepare maps for use by the Marines. October 7, Captain Clemens left Lunga with four Marines and three native police, reaching Aola late that night in a Higgins boat.

Early the next morning the little scouting party almost met disaster. A scout reported that a three-man Japanese patrol was coming down the beach toward the mouth of the Aola River. The Clemens party hurriedly tried to get the machine gun off the Higgins boat, but it got stuck, they had to abandon the boat on the beach and take to the bush with the prospect of the patrol's giving the alarm and leading a detachment of Japanese against them. Fortunately, however, the enemy patrol stopped at the mouth of the river and did not discover the activity in Aola.

On the 8th and 9th, Captain Clemens completed his reconnaissance and awaited the arrival of Lieutenant Colonel Hill's men, due to come that night at ten-thirty. It was almost one o'clock before a Higgins boat chugged out of the darkness, bringing Lieutenant Colonel Hill and twelve men. Misfortune had dogged the landing party. One Higgins boat, towed by one of the two Yippee boats, had come apart at the bows off Taivu Point and fifteen men were drowned. The consequent delay and the difficulties of the other Yippee boat in finding the rendezvous cost much precious time, and it seemed that the Marines would lose the element of surprise. The troops did not complete unloading until after noon on the 10th, in full view of any Japanese outposts that might have been watching.

Lieutenant Colonel Hill decided to move to the attack immediately, although it would take the main body, assigned to attack Koilotumaria, much longer to get into position than the detachment which was to attack Gurabusu. With two companies he set off on a night march on the inland trail leading behind Gurabusu and Koilotumaria. One company, commanded by Captain Richard Y. Stafford, was to attack

Official U.S. Navy Photograph

Henderson Field. This picture shows the Japanese-built runway shortly after it was captured. The Lunga River flows past the airfield to the west, entering the sea at Lunga Point (upper right corner).

Tulagi under bombardment, August 7. Hill 281, where Japanese resistance was concentrated, appears in the lower right corner. Beach Blue, where the Marines landed, is at the extreme left. The larger island in the background is Florida Island, and the small one between Florida and Tulagi is Makambo.

Official U.S. Marine Corps Photo

Gavutu and Tanambogo Islands. In the foreground is Gavutu as it appeared after aerial and naval bombardment, August 7. Across the causeway is Tanambogo. The small island, right center, is Gaomi, where Japanese sniper fire harassed Marine operations on Gavutu. In the background lies Florida Island.

Official U.S. Marine Corps Photo

The Ridge. This was the scene of the fierce fighting in the middle of September when the Japanese attempted to reach the airfield beyond the trees in the background. The knoll, left center, marked the Marines' reserve line where the main Japanese attack was finally stopped.

The beach at the Tenaru. The coconut-log tank obstacles in the center are on the sandbar that closes the mouth of the Tenaru River. The Japanese who attempted to cross the sandbar were encircled and annihilated in the coconut grove on August 21. The field shoes ('boondockers') in the foreground indicate that someone is in swimming.

Henderson Field from the east. In the foreground is a coconut plantation and the Tenaru River is beyond. Left center is the fighter strip, with planes dispersed near the runway. The Japanese-built bomber strip is in the upper right corner. Beyond it is the Lunga River. The line of grass-covered hills to the left is the Ridge. In the upper left corner is Grassy Knoll.

Japanese tanks at the mouth of the Matanikau. They attempted to cross the Matanikau River from the left bank and were knocked out by anti-tank guns and tank destroyers on the right bank. In the left background Point Cruz is visible, and in the far background Savo Island, whose waters were the scene of five night engagements between surface forces of the United States Navy and the Japanese Navy.

Crossing the Lunga River. A Marine patrol starts out at sunset.

Marines on the march. This shows the area just west of the Matanikau River.

After the Battle of August 21. Dead Japanese lie strewn on the beach near the mouth of the Tenaru River.

Official U.S. Marine Corps Photo

Japanese troop ship. This is one of the four transports that reached Guadalcanal November 15 and were sunk by dive-bombers from Henderson Field.

Major General Alexander A. Vandegrift. From this crude desk in his Guadalcanal tent, General Vandegrift of the Marine Corps directed the American forces.

Officers in conference on Guadalcanal, August 11. First row (left to right): Col. George R. Rowan; Col. Pedro A. Del Valle; Col. William C. James; Major General Alexander A. Vandegrift; Col. Gerald C. Thomas; Col. Clifton B. Cates; Lt. Col. Randolph McC. Pate; Commander Warwick T. Brown, USN. Second row: Col. William C. Whaling; Col. Frank B. Goettge; Col. LeRoy P. Hunt; Lt. Col. Frederick C. Biebush; Lt. Col. Edwin A. Pollock; Lt. Col. Edmund J. Buckley; Lt. Col. Walter W. Barr; Lt. Col. Raymond P. Coffman. Third row: Lt. Col. Francis R. Geraci; Lt. Col. William E. Maxwell; Lt. Col. Edward G. Hagen; Lt. Col. William N. McKelvy; Lt. Col. Julian N. Frisbee; Major Milton V. O'Connel; Major William Chalfant, III; Unknown; Major Forest C. Thompson. Fourth row: Major Robert G. Ballance; Major Henry W. Buse, Jr.; Major James G. Frazer; Major Henry H. Crockett; Lt. Col. Lenard B. Cresswell; Major Robert O. Bowen; Lt. Col. John A. Bemis; Major Robert B. Luckey; Lt. Col. Samuel G. Taxis; Lt. Col. Eugene H. Price. Last row: Lt. Col. Merrill B. Twining; Lt. Col. Walker A. Reaves; Lt. Col. John Dew Macklin; Lt. Col. Hanley C. Waterman; Major James C. Murray.

Aviation headquarters on Guadalcanal. After the Japanese artillery began firing on Henderson Field in October, headquarters were set up in the jungle. The shack was the home of Major General Roy S. Geiger.

Official U.S. Marine Corps Photo

Dead Japanese jungle fighters. They are half-buried in the tidal sands of the Tenaru River where they failed in a vicious night attempt to dislodge the Marines from Guadalcanal.

Lieutenant Colonel Carlson and some of his Raiders. They are resting in bivouac near the beach after their thirty-day operation in the jungle. Colonel Carlson is in the center of the first row.

Gurabusu at dawn the next morning, then set up a defense line facing Koilotumaria, and cut off the escape of any Japanese from that direction.

Captain Clemens led Captain Stafford's company into position. Silently they moved up on the sleeping Japanese encampment which stood on a little island in the mouth of the Gurabusu River. The company deployed on the banks of the river commanding the island. By the time they had got into position, it was later than the time originally set for the attack, but fortunately the camp had not begun to stir. At eight-thirty Captain Stafford gave the order to fire, the rifle platoons on the west side of the island moved up, and the machine guns opened up from the other flank.

The attack took the Japanese completely by surprise and they were mowed down in the leaf huts which served them as shelters. Twenty-six of them were killed in the bivouac area, four more were shot down as they tried to flee, and two more were killed near the beach. Only two sentries escaped, making off to the east after the Marines' first fusillade. The sleepy Japanese were able to return only a few shots, one of which struck and killed Captain Stafford as he directed his men in the forward skirmish line.

The Marines then moved onto the island, with one platoon taking up positions facing Koilotumaria to cut off the escape of Japanese which Lieutenant Colonel Hill's detachment might have flushed farther up the coast.

The Marines moving on Koilotumaria, however, had not been able to get into position until after noon. Meanwhile, the Japanese apparently heard the firing from Gurabusu, had taken alarm, and had fled to the south through the swamps. Consequently the Marines were closing the neck of an empty bag and found only three Japanese, whom they shot.

The raid, then, had been only half successful, but one prize caused the Marines particular satisfaction. Natives identified one of the dead Japanese as Ishimoto.

Ishimoto had been a shipwright at Tulagi before the war,

a carpenter and metal worker for the trading firm of Carpenters'. He became a general handy man, was sent out on many trips through the islands on company business, and learned to know the Guadalcanal area thoroughly.

He could speak pidgin English and knew how to get on with the natives. This humble worker left Tulagi as the war crisis grew in the Pacific, but when the Japanese began moving into the southeastern Solomons late in the spring of 1942 Ishimoto turned up again, in naval uniform. He informed the natives that he had been a reservist.

The Japanese, of course, had much work for one of Ishimoto's talents and knowledge. He selected sites for observation posts commanding the sea approaches to the southeastern Solomons. He tried to cultivate friendly relations with the natives and to win their acceptance of Japanese rule. He hunted down the local whites in the islands. With the arrival of Marines on Guadalcanal, Ishimoto's duties became more exciting. He conducted reconnaissance of American positions and strength, getting what information he could from the natives, and he helped to organize the landings of Japanese units sent to recapture Henderson Field.

Ishimoto was at the Marau Sound observation post when the Marines landed on Guadalcanal and his sampan was there bombed. He had to make his way across the island on foot, arriving at Taivu Point in time to help the Ichiki unit come ashore for their disastrous attempt to raid Henderson Field. With the Japanese force Ishimoto came westward and reached Koli Point. The rear guard of the Ichiki detachment, which had remained near Koli Point, moved back to Tasimboko near Taivu Point, still accompanied by Ishimoto. There they organized the landings of the Japanese forces which attacked the airfield in the Battle of the Ridge.

Ishimoto added to his reputation for ruthless terrorism by murdering two Catholic priests and two nuns from the Roman Catholic mission at Ruavatu. When Ishimoto and his party were at Tasimboko, they sent for the missionaries and held them prisoner in a hut. Then, when Ishimoto and his men moved to Gurabusu after the Battle of the Ridge, the priests and nuns were summarily put to death. The Japanese, it seemed, did not wish to be burdened with four useless people. After the raid on Gurabusu, the Marines found the vestments, altar cloths, chalice, and patten from the Ruavatu mission.

Two nights after the raid on Gurabusu, as the Marines waited at Aola for boats to take them back to Tulagi, they heard the dismal blast of a foghorn on a submarine, prowling along the coast between Aola and Gurabusu. The submarine was signaling to the dead men of Gurabusu. Ishimoto probably would not answer that signal again. Or perhaps the natives had not properly identified the body and Ishimoto would again light signal fires to guide in a Japanese landing party.

Chapter 7

Crisis in Mid-October

IN THE MIDDLE OF OCTOBER the Imperial Japanese Navy moved into the southeastern Solomons in great force. Its ships and planes threw a weight of steel and high explosive against the American beachhead that ripped the earth and everything on it and left the defenders reeling. But when the smoke of battle had cleared away at the end of the month, Henderson Field was still in our hands.

The latest Japanese land drive against Henderson Field had been temporarily stopped by the Marines' thrust beyond the Matanikau, but the Japanese rushed reinforcements to the island. For almost two months their night infiltration landings from destroyers and barges had continued. Now they were determined to bring down, for their final drive, the men and material which could only be transported by heavier shipping. Under cover of heavy aerial and naval bombardment the Japanese planned to land the remaining elements of a reinforced division, artillery, tanks, everything that would be needed for the final push. Then they would close in on the American defenders and drive them into the sea.

The Japanese had learned that a few thousand of the Emperor's finest could not dislodge the defenders. This time nothing would be left to chance. The pressure would be so

heavy and sustained, delivered by such overwhelming numbers of weapons and men, that resistance must end.

Up to October 1 Japanese surface craft had approached
Guadalcanal, probably to land troops on each occasion, at
least eighteen times. After the first of the month, the pace
of these operations quickened. The night of October 1 four
destroyers came in; the night of the 3d, nine destroyers and a
heavy cruiser; the night of the 5th, six destroyers; the night of
the 7th, five destroyers; the night of the 8th, a heavy cruiser
and five destroyers; the night of the 9th, two cruisers and four
destroyers. Well over five thousand Japanese soldiers might
have come on these warships to reinforce the thousands growing sick and weary in the jungle. Enemy strength to the west
of us was growing at an alarming rate.

The ventures of Japanese warships into the waters off
Guadalcanal did not pass unchallenged. We had planes, if
not surface ships, to oppose their coming, and day after day
striking forces went after the enemy ships as reconnaissance
planes picked them up. By now the Japanese were attempting to provide air coverage for their destroyer groups and our
planes had to fight their way through land-based Zeros and
float-planes before they could attack. They did not always
succeed in hitting the elusive destroyers, but in the first ten
days of October they took an impressive toll of Japanese
strength. One destroyer was sunk and three were damaged
by bombs. One heavy cruiser had suffered a direct bomb hit
and two torpedo hits and a second heavy cruiser had limped
back toward Buin burning badly after a torpedo hit and many
damaging near-misses by bombs. Two light cruisers had been
damaged. In these operations we lost one Wildcat, one Airacobra, and two Dauntless dive-bombers, while eleven Japanese float-biplanes and three float-Zero fighters had been shot
out of the air escorts. Despite such losses the Japanese per-

sisted. Our strength in planes and supplies was dwindling. Whatever feats the pilots of Henderson Field could and did perform, the war of attrition was telling against them. Japanese strength on Guadalcanal grew while ours diminished.

Such was the situation when the enemy's 'big push' began October 11. During the day the Japanese sent seventy-seven planes over Guadalcanal and that night the waters off the island swarmed with Japanese warships. The air raid, however, was a fiasco and the surface task force was battered by an American force lying in wait off the northwest tip of the island. It was an American day and night and felt much nearer to final victory. We were soon disillusioned. The Japanese had not even begun to throw their full weight against Henderson Field.

The preliminary air attack began just after noon on the 11th. In four waves the Japanese planes came over — first sixteen Zeros, then eighteen bombers, then sixteen bombers, and then thirteen more Zeros. Thirty-nine Wildcats and nine Airacobras rose to meet them. For two hours the sky was full of planes while we on the ground waited for the bombs to drop and for the sound of aerial fighting. Clouds had closed over the field and the enemy planes seemed to have difficulty in finding it. In any case, they circled the field again and again and finally dropped their bombs far to the east near Koli Point. Sixteen Grummans finally found the enemy planes in the cloud formations that massed and shifted over Henderson Field and shot down seven of the twin-engined bombers and four Zeros, with losses to our airmen of one Grumman (pilot saved) and one Airacobra. The net result for the enemy was a typically high loss in planes and nil results from bombing.

They had, however, accomplished one thing. About two-thirty in the afternoon, while the Japanese planes still circled over Guadalcanal, Douglas dive-bombers on a search mission spotted an enemy surface force of two light cruisers and six destroyers, covered by nine Zero fighters, two hundred miles out and headed for Guadalcanal. Our planes had been kept in the air so long by the protracted air-raid alarm that there was not time to refuel them and send them out to attack the approaching ships.

That night, however, a surface task force of the United States Navy did what the aircraft had been unable to do. For the first time since the Battle of Savo Island, August 8–9, our ships met the Japanese off the shores of Guadalcanal.

Just before midnight the camp was awakened by the sound of naval gunfire. From the ridges we watched the flashes on the horizon off to the northwest near Cape Esperance at the end of the island. We heard the booming of the big guns and saw great sheets of flame light the sky as ships burned or exploded. For half an hour the battle continued and our thoughts went back to the night of August 8–9. Then, too, we had seen and heard a naval battle near Savo Island and for two months we had felt the impact of its disastrous results. To us it seemed that every shortage in men, equipment, and supplies — shortages which had hamstrung us for weeks — could be traced directly to the defeat our ships had suffered in the night battle off Savo. What would be the results of this new encounter?

Before dawn our anxiety was quieted by the reports that began to come in from the scene of battle. A blue bulb burned dimly in the General's tent as Colonel Thomas came in with a dispatch telling the welcome news that the Japanese had been hard hit. Four of their warships had been sunk — a heavy cruiser and three destroyers — and a Japanese transport had been sent to the bottom. The gallant cruiser *Boise* had been damaged and later returned to the United States for repairs. The destroyer *Duncan* had been sunk, but the score was impressively in our favor.

Planes from Henderson Field took up the chase at dawn. They found two cruisers and four destroyers making their way back to Rabaul, and four striking forces of dive-bombers, torpedo planes, and fighters hit at them during the morning and early afternoon. They put a torpedo through one cruiser and scored several near bomb misses on the same ship, leaving her dead in the water and burning. They dropped bombs directly amidships on another cruiser and destroyer. The cruiser stopped dead and the crew were abandoning her when the pilots from Henderson Field headed back to base. The destroyer was set afire by the hit and several near misses and was about to sink when the fliers last saw her.

The Japanese, however, apparently had succeeded in landing some fresh troops and more equipment during the night, for fifteen new landing boats were sighted in the morning, at Kokumbona, Tassafaronga, and Maravovo. Airacobras bombed and strafed the new landing craft and near-by ground installations during the day.

Round one was clearly ours, but we soon learned that the enemy had been reserving his knock-out punch.

PURPLE NIGHTS — AND DAYS

I have mentioned that there were certain nights on Guadalcanal which everyone then there will always remember — the 'purple nights' when an impersonal danger filled the air and brooded over every one of the defenders huddled together within the defense perimeter around Henderson Field. The night of October 13–14 was splashed with deeper color than any of the others. We had been through 'purple nights' before, but they faded to dainty lavender compared to the events of this and succeeding nights.

The show began during the daylight hours. What the Japanese air raiders had failed to accomplish on the 11th, they succeeded in doing on the 13th. At noon a big formation swept over the field — twenty-four twin-engined bombers escorted by Zero fighters. Our fighters had got the warning too late, and although fifty rose to meet the raiders they hadn't time to climb as high as the enemy planes and the bombers dropped their loads of high explosive on the airfield without interruption. Two hours later, fifteen more twin-engined bombers, again escorted by Zeros, came over. Again they bombed the runways and again our fighter planes failed to gain altitude in time to break up the formation. The Japanese lost only two Zeros and one bomber, and we lost a Wildcat, but the pilot was saved. The raids had caused considerable damage. Both had blasted holes in the main runway and fighter strip, several planes on the ground had been damaged, and five thousand gallons of precious aviation gasoline had gone up in flames. It was not an auspicious beginning for the struggle that lay ahead.

Throughout the day disturbing reports came in of a powerful concentration of Japanese warships at Shortland Harbor, only three hundred miles away to the northwest. We were used to the constant threat of great enemy naval strength gathered not far from us. Ever since we first landed on Guadalcanal and Tulagi, Rabaul Harbor and the Buin area had teemed with Japanese warships, transports, and cargo ships. That fact had dictated our strategy in the ground fighting on Guadalcanal from the outset. But this new concentration was a closer and more immediate threat.

Despite the new menace, however, two American transports under naval escort had brought in an Army regiment, the first Army reinforcements to come to Guadalcanal. The new arrivals were the 164th Infantry under Colonel B. E. Moore, consisting largely of National Guardsmen from North Dakota and neighboring states. They immediately began to take up positions in the eastern sector of the defense perimeter, relieving the First Marines under Colonel Cates to reinforce our lines in the western sector toward the Matanikau. They got a foretaste of their future on Guadalcanal as they were landing and suffered several casualties from bombing raids as they concentrated in the coconut groves near Kukum after coming ashore. The ships that brought them escaped damage from the bombings that day, aimed primarily at the airfield, and succeeded in getting safely away from the island before we were engulfed in the inferno that began to blaze that night.

A hint of what was coming began at six-thirty in the evening. At that time a new sound was added to the din of Guadalcanal. It was the noise of Japanese artillery. We knew the Japanese had artillery on the island and from time to time our patrols had uncovered buried field guns and stores of ammunition in the jungle outside our lines. As early as the beginning of September the Japanese had begun to land these weapons, but they had never used them. For fire support they had relied upon naval gunfire. Never before October 13 had their artillery fired on the airfield. We knew, early in October, that the enemy had increased his quantity of artillery, but still it had stayed quiet.

When the first shell whistled over the Division Command Post and crashed on the western end of the airfield, there was a general scramble for the dugouts. We thought at first it was a bomb, from an airplane that had slipped over Guadalcanal unseen and unheard. It was a standing joke at the Command Post that Technical Sergeant 'Butch' Morgan, the General's cook, was exceedingly spry in catching up his helmet and making for shelter when the bombers came over. On this occasion Butch had joined in the dash for the shelters. I was standing at the entrance to one, near the General's tent, when another shell screeched overhead. The General listened thoughtfully, then said, 'Why, that isn't a bomb. It's artillery.' Butch took off his helmet in disgust. As a veteran of the First World War, he was used to this menace. 'Hell,' he said, 'only artillery! I thought it was a bomb.' And thereafter he refused to be disturbed by the intermittent shelling of the airfield, very close to the Command Post, by enemy artillery.

For about half an hour the Japanese guns, from positions near Point Cruz, fired at Henderson Field and at the beach area near the Naval Operating Base at Kukum. The Marines' push across the Matanikau had secured the airfield from shelling by light field pieces, but the Japanese had brought up fifteen-centimeter (roughly six inches) guns which could reach the field from well within their own lines east of the river. They fired a few rounds at the ships which had brought in the 164th Infantry, which were then preparing to leave Guadalcanal. The escort ships, Marine Coast artillery, and field artillery quickly answered, and when the Japanese guns grew silent after fifteen minutes of this heavy counter-battery, we dared to hope that at least some of the guns had been knocked out in this first exchange. We had no such luck. Throughout that night, and for weeks to follow, the Japanese artillery fired intermittently on the airfield, on ships unloading on the beach, on our front-line positions, and at other targets of opportunity. Firing from concealed positions in the jungle and behind the coral ridges west of the Matanikau, they proved very baffling to our counter-battery.

When the artillery began shelling the airfield at six-thirty that evening, some at Headquarters thought, 'This is the night!' Colonel Thomas expressed the hopes of Marines then ready and eager for a Japanese attack. 'It looks as though the Japs are getting ready to attack. Their ship losses the other night were heavier than they can take. Up the line there in Rabaul they've probably given these birds the word to shoot their piece while they've still got some rice. Well, if these babies want to play ball, that's good news. We're ready for them.'

There were signs, apart from the artillery fire that the Japanese were preparing to attack on land. Flares were reported by various observation posts, as though enemy units were signaling each other in the jungle night. An enemy plane circled the field at seven-thirty. Our searchlights caught him for a moment, but he got away. From the Matanikau front came the report of signs of hostile activity. A Japanese machine gun had opened up briefly on the left flank, by the Matanikau, then was silent. We waited tensely for the general attack, and the General warned all units to be alert.

The Japanese, however, refused to oblige with an attack.

They intended to land many more reinforcements before they again tried to puncture the line around Henderson Field.

Japanese planes were over at intervals throughout the night. No sooner did the sirens signal 'All Clear' than they wailed a warning that more Japanese planes were approaching. The enemy's fifteen-centimeter guns fired intermittently upon the airfield. We stumbled in and out of our foxholes and dugouts many times. We had an 'All Clear' about one o'clock in the morning, then, shortly after one-thirty, 'Condition Red' sounded again. It was Louie the Louse this time — the cruiser-type plane that spotted targets for naval gunfire. As always, he dropped a flare to mark the airfield. Then, as we watched from the mouths of our dugouts, there started the worst bombardment from the sea we had ever been through.

We had been shelled by cruisers and destroyers before. But this time a battleship — at least one — joined in the bombardment, standing off Savo Island twenty miles away. The combined force of battleships, cruisers, and destroyers opened up with everything they had. First fourteen-inch star shells burst into fantastic streamers of flame over Henderson Field, like a gigantic Fourth-of-July display. Then the high explosive came. Fourteen-inch, twelve-inch, eight-inch, and five-inch shells tore up the earth and set the ground trembling as though it was set in jelly. Throughout the bombardment Japanese planes came over in relays and bombed the airfield.

Captain Fred O. Wolf, an interpreter with the Marine forces, added to his great reputation as a wit by remarking, as the earth quivered under the bombardment, 'And you know it isn't the least bit habit-forming.'

The Division Command Post at this time was again located on the landward side of a coral ridge at the northwest end of the airfield. Salvo after salvo blasted the seaward side of the ridge and others pounded the roadway and coral hillocks scarcely fifty yards on the other side. The Command Post of the Eleventh Marines, a short distance away on the seaward side, suffered a direct hit from a fourteen-inch shell, a ton of steel and high explosive. It ripped through a reinforced concrete wall of a dugout excavated in the side of a coral hillock where many officers and men had taken shelter, but by some miracle all escaped with only minor injuries. Another shell blasted the crest of the ridge within a few feet of the Division Communications Center. Communications were disrupted. Everywhere wires were ripped up.

The only opposition we could offer to the surface force bombarding us was in the form of five-inch coast artillery and four motor torpedo boats which had arrived at Tulagi only that morning. The five-inchers scored hits on three Japanese destroyers which ventured too close to shore, but were powerless against the cruisers and battleship. The torpedo boats pluckily attacked a force of cruisers and destroyers. One torpedo struck home in a Japanese cruiser, but destroyers concentrated on the little patrol boats and chased them off the scene of battle.

For almost two hours the rain of steel and high explosives continued. Those who lived through that bombardment could only suppose that Henderson Field was left a shambles. Indeed, the destruction was great, especially in the dive-bomber squadrons. The morning of October 13 thirty-nine Dauntless dive-bombers had been in operating condition. After that night's rain of destruction, only four were in condition to take off. A Marine dive-bomber squadron which had just arrived on the island to relieve another lost its Commanding Officer, Executive Officer, Flight Officer, and two pilots. The fighter planes, based on the fighter strip east of the main runway, suffered relatively little damage.

After the naval bombardment stopped, bombers kept us in our shelters the rest of the night and at five-thirty the artillery opened up again, firing upon the airfield. At last, as day broke, we climbed from our dugouts and surveyed the damage. Wide-eyed men turning up bearing heavy base plates of fourteen-inch shells and huge shell fragments, proof of what we had only suspected as the shelling went on, that at least one Japanese battleship had joined in the bombardment. 'A most unenviable experience,' Henry Keyes, of the London *Daily Express* remarked, with British understatement.

That night was only the beginning. Again on the 14th we had two air raids. Twenty-five bombers came over at noon and dropped their bombs without interference and without losses. Our fighters had taken off on a false alarm earlier in the morning and after the second alert were unable to climb high enough in time to intercept the raiders. An hour later fifteen more bombers and ten Zeros came over the field. This time our fighters were there to meet them and the Wildcats shot down nine bombers and three Zeros. Throughout the day Japanese artillery fired intermittently on the airfield, gradually extending their range up the main runway. Air operations on that runway — the only one which came near to being an all-weather strip since much of it had been surfaced with steel matting — had to be suspended and operations were transferred to the grass fighter strip.

In the morning search planes picked up the Japanese convoy for which the previous night's bombardment was intended to clear a path. Six transports escorted by eight destroyers were making their way down the northern coast of Santa Ysabel. By four-thirty in the afternoon they were only one hundred and forty miles away, off the southern end of Santa Ysabel. A supporting force, consisting of one battleship, three cruisers, and four destroyers, was approaching Guadalcanal along the southern shore of Santa Ysabel. At four o'clock in the afternoon it was still one hundred and eighty miles away.

The Japanese had hoped, by their bombardment of October 13–14, to knock out the aircraft on Henderson Field so that the slow, vulnerable transports could close in to Guadalcanal unmolested by our planes. They all but succeeded. Only four or five bombers could be mustered to go after the Japanese transports in the first striking mission that afternoon. Ground crews on the airfield had worked feverishly all day to get planes into the air, but with the invasion force bearing down inexorably only that handful of planes could be sent to oppose them. They found the enemy transports just after five o'clock, dived in the face of heavy anti-aircraft fire, and planted a bomb on one of the transports. Ten more dive-bombers had been put back into commission in the course of the day and, after the first attack, nine Dauntless dive-bombers struck at the enemy transport group. Again they ran into a wall of anti-aircraft fire, but scored several possible hits and near misses on transports. One of the Japanese troop-carriers went to the bottom in flames. The others plodded steadily on toward Guadalcanal.

It was an anxious night for the defenders of Henderson Field. Our air force, the only weapon available to oppose the invasion, had been cut to pieces. No American surface task forces were in the vicinity to meet the invaders. By two o'clock the morning of the 15th, the enemy ships had arrived off Guadalcanal. The five transports that had survived the weak air attacks of the previous afternoon began unloading between Kokumbona and Cape Esperance while their screening warships again bombarded our position. This second successive night bombardment lasted for half an hour. Again it was concentrated against the airfield and did great damage.

Dawn revealed five transports brazenly unloading between Kokumbona and Doma Reef, only twelve to fifteen miles away, within sight of Kukum. Eleven warships screened the transports and a flight of Zero fighters and float-plane fighters provided air coverage. The Marines on land could do nothing but watch their enemies unload a few miles up the beach and wait for the day when they could come to grips with them on land. It is hard for men who had been fighting for two months in almost daily contact with the enemy to have to sit helplessly by while thousands more hostile troops pour ashore. Marines used to shake their heads and say, 'They are landing 'em faster than we can kill 'em.'

The two days and nights of bombing and naval shelling had

left us with only three dive-bombers able to take to the air as dawn broke that day. One plane fell in a crater while taxiing to the runway. Lieutenant Robert M. Patterson tried to take another off in the darkness just before dawn. Major Joseph N. Renner, Assistant Operations Officer, had inspected the runway, ripped and torn by bombs and shells, and had charted a course down the strip where a plane might be able to take off. As a little group watched anxiously in the darkness, Patterson's plane taxied to the end of the runway, roared up the strip to take off, then crashed into a fourteen-inch shell crater, a total loss. Lieutenant Patterson miraculously escaped injury and asked to take up another plane. Just at dawn he succeeded in getting the one remaining dive-bomber into the air and went on his lone mission against the powerful Japanese force a few miles west of us.

The ground crews worked feverishly to get more planes into the air. Lieutenant Colonel Albert D. Cooley, in command of bomber operations on Henderson Field, has called Lieutenant William L. Woodruff the real hero of the day. Lieutenant Woodruff was in charge of the maintenance section for scout bombers. He and his ground crews, who worked throughout the hurly-burly of those days without rest for seventy-two hours under shellings and bombings, put more and more planes into the air as the day wore on and the little group of fliers achieved results all out of proportion to their numbers.

Six Wildcats which had gone out on patrol as the sky began to brighten had first spotted the enemy ships. Two of them swung low to strafe the transports and were attacked by float-plane fighters. One of the Japanese planes was shot down, but we lost a Wildcat. As dive-bombers were put into operating condition, they took off to bomb the ships and before seven o'clock in the morning single bombers, operating alone in a sky full of anti-aircraft bursts and enemy fighter planes, made four attacks on the transports and scored two hits.

Then General Geiger decided to stop the single-plane attacks and hold all planes until a striking force could be assembled. Every available plane was thrown into the attack, including the General's Catalina flying-boat. Major Jack R. Cram had just flown it in with a cargo of two torpedoes. He volunteered to take up the big, slow plane and attack the transports. All available dive-bombers and fighters took off to rendezvous fifteen miles east of the airfield and Major Cram joined them. They gave him a lead as they wheeled to the west to move in on the Japanese transports, so that his slow lumbering plane would not be left behind by the faster bombers and fighters. Then they attacked. Major Cram put the Catalina into a steep glide, swooped low over a transport, released his torpedoes, then barely cleared the superstructure as he climbed through heavy anti-aircraft fire. At full speed he headed back for Henderson Field with Zeros diving on him all the way. One had just got on his tail as he came over the edge of the field, then dropped away as Cram gained the protection of our anti-aircraft defenses. Zero pilots had learned to respect the gunners of the Special Weapons Battalion (Lieutenant Colonel Robert B. Luckey) who dotted the airfield. Already that morning Japanese strafers had been shot down as they came in low over the field and thereafter the Zeros gave it a wide berth.

Flying Fortresses based on Espiritu Santo appeared on the scene just before noon and scored hits on a transport and a warship. By noon two of the transports were ablaze and beached. Just after noon twenty-seven enemy bombers came over and dropped their bombs without interception — our few planes were too busy attacking the Japanese landing force. The anti-aircraft, however, got three of them. The attacks on the Japanese ships continued and by mid-afternoon two transports had been sunk, another was burning on the beach, and the other two had been hit, but were making for the open sea. Our fliers pursued them and late in the afternoon, catching up with them sixty-five miles from Guadalcanal, set one on fire and scored a near miss on the other.

In a day's constant aerial combat, as Zeros and float-biplanes attacked our dive-bombers, as our Wildcats pursued the Zeros and strafed the enemy ships, and as our Airacobras strafed the enemy's landing beach, one Zero and five Zero float-planes were shot down. We lost three dive-bombers, one Wildcat, and one Airacobra. Six new dive-bombers arrived at Henderson Field — pathetically small, but highly welcome reinforcements for our battered air force.

The Japanese had paid for their landing with the loss of four transports and damage to the other two, but they had succeeded in landing thousands of men and much equipment. It was a discouraging day for the American forces around Henderson Field. Most disheartening of all, there was no immediate prospect of a turn for the better. The Japanese Navy commanded the waters around Guadalcanal. It seemed there was nothing to prevent their continuing to shell our position at their pleasure.

As if to confirm our forebodings, Japanese warships shelled the airfield area for the third successive night. Enemy bombers were over in relays throughout the night, dropping bombs intermittently and keeping the garrison awake. At twelve-thirty the surface craft opened up and for an hour pounded the area. They were gradually cutting down our remaining air strength, and of the powerful concentration of aircraft that crowded Henderson Field only three days before, only nine Wildcats, eleven Dauntless dive-bombers, and fourteen Aira-cobras (half of them not equipped for high-altitude work and therefore almost useless as fighter planes) were in operating condition the morning of October 16. All the Avenger tor-pedo bombers had been knocked out.

The shrunken air force, however, never let up in its attack on the newly landed Japanese to the west of us. They made seven attacks on enemy positions during the day, bombing and strafing new landing boats, supply dumps, bivouac areas, and the beach area. They continued to carry out their usual search missions over the Solomon Islands. They provided air coverage for the destroyer *Macfarland* which arrived with a precious load of aviation gas at noon.

It was a quiet day, as days went on Guadalcanal, though full of feverish preparations for the next round. There were three air alerts, but nothing came over, and in the evening air reinforcements arrived in the form of twenty Wildcats and twelve Dauntless dive-bombers. As they circled the field, to the cheers of bomb-battered, shell-battered Marines and soldiers, eight Japanese dive-bombers slipped in at low altitude to attack the destroyer *Macfarland*. No more urgently needed cargo had ever arrived at Guadalcanal than that carried by the *Macfarland* and it sickened us when the Japanese raiders succeeded in scoring a hit which sent her limping to Tulagi. The enemy paid, however, with a loss of four dive-bombers, all shot down by Lieutenant Colonel Harold W. Bauer, commanding the new Marine fighter squadron coming to Guadalcanal. He spied them out of the corner of his eye as his formation of Wildcats circled the field and alone chased the whole flight out toward Savo Island. He knocked them off one by one until he ran out of ammunition and fuel. That was one episode in the struggle to supply Guadalcanal with aviation gas during that critical period.

'NO MORE AVIATION GAS'

The morning of October 15, when the Japanese transports were unloading a few miles west of Kukum, with our air power shattered by the steady pounding from Japanese naval guns and bombs, a stunning announcement came from the Air Command on Henderson Field. 'We have no more aviation gas.' They said that after our few planes then in operating condition were fueled, the supply of gasoline would be exhausted. It seemed there was nothing to do but to direct the aviators to use every drop they had, then put the planes at the far end of the main runway out of range of Japanese artillery, and secure. It was a heart-breaking situation. No group of fliers had ever done a more magnificent job than this based on Henderson Field. Now, just when they were most desperately needed, they must be grounded for lack of fuel.

As it turned out, a small supply of aviation gas still remained at the airfield, but the shortage was nevertheless grave. No drop of gasoline was ignored in the frantic search that followed. An urgent request was radioed for gas to be flown to Guadalcanal by air transports, in as steady a stream as possible. All gas was siphoned out of abandoned wrecks on the field. Driblets were drained out of wrecked Wildcats. A Flying Fortress, shot up by naval gunfire, served as a bigger reservoir.

Marine officers set out to find small dumps of aviation gas, scattered about our position, which might have been overlooked. The gasoline had been dispersed in small dumps over a wide area, most of them partly under the surface and covered with earth, and it was quite possible that a thorough search would reveal isolated groups of drums. Lieutenant Colonel John D. Macklin, who had supervised the movement of aviation gasoline to the airfield after our original landing, when we expected aircraft to arrive at any moment, located more than one hundred drums. He took Major Holmes of the Supply Section with him so that in case anything happened to one the other would know where the precious dumps were spotted. The Pioneers found about two hundred drums in their area, Colonel Whaling found one hundred at the new fighter strip then being developed near the beach south of Kukum. Lieutenant Colonel Macklin located another lot of forty drums, then twenty-five more. By the end of the day well over four hundred drums had been located. That night two Yippee boats — converted tuna fishing vessels — slipped over from Tulagi and unloaded two hundred drums of gas before the enemy started his third successive night naval bombardment of our position.

The next day, October 16, the destroyer *Macfarland* came in with several thousand gallons. She arrived at noon, to the immense relief of everyone aware of the critical shortage, and began unloading drums of gasoline. Three hundred drums had been unloaded when the eight Japanese dive-bombers staged their surprise attack and sank a barge that was being loaded with gas to transfer ashore. The *Macfarland*, too, was hit in the stern, but made safety in Tulagi Harbor where she continued to unload.

Meanwhile, transport planes maintained a shuttle service back and forth between Henderson Field and American bases to the southeast. Each brought in a tiny but priceless load — little lots of six or eight drums. By such expedients we were able to get barely enough fuel to keep our planes in the air.

We anxiously awaited another shipment of aviation gas which we knew was on the way. A tug, with a large seagoing barge full of gas in tow, escorted by the destroyer *Meredith*, was three days overdue when we learned the fate of these vessels October 18. On the 15th, as the little convoy approached Guadalcanal from the southeast, they were attacked by Japanese dive-bombers. The *Meredith* was sunk, leaving the tug and barge unprotected. But they continued on. Again, on the 16th, they were attacked by dive-bombers. The tug was disabled and left dead in the water, but the barge, with its load of gasoline, ammunition, and landing-mat, was still afloat. An escort of destroyers was dispatched to pick them up and finally on the 23d the cargo reached Guadalcanal.

Destroyers with deckloads of gas drums began coming to Guadalcanal. Another large seagoing barge was brought safely to port on the 19th, and the gas crisis was relieved for the moment.

GETTING READY FOR ANOTHER CLASH

Those were the days when the newspapers in the United States carried lugubrious headlines, when editorials began preparing the public for disaster in the Solomons, when radio

commentators and press dispatches told a gloomy tale of in-
exorable Japanese pressure on the defenses of Henderson
Field.

Headlines in American newspapers in mid-October told of
strong Japanese forces moving in for the kill. 'Japs Land in
Force, Shell Guadalcanal,' 'Japs Believed to Rule Sea in
Solomons'; 'Japanese Fleet Massing North of Guadalcanal as
Decisive Battle Rages'; 'Fate of U.S. Airfield on Island in
Doubt.' Editorials warned gravely that the Japanese were
launching a major drive which might overwhelm the defend-
ers of Henderson Field and began to speak as though Guadal-
canal would be added to the list of American defeats in the
Pacific.

October 16 the *New York Times* said in an editorial:

> We know that these American young men will do all
> that humanly can be done to stand their ground and to
> advance. While we at home work, sleep, amuse ourselves
> — and what else can we do? — they fight . . . Guadal-
> canal. The name will not die out of the memories of this
> generation. It will endure in honor.

On the 20th the *Times* again commented on the growing crisis
in the Solomons:

> The time had to come in this area when the Japanese,
> with all the striking power they could muster, would come
> against the Americans, with all the defensive and offen-
> sive force our side can bring to bear. Of the ultimate
> issue in the Pacific not one American will have doubts.
> For the immediate result at Guadalcanal we can hope
> and pray, and that is all we can do — aside from working
> harder and making sacrifices to help the cause along.

The New York *Herald Tribune*, on the 16th, remarked that

> The shadows of a great conflict lie heavily over the
> Solomons — all that can be perceived is the magnitude
> of the stakes at issue.

The *Washington Post* on the 17th prepared its readers for grave news from the Solomons:

> The latest news from the Solomons is far from hopeful. On the contrary it is ominous. The possibility cannot now be ignored that our forces may be dislodged from the precarious foothold they obtained on Guadalcanal Island at no small cost last August. It is a military axiom that any objective can be attained if there is a readiness to pay the price that may be necessary. The Japanese know that, even if we don't. Into the renewed Battle of the Solomons the Japanese have thrown everything they have. They have been prodigal of man-power and materiel.

At a press conference October 19, Secretary of the Navy Knox was asked if he thought the island would be held. The papers quoted him as replying:

> I certainly hope so. I expect so. I don't want to make any predictions, but every man out there, ashore or afloat, will give a good account of himself.

The echoes of this sombre chorus reached George on Guadalcanal. In the evening he listened to the news from San Francisco if he was lucky enough to be near a radio, and heard the note of pessimism creeping into the news announcer's and commentator's voice. Perhaps for the first time he began to have doubts of the outcome on Guadalcanal himself. He began to see what he could not see from his spot on the island — that strong Japanese forces were moving all about the island and that the outcome of the struggle for Guadalcanal might be decided far from its shores. However well he might fight, he would lose in the end if the Japanese gained complete supremacy on the seas.

For two months George had worked and fought with little rest. One night he would lie in a foxhole at the front line. The next day he might be sent down to the beach on a working party to labor all day under a hot sun unloading supplies from a ship that had come in. Back to the front at night, then next morning he might struggle through the jungle on patrol. He was sick. Malaria, dengue, intestinal diseases, malnutrition had left him weak. His recreation was an occasional bath in the Lunga River or at the beach, where he threaded his way through the barbed wire for a dip in the lukewarm Pacific. Even when there were no major actions on land, he was constantly on the alert. Day after day he had burrowed into the ground as the bombers came over and many nights he had returned into the ground as Japanese ships shelled him.

In these latter days the strain had become even greater. George had long since become a veteran in the matter of bombings and was so little disturbed by them that he seldom went into a shelter until our anti-aircraft opened up, a sign that the bombers were almost overhead and that the bombs would soon whistle down. Fourteen-inch shells were another matter. George began to show a preference for sleeping underground. Sleep had become a major problem in his life. He caught it in snatches as he could, day or night, during lulls in the noise that beat against his ears. If he crept underground at night, he might be able to sleep through a few light bombings. If the ground were muddy and the dugout full of mosquitoes — well, that didn't matter much if he could just sleep.

George had seen friends collapse under the strain, not many, but enough to impress upon him what a hell he was going through. One friend had a vacant stare in his eye. He did not listen when George spoke, and his ears seemed to be hearing something in the sky. He was sent away on a plane. Another fell to the ground one day, clutching his stomach in agony, though the air was quiet and nothing had struck him. He, too, was sent away.

The Press Club, where the correspondents lived, had a jeep driven by Private Giralamo Grande whom we called 'Jerry.' Jerry had instructions to stop by the Press Club each evening before he returned to the Motor Transport area, to pick up any press dispatches ready to go out by plane. One evening, when nerves were at their tautest, Jerry stuck his head in the tent to ask if there was anything to go out. I told him there was nothing, that he could go on back to camp. Then, as he went down the hill to his jeep some hundred yards away, I found there was some materiel that should go immediately and ran after him. In those hectic days it had become an unwritten rule that no one should run; too many men were upset by a haste that might indicate bombers were coming over. I not only ran, but I shouted out, 'Jerry, Jerry!' which, to overwrought nerves, sounds very much like 'Air raid! Air raid!' A group of officers was standing near the jeep park as I ran past shouting, and with one accord they put on their helmets and dashed for a shelter. Quite properly I was 'read off' by every superior officer in the camp.

It is strange how quickly one bounces back from such a pounding as the defenders of Henderson Field took in the middle of October. Inexplicably, the Japanese did not follow up their smashing three-day bombardment as relentlessly as we had expected and life returned pretty much to normal.

There was a lull as both sides prepared for the approaching clash of ground forces. It was a 'lull' only in the sense that the bombardment let up somewhat. We were not again shelled from the sea except for a short and ineffective bombardment just after midnight of the 17th. Japanese aerial activity, however, continued unabated.

At dawn of the 17th two American destroyers began to shell the Japanese positions along the coast to the west of Kokumbona. For three hours they raked the shoreline and the area for some distance inland where Japanese supplies and equipment were presumably concentrated. Several large fires, and the thick black smoke which tells of burning supplies, rewarded this intensive shelling. Fifteen Japanese dive-bombers attacked the destroyers as they were performing their mission, but the ships escaped damage, and Wildcats from Henderson Field shot down eight of the bombers and two of the escorting Zeros. Anti-aircraft fire from the destroyers brought down six more Japanese dive-bombers, while we lost only one Wildcat.

In the afternoon another flight of bombers, sixteen twin-engined Mitsubishis with a Zero escort, bombed the airfield. The Wildcats did not get high enough soon enough to intercept them, but our anti-aircraft batteries shot down two of the bombers. In the week that followed, there were seven air raids and the enemy formations sustained very heavy losses. At a cost to us of seven Wildcats and six pilots, forty-six Zeros, nineteen dive-bombers, and fifteen twin-engined bombers were brought down. The next enemy daylight air raid came on the 25th — 'Dugout Sunday'; but that is a story in itself, which will be told later.

Throughout this period both Japanese and American planes were active at night. As the moon grew bright over Guadalcanal, planes droned through the air every night. Some were ours, some were Japanese, as each belligerent sought to harass the other's troops with strafing and bombing. The purists will say that the Japanese night-bombers — usually four-engined Kawanishi flying boats or twin-engined bombers — should be called 'Washing Machine Charlie,' so named from the distinctive sound of the big planes' engines, as distinct from 'Louie the Louse,' the cruiser-based planes which acted as spotters for naval bombardments. 'Louie the Louse,' however, was the name favored for any Japanese plane that disturbed our sleep. Our own planes flying over Japanese lines at night were gratefully named 'Saint Louis.' Every night after October 17 the comforting drone of 'Saint Louis,' in the form of dive-bombers or big naval patrol bombers, could be heard shuttling back and forth over the enemy positions to the west. We often heard the more ominous and distinctive drone of Louie the Louse over our own position. He showed a predilection for coming soon after nightfall, but we never knew at what time of the night we would have to take to our shelters while he cruised over the field.

Every day and many nights our own planes from Henderson

Field bombed and strafed the Japanese positions to the west, hitting at their supply dumps, landing boats, bivouac areas, and gun emplacements. A shortage in bombs developed and somewhat hampered this steady pounding of the enemy, but he had little peace as he tried to get his forces into position for the big push on land. At night our planes patrolled the coast-line of Guadalcanal on the lookout for Japanese warships which continued to come into near-by waters, though they did not shell us. At two o'clock the morning of October 20 a Catalina flying boat on patrol found an enemy cruiser off Lunga Point and scored a near miss and a hit on the Japanese ship. She was dead in the water, smoking badly.

During the ten-day period that elapsed between the time the Japanese began to shell Henderson Field and the first attack by their ground forces, enemy artillery continued to fire intermittently. The airfield and the Naval Operating Base were the primary targets. By October 15 they had forced abandonment of the Naval Operating Base at Kukum, where our supply ships had been unloading up to that time, and thereafter ships unloaded at Lunga Lagoon, about two miles east of Kukum. Even there they were not immune from enemy artillery, and an occasional shell screamed over the Lunga to splash in the sea off the lagoon.

The shell-bursts crept farther and farther up the main runway of Henderson Field. They consistently hit on the western end of the strip and sometimes much farther up. In later days the Japanese artillery even reached as far as the new fighter strip. Operations on the main runway became increasingly hazardous and were shifted, as much as possible, to the fighter strip, still simply a dirt runway bound together by its native grass. The Air Command had to abandon the 'Pagoda,' the Japanese style building on a mound overlooking the main runway which the Japanese had built and which we had taken over as headquarters for air operations. The buildings at Kukum and the Pagoda were razed. The main radio direction-finder station on Pagoda Hill had been demolished in the mid-October bombardment. The disappearance of these familiar landmarks did as much as bombing and shellings to give us the feeling that we were under siege.

Pistol Pete, the six-inch Japanese naval gun (or guns) responsible for this harassment, was hated with a special bitterness by the airmen of Henderson Field. He had little ammunition and could only fire at odd moments of the day or night, but no one on the airfield ever knew when he might open up. Several times Pistol Pete kicked up the earth behind planes warming up at the end of the runway to take off. Time after time the fliers took off to attack the gun as a new report of his location came in. It was, however, well emplaced and well concealed, and it was many weeks before Pistol Pete was finally silenced. He fired from positions outside the range of our own artillery, near Kokumbona. As we had nothing larger than a 105-millimeter howitzer at that time, counterbattery was out of the question.

After the 'purple nights' of mid-October, when the Japanese had made big landings west of us, we got air reinforcements, material shortages were made up as much as possible, and the Marines with their Army reinforcements made ready for the fighting on our jungle defense perimeter which was bound to follow soon. As the Japanese moved their forces toward the Matanikau River, that front became more and more active. Ten days after the Japanese drive began, the battle for Henderson Field started.

Chapter 8

Smashing the Sendai Division

T HE JAPANESE, it developed, planned to recapture
Henderson Field by a classic maneuver — a holding
attack along the coast in the west with the main attack in the
form of a wide envelopment aimed at the southern defense
sector. The undertaking was entrusted to a reinforced division, the Sendai or Second Division of the Imperial Japanese
Army, plus attached units of artillery and special troops. The
division was commanded by Lieutenant General Maruyama
and consisted largely of veterans of campaigns in China,
Malaya, the Philippines, and Java, men who had never known
defeat and who had pushed the European steadily backward
throughout the western Pacific.

Undoubtedly they hoped that the holding attack, led by a
company of medium tanks (fourteen to fifteen tons), against
our forces on the line of the Matanikau River would draw our
reserves in that direction, while the main attack drove through
from the ridges and jungle south of the airfield. The Japanese
would have been interested to know that our 'reserves' consisted of only one understrength battalion, the hard-worked
Third Battalion, Second Marines, under Lieutenant Colonel
R. G. Hunt. There were signs that the Japanese also considered another holding attack in the form of a frontal assault on
our beach defenses near Lunga Point, launched from the

161

landing craft which they had been sending to the western part of the island.

In preparation for their attack, the Japanese had long been hacking trails through the jungle west and south of us. The naval forces comprising their original garrison on Guadalcanal, which had withdrawn westward beyond the Matanikau when we occupied the airfield, had long since been reinforced by troops and laborers engaged in getting ready for the day when overwhelming Japanese forces could encircle and assault the airdrome. Deep into the jungle south of Kokumbona they had cut trails over which men and equipment could be moved. Inland, to the south of the Mambulo and Mount Austen, the network was extended. Hidden by the dense mat of jungle vegetation, the Japanese soldiers who had landed from destroyers and transports throughout September and October moved up to jump-off positions near our lines in several sectors.

After October 15, when the large-scale landing was made from transports, eight days passed before the enemy was ready to launch his assault. Early in the evening of the 20th a Japanese combat patrol, feeling out our lines at the mouth of the Matanikau, tried to cross the river, but was driven back with the loss of an armored vehicle. Again on the 21st the enemy was active west of the Matanikau. Several tanks were brought up close to the river, but were driven back by heavy artillery fire. As the brief tropical twilight deepened, planes strafed our front-line positions at the Matanikau. For a while it looked as though the Japanese were ready to attack in force, but as the night wore on nothing happened except that a bomber came over at nine o'clock on a nuisance raid, just in time to give a sixteen-bomb salute to the Commandant of the Marine Corps, Lieutenant General Thomas Holcomb, who had arrived by airplane that evening. The next day Japanese artillery fired intermittently as the Commandant and his party toured our area and visited front-line positions, but the night passed quietly.

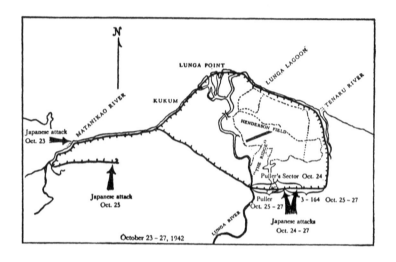

N

LUNGA POINT

LUNGA LAGOON

TENARU RIVER

KUKUM

MATANIKAO RIVER

HENDERSON FIELD

Japanese attack
Oct. 23

"THE RIDGE"

Puller's Sector Oct. 24

Japanese attack
Oct. 25

Puller
Oct. 25 – 27

3 – 164   Oct. 25 – 27

Japanese attacks
Oct. 24 – 27

LUNGA RIVER

October 23 – 27, 1942

THE DRIVE AGAINST HENDERSON FIELD

At dawn on the 23d the Commandant, accompanied by Major General Vandegrift, took off from Guadalcanal and went to South Pacific Headquarters for conferences. Brigadier General Rupertus took over command of the First Marine Division, Reinforced, in the absence of Major General Vandegrift. The Japanese chose that day for the beginning of their drive against Henderson Field. During the day enemy air attacks continued. This time they sent over sixteen twin-engined bombers escorted by twenty-five Zeros. The Wildcats concentrated on the Zero fighters and shot down twenty of them, and the bombers jettisoned their load on the shoreline far from the airfield. One of the bombers was also shot down and three left smoking, while all of the Wildcats returned to the field with no losses except for bad damage to one from Zero gunfire.

Enemy artillery was active throughout the day and succeeded in forcing us to abandon the naval operating base at Kukum. They were also hitting far into the airfield and some shells reached as far as the fighter strip east of the main runway. At dusk the intermittent fire of enemy artillery, by then one of the familiar sounds on Guadalcanal, grew steadier and more purposeful. Every artillery piece the Japanese had seemed to concentrate against the Marine positions on the right bank of the Matanikau. Mortars and machine guns joined with six-inch guns and seventy-five-millimeter howitzers in pounding our lines in that sector. The preparation was first laid on our front-line positions. Then the enemy's fire dropped back to where he thought our command posts were. Then he increased his range and started shelling the airfield. The Eleventh Marines immediately replied with counter-battery.

As reports came in from the Matanikau sector, Staff Officers at the Division Command Post concluded, 'This is the night!' The artillery preparation seemed a certain sign that the Japanese were about to launch the long-expected attack, and in fact they were.

In the twilight Marines manning the defenses on the right bank of the Matanikau could see Japanese tanks milling about on the opposite side of the river. Two 'half-tracks' — tank-destroyers mounting seventy-five-millimeter guns — had been dispatched to the Matanikau to meet a possible tank attack.

The leading enemy tank rumbled up the coast road toward the mouth of the river, sped out on the sand bar which almost closes the Matanikau at this point, and started across. It was knocked out by a thirty-seven-millimeter anti-tank gun of the Special Weapons Battalion. Another tank dashed out of a hidden track the Japanese had cut in the jungle toward the southeast from the river's mouth. This tank, coming from an unexpected quarter, took the defenders by surprise, sped across the sand bar before it could be stopped, overran a machine-gun emplacement, then stopped dead as it struck a tree stump. For a moment it was disabled and vulnerable — time enough for the half-track stationed near the river mouth to swing about into position and bring its seventy-five milli-meter gun to bear. It was then that Private First Class Joseph D. R. Champagne distinguished himself by helping to knock out the tank. He had crouched in a foxhole, directly in path of the tank, and when it stopped momentarily abreast of him, he calmly stood up, placed a grenade in the track, and wrecked the treads on one side of the tank. Its engine was still running, but as the tank backed away from the obstruc-tion at full speed, the half-track opened fire at point-blank range and drove the tank twenty yards into the sea where it stopped, a total wreck.

Two more tanks made up the first wave of four that tried to force a crossing of the river. They, too, were knocked out by the half-track and thirty-seven-millimeter guns. Soon five more tanks started across and again the defenders stopped the entire group. In the course of the action Second Lieutenant Thomas C. Mather, in charge of the half-tracks, was knocked unconscious by concussion from a mortar explosion. When he recovered consciousness, he continued to lead the fight against the tanks, mounted the only half-track which was able to fight effectively in the cramped clearing at the mouth of the river, and disabled five of the fifteen-ton tanks which tried to force a crossing.

Meanwhile, the Eleventh Marines had begun to lay down the heaviest series of artillery concentrations in Marine Corps history. Their fire was directed, not against the tanks at the mouth of the river, but against the infantry which were concentrated behind the tanks near Point Cruz, ready to exploit any breach of our lines the tanks might make. More than six thousand rounds were fired into that tiny area and the Japanese infantry massed there were completely destroyed or demoralized. A few days later, when Marine patrols were able to operate west of the river again, they found the remains of about six hundred enemy soldiers. Early in the battle dive-bombers from Henderson Field attacked the Japanese infantry, and Marines on the opposite side of the river could hear their screams and groans as the bombs and shells struck home.

Until midnight the battle and alarms continued. Always, in the course of such a battle, ears and eyes strained to catch new signs of enemy activity start alarms that turn out to have little basis in fact. About nine o'clock that night it began to rain. The sky to the northwest, out toward Savo, was full of lightning flashes. Bursts of artillery and mortar shells filled the jungle night with noise. In that chaos of flashes and explosions front-line observers fancied they saw Japanese ships standing in toward Guadalcanal from Savo, firing on our positions at the Matanikau. Some thought the Japanese were attempting to land behind our forces at the river line, between them and our main line of resistance farther east toward Kukum. That was a very weakly held and vulnerable stretch of beach and the Division reserve was put on the move to help oppose a possible landing. Lieutenant Colonel S. G. Taxis, Operations Officer of the Third Defense Battalion in charge of coast defenses in the Lunga Point area, made the comforting report that he could see plenty of shooting stars, lightning, and artillery fire, but no ships, and in fact the enemy did not attempt a landing that night.

Early in the evening there had been activity at the elbow in the Matanikau River, about one thousand yards from the shore. Some Japanese tried to cross there, but were driven back. Again, about midnight, observation posts reported signs of new enemy activity at this point. The Third Battalion, Seventh Marines (Lieutenant Colonel W. R. Williams), occupying the sector on the left flank of Lieutenant Colonel McKelvy's battalion were alerted to meet a possible enemy attempt to outflank the defenders at the river's mouth after their unsuccessful attempt to cross the sand bar. By one o'clock, however, all was quiet and remained so the rest of the night except for occasional artillery fire.

The Japanese attempt to force a crossing of the Matanikau had failed completely. The enemy forces engaged in that sector were so shattered that they could not again launch a holding attack there to divert our forces from the main attack, which was to come south of the airfield. That assault had not yet materialized and, thanks to the failure of the Japanese to co-ordinate the two, the Marines could concentrate all their energies to meet the main effort which started the next night.

THE MAIN ATTACK

The Japanese had done well in concealing their movements through the jungle south of us. Swinging far to the west and south of our defenses, cutting through a tangle of underbrush and dense woods across hilly difficult terrain, they had succeeded in eluding patrols sent out from our lines.

Shortly after dawn on the 24th a Japanese column was observed moving around our left flank at the Matanikau near the sector held by Lieutenant Colonel Williams' battalion. Our planes attacked the Japanese and our lines in that sector were reinforced by the Second Battalion, Seventh Marines,

under Lieutenant Colonel H. H. Hanneken. As they moved
in to fill a gap about nine hundred yards long, they suffered
thirty-three casualties from Japanese artillery fire. The
enemy movement in that sector indicated that the battle near
the Matanikau would start again, and the night of the 24th a
platoon of Japanese, about seventy strong, hit against a part
of the Marine ridge-top line held by twenty-five men. The
attack was repulsed, with enemy losses of twenty-five dead and
one machine gun captured, and at daylight the Japanese
withdrew into the tangle of trees and brush in the ravine below the Ridge.

The enemy's main effort the night of October 24–25 developed south of the fighter strip, near the Ridge, although patrols had seen no signs of enemy activity there throughout the
day.

Along the southern line of our defense perimeter the First
Battalion, Seventh Marines (Lieutenant Colonel Lewis B.
Puller), occupied a sector about twenty-five hundred yards
long, extending from the Lunga River westward to a grassy
field southeast of the fighter strip. The grassy plain borders a
flat stretch of thick jungle. Dense underbrush and creepers
cover the ground below towering trees. Farther west a steep
ridge rises from the jungle and runs westward to the north-
south Ridge where the Japanese attacked September 12–14.

It was a long line through forbidding terrain for one battalion to hold and Lieutenant Colonel Puller's men were
spread very thin. During the day patrols had pushed southward for a distance of three to four thousand yards in front of
his line without finding any sign of the enemy. That night,
however, the enemy fell upon them in a series of fierce assaults.

The first enemy attack started about ten o'clock at night,
against the Ridge. A torrential tropical rain beat down,
obscuring a moon that was almost full. A listening post of
forty-six men, under Platoon Sergeant Ralph Briggs, Jr., was
on a grassy knob fifteen hundred yards in front of Lieutenant
Colonel Puller's barbed wire. Through the heavy rain pelt-

ing against jungle thickets the men in the outpost thought they heard voices and movements about the hill where they were watching. At first they were uncertain what was causing the noise, then the Japanese swarmed about the hill.

Briggs immediately notified Lieutenant Colonel Puller, but the Japanese were already attacking the First Battalion's lines. The Colonel wanted to give his forty-six-man outpost a chance to return inside our defensive lines before opening fire and he ordered his men to hold their fire until the outpost was safely back.

The Japanese, however, had already begun to cut the barbed wire in front of our lines, and as Briggs and his men left their isolated hilltop and started to make their way through the jungle toward the Army lines, the Marines could delay no longer in meeting the Japanese attack. Lieutenant Colonel Puller ordered his men to open fire. The Japanese made charge after charge, and the Marines repulsed each. The fighting would be heavy for ten or fifteen minutes as the Japanese, massed along a narrow front, tried to clear an opening with mortars and machine guns, then charge against the Marine lines. Then there would be a lull as the enemy withdrew to organize another assault.

Sergeant John Basilone, in charge of two sections of heavy machine guns, won the Congressional Medal of Honor for his gallant fight that night. Japanese mortars had found the machine-gun positions of one of his sections and had knocked out all but two men in the gun crews. Basilone, under continual fire, moved an extra gun into position, placed it in action, repaired a second gun, manned it himself, and held the line until replacements could come up.

Later in the battle, his gunners desperately short of ammunition, the Japanese had broken through the Marine line near-by, cutting Basilone off from his supply. He fought his way through the attackers and succeeded in returning with the ammunition so urgently needed by his gunners.

In the midst of the attack, a machine gun manned by two

Privates First Class, Edmund J. Dorsogna and Jack Sugarman, broke down, but the two men repaired it under heavy fire and put it back in action. Three more times the gun jammed, but each time the two stayed by it, repaired it, and continued to resist the Japanese.

Private Theodore G. West was wounded early in the battle, so badly hurt that he could not fire his rifle, but he stayed in his position in the front line, helped place two rifle squads in a most advantageous position where six hours of fighting had made the Marine line very weak, and helped direct their fire. He refused to leave the front line for nearly six hours after he had been wounded.

As the attacks continued unabated, Lieutenant Colonel Puller began to wonder if his line could hold intact throughout the night. He called for reinforcements, and about one o'clock in the morning an Army battalion began moving up through the jungle to strengthen his line. The 164th Infantry, U.S.A., had landed on Guadalcanal only eleven days earlier. Throughout that time they had been pounded by the worst series of naval shellings and bombings that the Japanese had yet thrown against American positions on Guadalcanal. They had not yet met the Japanese in battle. They were unfamiliar with the terrain. That night, however, the Third Battalion, 164th Infantry (Lieutenant Colonel R. K. Hall), proved their worth.

Along jungle paths deep in mud the soldiers moved southward, toward the sound of battle, and by three o'clock they had moved into the Marine lines. From ten o'clock at night until the arrival of the Army reinforcements the Marines had hurled back six enemy charges. At five-thirty, just before dawn, the last desperate assault began. This time the Japanese succeeded in driving a salient into the line about one hundred and fifty yards deep and one hundred yards wide. That was the biggest penetration they had made of American lines, but they could not exploit the break-through. As the sky grew light, the Marine and Army defenders began to clean out the pocket of Japanese. Cross-fire from the sides of the salient killed all but a few who made a break toward the south. Thirty-seven dead Japanese and three of their machine guns were found in the salient and two Marine machine guns which had been overrun were recovered. Fifteen more Japanese were killed as they tried to get back across the wire. Some rose from thickets where they had been hiding, dashed a few yards, fell to the ground again, then sprinted again for the break in the wire. They were picked off one by one as they tried to escape.

Planes joined in the fight with the coming of daylight and pursued the Japanese force as it withdrew southward into the jungle. Back of our lines, in the lines, and in front of the barbed wire more than three hundred enemy dead, including from twenty to thirty officers, were found during the day. Many more must have been killed far in front of our lines by mortar fire and by the artillery which maintained a heavy fire throughout the night battle and the following day.

THE LOST OUTPOST [1]

Upon getting their orders from Lieutenant Colonel Puller, Platoon Sergeant Briggs and the others in his outpost started down through the jungle to try to make our lines. The Colonel had told them not to try to come through his sector; the Japanese were already attacking there. Instead they headed eastward, down the hill, through the jungle, toward the grassy field where the Army had dug in.

The jungle around them was full of the noise of battle and a pelting rain added to the confusion. Some got lost in the darkness and some had taken cover when the Japanese first swarmed about the listening post. The main body, however,

---

[1] It is beyond the purpose and scope of this book to tell the many personal adventure stories that might be told of the fighting on Guadalcanal. The adventures of the men in Lieutenant Colonel Puller's listening post, however, deserve a full account and may be taken as typical of the experiences of many men who fought the jungle and the Japanese on Guadalcanal.

pushed on through the underbrush until they reached the clearing which marked the end of Puller's line. There they paused. As Briggs at the head of his men stepped into the open field, he heard a large force of Japanese approaching. Quickly he passed the word to the men not to make a sound and together they crouched in the woods at the edge of the clearing as the enemy swung by.

First a point of two squads passed, almost within arm's length of Briggs. Then a whole battalion, about seven hundred strong, filed along the edge of the field. One brushed the edge of Briggs' bayonet. Another tripped on the helmet of a Marine lying on the ground.

'I don't know why they didn't stop to get us,' Briggs said. 'They must have known we were there. It was the most unreal experience I've ever had — like a dream. That whole battalion of Japs swinging by — singing, jabbering, shouting, "U.S. Marines, you going to die tonight." And the smell was terrific.'

As the enemy appeared all around them in the field, the Marines knew they were cut off from the Army lines as well as their own, and they hid in the jungle all night while the battle raged about them. Our own artillery hit close as it opened up on the Japanese moving up to attack.

At daylight the men decided to make a break for it across the grassy field. Briggs suddenly remembered that in their haste to get out of the outpost they had forgotten to put their machine gun out of commission. He didn't want that to fall into enemy hands, so with Private First Class Gerald P. White he retraced his steps through the jungle and up the hill to the outpost. There they removed the base plate and bolt of the gun and then made their way back to our lines.

The others started through the grass — tough, sharp, shoulder-high grass. Several Japanese machine guns commanded the field and every time the Japanese saw a movement in the grass, where Marines were crawling along the ground, they opened fire. Other Marines were caught by snipers as they came out in the woods on the other side. Two were killed and ten were wounded in this break for our lines. Three times Corporal Mike Orloski, Jr., leader of a mortar section, crossed the grassy plain under fire to bring in wounded. On his last trip he made a mad dash across the grass in a jeep to bring in a last load of wounded.

Thirteen men were still unaccounted for. During the next two weeks they turned up — those who survived — singly or in little groups with amazing stories of their fight for survival.

October 29 an Army patrol operating in the coconut groves east of our lines came across six exhausted, hungry, and jungle-wise Marines. Their hard-won knowledge of the jungle came from living in it five days with little water, no food, in the midst of the enemy, and under our own artillery fire.

The six men, who had become separated from the others in the outpost were Pharmacist's Mate Homer H. Berry, Privates First Class Richard Hollinger, Edward C. Rothman, Matthew Constantine, and Privates George E. Safley and Cecil Bazzell.

As they had started down from the listening post in front of their own sector, they were caught in a concentration laid down by our own artillery. The Japanese were all around them and they spent the night hugging the ground and playing dead.

'At least it fooled the Japs,' Berry said. 'One of them jumped right over me. When day came, I whispered to one of the other guys lying near me and we decided we'd better move on.' As the sun sucked up the rain that had poured down the night before, a mist filled the jungle in the early morning — a mist which the Marines welcomed as they moved cautiously through the jungle. Berry found four other Marines near-by and the six decided to strike for the Lunga River and work down it toward our lines.

'Once on a hill,' Berry went on, 'we ran into a small Jap patrol. Dick Hollinger shot two of them, then we ducked and tried to get around the rest of them. Sometimes we ran into others. By shouting and putting up a bluff, we thought we might fool them into thinking we were just the point for a big patrol. It seemed to work.'

Water was the biggest problem for these six against the jungle, as it was for the other little groups of Marines who were trying to get back to our lines at the same time. They had only five canteens of water, since one of the boys had lost his. They rationed out a mouthful at a time for each man whenever their mouths got so dry they thought they couldn't go on. Even so the water didn't last long. Berry, a pharmacist's mate, devised an ingenious way for getting water. He cut a rubber tourniquet into six pieces and gave one to each man. He would stick one end down the stem of a jungle plant and suck up the water.

For five days the boys tramped through the jungle, wandering in circles, trying to keep each other's spirits up, wondering if the Marines back at camp had given them up, and imagining the feasts they would eat when they got back to safety. One of the boys almost broke down at one point, ready to give up a struggle that began to seem hopeless. The others gathered around to encourage him, told him they would carry him rather than leave him alone. He stuck with them.

On the fifth day they came into the coconut grove near the shore east of the Tenaru. There they ran across the Army patrol that gave them cigarettes, food, and water and brought them back to our lines.

Another man in the outpost was picked up alone by a Marine patrol up the Lunga River after he had roamed the jungle for six days. Private First Class Charles G. Owens had begun his adventure with two others after he had become separated from the main body of the platoon on the first morning. He had taken shelter behind a log when approaching Japanese had caused the men to scatter. He found two other Marines there. All day they hid out behind the log, fearing to move because our artillery was pounding the area and our planes were bombing and strafing it. Toward the end of the day they started out to find the Lunga River. Owens could hear the others just ahead of him, but couldn't see them through the dense underbrush.

'Suddenly I heard one of them shout out, "Oh, God! Help!" and could hear him gasp. I guess a Jap had bayoneted him. Then the other guy fired his rifle and two Japs ran past me up toward the noise.'

Owens continued on alone and spent the night on a hilltop. The next day he heard enemy soldiers chopping trees and vines and moving about below him and he stayed on in his hideout at the top of the hill. The Japanese were carrying wounded and equipment back through the jungle. After three costly drives against our lines in that sector, the Japanese were withdrawing toward the interior.

On the third day Owens ran into a Japanese soldier and shot him. He was trying to make a grassy field that lay ahead when he saw another Japanese, who seemed to be wounded. Owens avoided him and worked his way to the other side of the field, when another enemy soldier suddenly jumped up out of the grass and shouted. 'I let him have it.'

The next day he shot a wild fowl, tore off its skin and ate the breast and legs. It was the first food he had had in the four days since he had left the outpost.

Owens devised his own methods of extracting drinking water from the jungle. To conserve the little water left in his canteen he sucked the dew from grass and leaves early in the morning. On the fifth day it rained and he wrung the water from his soaked shirt into his steel helmet. He also found a tree whose bark had been broken by ants. Tearing more of the bark away, and using a leaf as a funnel, he held up his helmet to catch the water as it trickled down. For food he ate some red berries with a stone center.

On the sixth day Owens crossed an open field and crawled through some dense underbrush which turned out to grow along the Lunga River. At the river he washed and drank and lay down behind a log to await night, when he planned to try to get down the river to our lines. Then he heard voices, speaking English. It was a Marine patrol. They gave him chocolate and food and sent him back to our lines.

Private First Class Howard M. McKee spent five days hiding out in the field of grass which the men in the outpost had to cross to reach the Army lines. McKee was separated from the others in their attempts to cross the field the morning of the 25th. Counting on the battle's being over soon, McKee decided to dig in where he was, in no-man's-land. He used his helmet as a shovel and dug several foxholes at various points on the field. He had no food or water all that time. Several times our artillery fired on the field and McKee was showered with dirt from close hits.

On the fifth day the Japanese fired the grass to rout out any Marines who might be hiding there. McKee cut down the grass near the edges of his foxhole to keep the flames from reaching him. After the fire some Japanese soldiers came out to search the field, but only ran away at sight of him. He then moved on and ran into an Army truck which picked him up and brought him back to his own outfit.

Private First Class Wallace E. Wynn was the last man of the outpost to return to the relative safety of our position. He spent two weeks in the jungle.

When the Japanese first started coming up the hill toward the outpost, Wynn and two others found themselves separated from the rest of the platoon. They started out alone through the jungle and hid behind a log.

'Two Japs came up to the log and I could hear one of them mumble something. One reached down and touched me, but I guess I was so stiff with fright that he thought I was dead. Anyway he crossed the log and went on.

'I stayed all night in the bushes. Shells from our artillery began to burst around me and I couldn't do anything but lie there and hope the shrapnel wouldn't hit me. In the morning I began looking around and saw two other heads peeking out of the tall grass. At first I thought they were Japs, but then I saw they were my two buddies. We got together and admitted to each other we were really scared.

'We decided to stay there awhile. Later in the day some Japs came up searching the woods. One was very close. I whispered to my buddy that we'd better get him before he got us, so I raised my rifle, took careful aim, and shot him through the head.

'Three other Japs came running up to see what it was all about. The one I had shot seemed to be signaling where we were, so the three of us decided to take off. We ran through the bushes and came smack onto six more Japs. Three of them ran away, but the other three started to rush us with fixed bayonets. One of them got me all right, in the chest, but luckily I had turned away just as he thrust and only got a cut of about three inches. Before he could finish the job, I shot him.

'One of my buddies was running with two Japs after him. He had lost his rifle — I guess he lost it in the skirmish. One Jap caught up with him and drove the bayonet through his back. I could see the blade go right through him. Then I shot the Jap as he bent over him. The third took off.

'I ran farther on into the woods and came upon a clearing where about a dozen Japs were eating. I didn't know what to do, but on the spur of the moment raised up, motioned with my right arm and shouted, "Come on, boys — let's get 'em." The Japs cleared out when they heard my command to my imaginary army. I let loose with my rifle, trying to keep up a steady fire to keep their heads down, and then turned and ran, for a long time. Finally I just dropped in the underbrush and stayed there while the Japs started moving about looking for me. I stayed there all night never daring to move.'

For days Wynn continued to roam through the woods, trying to get back to our lines. For water he squeezed out soaked, rotten wood and for food he found some cane that looked like cabbage. He lost all track of time and days. At last he climbed a hill, spotted the way back to the Marine position, and ran into a Marine patrol which brought him safely back.

Wynn's return accounted for the last of the thirteen men lost in the jungle from the little outpost. Nine had returned. Four would never return.

'DUGOUT SUNDAY'

The Japanese offensive reached a climax Sunday, October 25, a day marked by the most intensive aerial fighting of the campaign, by the appearance of enemy naval units in the waters off Guadalcanal during daylight hours, and by a renewal of enemy attempts to break through on the land front. Far at sea to the northeast powerful United States and Japanese naval task forces were moving toward each other to exchange aerial blows.

It had rained hard the night of October 23 when the Japanese had tried to push tanks across the mouth of the Matanikau. It rained again the next night, in torrents. The fighter strip, then just a dirt field bound together by the grass that grew on it, was a morass at dawn. The bomber strip was under harassing fire from enemy artillery. The Japanese chose the day, so inauspicious a one for the defenders, to throw their aerial strength against Guadalcanal.

In two and a half months of fighting in the Guadalcanal area, before October 25, planes based on Henderson Field had shot down three hundred and fourteen Japanese planes and had bombed or torpedoed twenty-nine ships. We had lost only thirty-two pilots in the operations which resulted in that terrific toll of Japanese strength. One hundred and forty-three Zero fighters, one hundred and twenty-two twin-engined Mitsubishi bombers, twenty-nine float-biplanes, nine Aichi dive-bombers, nine float-Zeros, one twin-tailed, twin-ruddered bomber, and one Kawanishi flying-boat had fallen to the guns of our fighter planes and gunners on bombers. Seven Japanese ships had been seen to sink, four others were believed to have been sunk, and eighteen others had been damaged by our dive-bombers and torpedo planes. As Rear Admiral McCain, Commander of Aircraft, South Pacific, had prophesied, Guadalcanal had become a sink-hole for Japanese air power. The feat had been accomplished with amazingly small forces. On the 25th the Japanese poured more planes down the sink-hole. Early in the morning a Japanese twin-engined reconnaissance plane, escorted by several Zeros, began cruising about over our position. Because of the mud on the fighter strip, not a plane could take off to shoot down the impudent visitor. For about an hour the Japanese plane continued its reconnaissance mission, then it grew too daring, swooped low over the field, and was shot down in flames by anti-aircraft fire.

At last some of our fighters managed to get into the air to attack the Zeros which had been circling the field at their pleasure since dawn. There then began a series of dogfights that lasted throughout the day. Although 'Condition Red' ('Enemy planes overhead') was in effect almost all day long, the name 'Dugout Sunday' was a misnomer in a sense. Enemy bomber formations came over only twice and Marines and Army troops soon began climbing out of their dugouts and foxholes to watch the spectacular show in the sky. Seventeen Zeros were shot down during the day. We lost only two Wildcats and the pilots of both bailed out and parachuted to safety.

No sooner would the remnants of one flight of Zeros, shattered by our fighter planes, make off for their base than another would come in. This was the day when Captain Joseph Foss, who later built up a record of twenty-six planes to his credit, shot down four enemy aircraft. In the afternoon two formations of enemy bombers came over and bombed the airfield. It was five-thirty in the afternoon before 'Condition Red' at last ended.

A log for an hour of the air battle may give some idea of the furious activity in the sky over Guadalcanal that day.

2:23 (P. M.) Condition Red. 16 bombers five miles out, at 20,000 feet altitude.

2:24 Enemy planes split into 2 groups. 16 bombers coming over in a straight line.

2:30 Bombs dropped along beach near Kukum.

2:34 1 bomber shot down.

2:35 Another bomber with motor shot out.
Bombers going out.

2:36 2 Zeros shot down over field.
Another bomber coming down. (5 shot down altogether)

2:42 Another enemy formation coming in.

2:50 Dogfights overhead.

2:51 1 Zero shot down.

2:52 Another flight coming in, very low, 10 miles out.

2:56 Zeros strafed airfield.

2:57 3 Zeros coming in, 5 miles out.

3:00 9 dive-bombers over field; bombed 'graveyard' of wrecked planes. (Major General Geiger chuckled when he heard what the Japanese bombers had picked for a target. 'Right in my bone-yard! I couldn't have picked anything I'd rather have them hit.')

3:01 8 Zeros to the southwest.

3:03 2 groups of enemy planes going out. A few Zeros still prowling around.

3:07 6 Zeros coming in at 4000 feet. Strafe field.

3:08 3 groups of planes going out.

3:16 Condition green.
(Within twenty minutes there was another condition red and the dogfights began again.)

Meanwhile, the Dauntless dive-bombers were having as busy a day as the fighter planes. While strong surface forces of the United States and Japanese Navy were steaming toward each other far from Guadalcanal to join in the engagement known as the Battle of Santa Cruz, other Japanese warships approached Guadalcanal.

Early in the morning three Japanese destroyers came into

the channel between Florida and Guadalcanal in one of the few daylight ventures enemy warships made into our waters while we had planes on Henderson Field. They closed in, shelled and sank the tug *Seminole* and a Yippee boat unloading supplies from Tulagi, then laid a smoke screen and put out to sea again as our five-inch coast-defense guns opened up and scored three hits on one of the destroyers. Four Wildcats joined in the attack (no dive-bombers had yet been able to take off from the muddy airfield) and strafed the decks of the destroyers.

Three other Japanese destroyers were just north of Florida Island, and about one hundred miles away, off the northern shore of Santa Ysabel, there were a heavy cruiser, a light cruiser, and four destroyers, while near-by two other destroyers protected two transport ships. For a while it looked as though our air defenses could not turn back this concentration. At nine-thirty in the morning the Commanding General had had to inform the Commander for Air in the South Pacific that Henderson Field could not be used because of the mud and had asked for an air strike to be sent against the Japanese ships from other bases. Moreover, we had only twelve Avenger dive-bombers left in operating condition. The Commander for Air said he would send in seven more Wildcats and three dive-bombers. That meant scraping the bottom of the barrel; no more aircraft reinforcements for Guadalcanal were available in the South Pacific.

Our few planes, however, performed wonders. At eleven-thirty in the morning one Dauntless dive-bomber managed to get in the air and fifteen minutes later two more joined him. At one o'clock four of them attacked the Japanese heavy cruiser and light cruiser, then only forty miles from Guadalcanal in company with four of the destroyers. They hit the heavy cruiser with a thousand-pound bomb, scored a damaging near miss or possible hit on the same ship with a five-hundred-pound bomb and two near misses on the light cruiser. This damaging attack turned the Japanese ships back, and an hour later three Airacobras, being used as light bombers, found them on a course toward the northwest. They attacked without scoring any hits. At four-thirty four Dauntless dive-bombers again attacked and scored near misses on both cruisers, and at five four more dive-bombers and the three Airacobras made a final attack. One Airacobra hit the heavy cruiser with a five hundred-pound bomb and a dive-bomber scored a near miss on the light cruiser. By now both cruisers were making very slow way, trailing large oil slicks. They had been crippled by a small force of eight dive-bombers and three Airacobras which had been forced to make their attacks without any fighter protection. Our fighters were far too busy that day over Henderson Field to be available for escorting the bombers.

All in all, it was an exceedingly good day in the air. As so often happened on Henderson Field, an air force which began the day with the odds seeming to be hopelessly against them had achieved a brilliant triumph from inauspicious beginnings. Japanese losses for the day were seventeen Zero fighters and five twin-engined bombers, with a heavy cruiser and a light cruiser very severely damaged. Our losses in aircraft were two Wildcat fighters, both pilots saved.

As the battle raged in the sky and sea around Guadalcanal, Marine and Army ground forces were getting ready for a renewal of the fight on the defense perimeter. The line in the Seventh Marines sector south of the airfield was strengthened. The Third Battalion, 164th Infantry, U.S.A., which had filled in Lieutenant Colonel Puller's line the night before as reinforcements, was assigned the eastern half of the twenty-five hundred-yard line formerly held by Puller's battalion. The Third Battalion, Second Marines, constituting the Division Reserve, was moved up to the Engineers' bivouac area at the edge of the airfield north of the Ridge. The Japanese had pulled back into the jungle, beyond mortar range, to await the coming of darkness.

The fighting flared up again that night. The Japanese

struck again at the line south of the fighter strip, now defended by the Army battalion under Lieutenant Colonel Hall. They hit at the Company K line after midnight. They found no soft spots, but just before daylight, at four-thirty, they launched a determined assault against the left flank defended by Company L. For the second successive night they tried to break through near the point where the jungle meets the grassy plain. The Third Battalion, Second Marines (the Division Reserve), had been called up for support and although one infantry company and a machine-gun platoon were committed, the Army defenses held firm. Although a few Japanese filtered through the L Company line, the attackers never got within a mile of the fighter strip. Enemy losses were heavy and in the morning six hundred dead were found in front of the Army battalion's position — two hundred in front of Company K and four hundred in front of L.

That same night the Japanese tried to break through our lines in another sector, some four miles to the west. There the First Battalion, Seventh Marines (Lieutenant Colonel Herman H. Hanneken), had reinforced the Ridge line extending eastward from the Matanikau, a sector held by the Third Battalion, Seventh Marines (Lieutenant Colonel W. R. Williams), alone on the night of the Matanikau tank battle.

The Marines had heard enemy soldiers in front of their lines, jabbering as they came up the trail in the heavily wooded draws below the Ridge. At one o'clock in the morning the Japanese opened up at the east end of the Ridge and the Marines replied with mortar fire which seemed to silence the attackers. The heavy firing in the Army sector, far to the west, indicated that the main Japanese force might have passed by Hanneken's position.

All was quiet for two hours. Then the Japanese attacked strongly on a three hundred-yard front. The enemy, as usual, had massed his troops in a fairly small area, driving hard against a short segment of the defense line. Hanneken's left flank on the Ridge took the brunt of the attack. Some Japanese had climbed into tall trees on the steep southern slope of the Ridge where they could direct plunging fire into the defenders on the crest. They charged up the Ridge and gained the top with three heavy machine guns, five light machine guns, and Tommy guns. Scores swarmed up the seventy-foot cliff. On the crest they captured two Marine machine guns and turned them against the Marines.

Platoon Sergeant Mitchell Paige, commanding a section of machine guns, was one of the few defenders left on the Ridge top, of a force that had numbered only about thirty even before the fighting started. He and his comrades had about three hundred grenades which they kept throwing over the cliff on the Japanese scrambling up toward them. When the Japanese had gained the top, climbing right into the foxholes and gun emplacements with some Marines, Paige kept on firing the machine guns. When all of his men had become casualties, he carried on alone, moving from gun to gun to keep them firing. While he was fixing the feed mechanism on one gun that had broken down, it went out of action. He manned a second gun, then lost that. This left the defenders in that particular sector with only one machine gun. Paige ran over to the unit on his flank, borrowed another gun and some ammunition, returned to his position through heavy fire, and continued the fight.

Meanwhile, Major Odell Conoley led reserve troops into the breach. The Marine counter-attack, in which Platoon Sergeant Paige joined, started at five-thirty in the morning, and for forty-five minutes the Marines pressed the Japanese hard, gradually pushing them back over the cliff. Private James E. Sands was one of the Marines in the little group that counter-attacked. Armed with hand grenades he rushed several Japanese emplacements on the crest of the Ridge and knocked out one heavy and one light machine gun. Even after he had been wounded in the hip, he refused medical aid until the Marines were thoroughly established in their old position. Ninety-eight Japanese bodies were found on the

Ridge when morning came and two hundred more were found down in the ravine.

The daylight hours of the 26th were quiet in all sectors on Guadalcanal, but far out at sea an aerial engagement was being fought which would have a great influence on the island's fate. For many days powerful naval task forces of the United States and Japan, including carriers on both sides, had been moving toward each other. On the 26th the planes of each force attacked the ships of the other and long-range blows were exchanged which determined the balance of naval power in the South Pacific for the immediate future. We lost two ships in the engagement — the carrier *U.S.S. Hornet* and the destroyer *U.S.S. Porter* — and other ships suffered damage. The Japanese in turn suffered damage which pared down their superiority in the area, and to that extent relieved the pressure on Guadalcanal. Two Japanese carriers were damaged by bomb hits, one severely. One battleship of the Kongo class was hit with two heavy bombs, three heavy cruisers, and two light cruisers were damaged. The Japanese definitely lost more than a hundred of their carrier-based planes and probably lost as many as one hundred and fifty. After this exchange the two forces turned about and steamed away from each other.

Meanwhile, the ground forces on Guadalcanal were preparing for another night of fighting. Two platoons of the Third Battalion, Second Marines, which had gone into the Army line to reinforce it during the night battle, were withdrawn back to reserve position and replaced by Army units. One company of the Engineer Battalion was sent to reinforce the Seventh Marines in the Matanikau sector.

In the evening the Japanese began shelling Lieutenant Colonel Williams' position in the Matanikau sector, but no attack developed there. Instead, the battle was resumed behind the fighter strip, but in much less strength than on the two previous nights. The Japanese hit against the left company of Puller's battalion, on the steep eastern spur of 'the

Ridge.' The first assault was driven back, but about seven-thirty another was launched against Puller's left and the Army's right. The fighting came in spurts as the Japanese charged against the wire with grenades, knives, and bayonets. The hardest and final push started at two o'clock in the morning and lasted for half an hour. It, like the earlier charges, was repulsed. Army mortars brought an enemy concentration under heavy fire and in the morning they found they had wiped out a heavy weapons company of mortars and machine guns. More than two hundred dead Japanese were found the next day.

The Japanese attacks of October 23–26 constituted the last major effort of the enemy to break through the defense perimeter around Henderson Field that month. The night of October 27–28 the fighting flared up again south of the airfield and farther west in Hanneken's sector, but it did not assume major proportions. At eight-thirty it looked as though the Japanese were trying to push down the river, between Puller's battalion on the right bank and the First Battalion, First Marines (Lieutenant Colonel Cresswell), on the left. The much-worked and much-traveled reserve battalion (Third Battalion, Second Marines, Lieutenant Colonel Hunt) was rushed to the Pioneers' Bridge on the Lunga River, but the fighting died down and the Japanese never launched a serious attack.

The plight of Lieutenant Colonel Hunt's battalion in that week of bitter fighting was symbolic of the problem facing the entire First Division. Rushed from point to point on the defense perimeter as this or that sector became threatened, its strength constantly reduced by casualties and disease, the reserve battalion had no rest. So it was with the whole division. There was no place in the fourteen square miles then held by the Marine and Army defenders where men, worn out by repeated poundings from air and sea, by fighting or continual alerts, by lack of sleep and by disease, could rest their tired bodies and strained nerves.

Moreover, they had no immediate prospect of reinforcements or relief. No ground reinforcements had arrived since the major enemy landings in the middle of the month. October 26 the Commanding General called this fact to the attention of the Commander of the South Pacific Area and pointed out that our forces were spread thin around the defense perimeter trying to defend the airfield with only one understrength battalion as a completely inadequate Division reserve. 'The Japanese,' he concluded, 'can be stopped if help is received in time,' and he urgently asked that air and ground reinforcements and replacements be sent to Guadalcanal without further delay.

As it turned out, the Japanese had already been stopped. Crises and moments of great peril to the American hold on Henderson Field lay in the future, but after the bitter fighting late in October Japanese ground forces never again were able to launch a serious attack against the airfield.

Chapter 9

Crisis in November

THE JAPANESE SENDAI DIVISION and attached units had been shattered in its futile attempts to retake Henderson Field between October 23 and 28. It ceased to be effective as an offensive force. Now we were to learn whether it retained much strength on the defensive.

Plans were quickly developed to drive the enemy out of the battle-scarred area between Matanikau and Kokumbona, to destroy as many Japanese as possible and push the remnants beyond the Poha River, out of artillery range of the airfield.

The First Marine Division, Reinforced, was not in good moral or physical position to attack. For three months, almost without rest, the men had been subject to the strain of bombing, shelling, and battle. Disease was beginning to take a heavy toll. We were short of ammunition. But the need of making the airfield secure led the command to accept the risks involved and make a limited attack immediately.

Another purpose impelled the decision to attack. As Colonel Thomas said, with a nod toward the northwestern Solomons, 'We want to give them a sense of futility, especially that concentration up at Buin.' The Japanese had suffered enormous losses in every attempt they had made to recapture Henderson Field. Surely they would eventually give up their efforts to seize the important air base. As it turned out, however, the Japanese had not yet come to think that their efforts were futile.

MARINES ATTACK ACROSS THE MATANIKAU

The Marines' offensive was to begin at dawn November 1. The terrain ahead of them was difficult and the enemy well dug-in. Beyond the Matanikau, to the west, the coral ridges characteristic of Guadalcanal lie very close to the shore, in some places less than one hundred yards from the beach. These grass-covered ridges rise steeply from the thin coastal strip and describe intricate patterns for a distance of a mile and a half to two miles inland, where the grassy ridge slopes give way to the almost unbroken blanket of jungle covering the foothills of the mountains to the south. The draws and gullies that lie between the coral ridges are choked with a tangle of trees and underbrush fed by the streams and water-courses that run through the depressions. (See map, p. 194.)

The Marines' route of advance lay across this network of ridges and draws. The enemy had concentrated his defenses in the jungle-filled gullies where he had emplaced machine guns in caves and holes in the coral, often concealed by the luxuriant green vegetation. Our operation plan called for an advance from ridge-line to ridge-line toward Kokumbona, with the Poha River, well beyond Pistol Pete's range of the airfield, as the eventual objective. Two regiments would take part in the initial attack, supported by artillery of the Eleventh Marines and by aircraft based on Henderson Field and Flying Fortresses based in other islands.

October 31, the day before the attack, the Third Battalion, First Marines, patrolled the area west of the Matanikau and during the night one company of that battalion outposted the high ground just west of the river. Patrols beyond the Matanikau had destroyed two Japanese field pieces October 30 and had met some resistance on the 31st. Patrols operating several thousand yards in front of our lines in other sectors had made no contact with the enemy.

Late in the afternoon of the 31st the Fifth Marines (Colonel Merritt A. Edson) and the Second Marines (Colonel J. M. Arthur) began moving up to assembly areas near the Matanikau. Long lines of men in green and trucks full of ammunition and food crowded the beach road west of Kukum in a steady stream. The Fifth Marines were to make the assault on the morrow. The Second Marines (less the Third Battalion which had gone to Tulagi for a well-earned rest) would closely support them and launch an attack in depth if strong resistance was encountered. During the night the Engineers threw four assault bridges across the Matanikau.

At six-thirty in the morning, November 1, the attack began with a heavy artillery preparation. Nine batteries of the Eleventh Marines laid down concentrations on the terrain over which the Fifth Marines were to advance. Ten minutes later Flying Fortresses swept over and in the next two hours nineteen of them bombed and strafed the Kokumbona area.

As the artillery barrage lifted, the Fifth Marines advanced across the assault bridges. The First Battalion (Major W. K. Enright) was on the right, along the beach, the Second Battalion (Major L. W. Walt) on its left, and the Third Battalion (Major R. O. Bowen) in reserve. By eight o'clock the Second Battalion had reached its first objective, a ridge line running inland from Point Cruz. Colonel Whaling, in command of a detachment consisting of the Third Battalion, Seventh Marines (Lieutenant Colonel W. R. Williams), and Whaling's Snipers had moved inland on the left flank of the assault troops to secure that flank. His group also soon reached the first objective. The First Battalion, Fifth Marines, was held up by a strong pocket of Japanese resistance near the base of Point Cruz. Well-emplaced machine guns and thirty-seven-millimeter anti-tank guns commanded their line of approach and also harassed the Second Marines as they moved up on the east bank of the Matanikau. The Second Battalion and the Whaling Group continued on to the ridge-line which was their second objective, but the First Battalion was held up during the day by the pocket of resistance at Point Cruz.

Company C, whose line of advance led frontally against the Japanese strong-point near the base of Point Cruz, suffered the heaviest casualties in the westward push of the Fifth Marines. Going forward through machine-gun fire on November 1, Sergeant Carl W. Weiss knocked out a Japanese gun set up on the crest of a ridge and set up his own machine gun. Three times Weiss and his gunners threw back Japanese who charged up the hill to retake the position, but on the last assault one of his men, wounded in the action, rolled in front of and under the gun. Although it meant exposing himself to heavy fire, Weiss pulled his comrade back to safety and continued firing. His company later withdrew from the forward position, but the next day Weiss again crawled up the crest of the ridge to set up his gun. A Japanese machine gun opened up on him as he inched forward. He threw a grenade and crawled on. As he was raising his arm to throw a second grenade, the enemy gunner found his mark and Weiss fell dead.

Private William F. Seiverling, Jr., another member of Company C, also gave his life in the Fifth Marines' attack. When the order came to fire on an enemy position in a ravine, Seiverling ran down the hill, killed a sniper, and possibly hit another. His platoon suffered heavily in the assault and withdrew to reorganize, while Seiverling covered the evacuation of wounded. Then Seiverling, hearing that his company's second platoon was in difficulties on the left flank, ran between the Japanese positions and the second platoon, covering its withdrawal. He killed several Japanese before he was hit by an enemy bullet. Then, though painfully wounded, he kept on firing into the Japanese positions and had started back across the ridge when he fell mortally wounded.

Company C was forced back in its frontal attack. Corporal Terrence J. Reynolds, Jr., of Company D, gave his life helping to cover the withdrawal. He picked up a light machine gun and ammunition belt, rushed out in front of the Marine line, firing from his hip to stop the Japanese pressure. While he was still well forward he was killed trying to throw back an enemy rush.

The Japanese pocket at Point Cruz was the main center of enemy resistance and it was decided to by-pass it, encircle it, and gradually reduce it rather than to attack frontally. Accordingly, after Colonel Edson had conferred with the Chief of Staff and Operations Officer late in the day, it was decided that the Second Battalion, Fifth Marines, should move toward the beach behind the Japanese strong-point and the Whaling Group should shift northward at daylight to take over the Second Battalion's zone of action. The Second Marines, which had been held in reserve during the first day's action, were to pass through the Fifth Marines and continue the attack westward.

November 2 the Whaling Group moved northward as planned and established contact with the Second Battalion, Fifth Marines, as that battalion closed in on the Japanese just west of Point Cruz. The attack against this position continued throughout the day. The Japanese were gradually pushed back into a narrow area between the beach road and the beach beyond Point Cruz. They had well-concealed emplacements in a draw at that point — machine guns in cliffside holes that could only be knocked out by a direct hit on the aperture or by approaching them from behind and blasting the emplacement with grenades. It was Tulagi all over again.

Private Charles M. Shepperd distinguished himself in the Fifth Marines attack November 2 by staying on the front line as his platoon withdrew to permit Marine mortars to fire into the area. Firing an automatic rifle at a Japanese machine gun nest, he killed five of the gun crew, captured the gun, and brought it back to our lines.

Captain Willard W. Keith, Jr., was killed that afternoon leading a platoon against a strong Japanese machine-gun and rifle-platoon position concealed by the jungle. Marine artillery and mortar concentrations had already been laid on the area in vain attempts to dislodge the defenders. Finally Captain Keith led bayonet and grenade charges, and although the Marines succeeded in overrunning the Japanese position and destroying the enemy, Captain Keith was killed.

The Marines dug in for the night of November 2–3 along a line about twenty-five hundred yards west of the Matanikau. The Second Marines had moved forward during the day. Their Second Battalion (Lieutenant Colonel O. K. Pressley) was on the right flank of the Marine line, its right resting on the beach. The Third Battalion, Seventh Marines, was on the left. The First Battalion, Second Marines (Lieutenant Colonel R. E. Hill), was between them and just behind them, ready to jump off at dawn the next day.

At seven on the 3d, in a gesture of defiance of the forces moving up to capture it, Pistol Pete, the enemy long-range gun, opened up from near Kokumbona, fired eight or nine rounds on the airfield, then was silent. The First Battalion, Second Marines, now the assault battalion, moved westward along the beach, while behind them the Second Battalion, Fifth Marines, continued to reduce the Japanese pocket of resistance at Point Cruz. By ten o'clock the Fifth Marines had captured two seventy-five-millimeter and nine thirty-seven-millimeter guns in that position. Some Japanese, pushed into a narrower and narrower space along the beach, were trying to escape by swimming out to sea. Enemy artillery concentrated on the Marines who were attacking the little Japanese pocket.

Second Lieutenant Paul Moore, Jr., led a platoon in the series of charges that forced the Japanese to the shoreline in the face of an artillery barrage. He received serious wounds, but although he was forced to his back he continued giving orders to his men until he finally lost consciousness.

Corporal Weldon F. DeLong of Company K had played an important part in the Fifth Marines' advance November 2. With two other Marines he had rushed a Japanese thirty-seven-millimeter gun which had been firing at them point-blank, killed the crew, seized the gun, and put it out of action. The next day, as the Japanese were pushed back to the beach, DeLong was fatally wounded in a Marine bayonet charge against enemy positions.

Meanwhile, the Third Battalion, Seventh Marines, under Colonel Whaling, had run into another pocket of enemy resistance as they approached the ridge-line marking the third objective of the operation, about thirty-five hundred yards west of the Matanikau. The Second Battalion of the Second Marines had also reached the objective line by noon. The First Battalion, Second Marines, moved up in reserve.

The First Battalion, 164th Infantry (Lieutenant Colonel F. Richards), also moved up to relieve the Third Battalion, Seventh Marines, which returned to their position in the defense perimeter as part of a move to meet a new crisis.

SECOND FRONT IN THE EAST

No sooner had the Marines' attack in the west got well under way than the Japanese began landing to the east of us, hindering the continuance of the attack beyond the Matanikau and threatening to create a serious situation on the eastern flank.

The events of the first two weeks in November graphically show the difficulties facing the Marine and Army defenders of Henderson Field. They had at all costs to hold the defense perimeter around the field. At the same time, with limited forces, they had to try to knock out Japanese detachments still on the island before the enemy forces grew to overwhelming numbers, and they must try to keep the Japanese out of artillery range of Henderson Field. As we struck out in one direction, the Japanese threatened from another. Tired troops who were relieved from assault forces in one sector were immediately called upon to meet a blow against another sector. It was a situation to try the ingenuity and patience of the

High Command and the staying power of the boys in the front line. There were rapid changes in the disposition of units. Each hour of those days brought a new problem for the Command. Nothing was predictable. Each new move had to succeed, else the whole framework of defense might collapse.

The Japanese had not landed any considerable force to the east of us since early September, when they put ashore at Taivu Point Major General Kawaguchi's brigade which met disaster in the Battle of the Ridge. There were signs, however, that they might soon again resume landings on our eastern flank.

November 1, the day the offensive west of the Matanikau began, the Marine Command decided it must send the Second Battalion, Seventh Marines, under Lieutenant Colonel H. H. Hanneken, out toward Koli Point to greet any Japanese who might land in that neighborhood. The expedition was beset with difficulties from the outset. First, there was the problem of transporting the battalion to the spot where it was needed. The original plan called for a movement in landing boats, but all the craft were busy supplying the troops attacking in the west and not enough could be spared to move men to Koli. So the Second Battalion, Seventh Marines, was instructed to move up to the Ilu by trucks that afternoon, bivouac there for the night, then proceed on foot to Koli, November 2.

At six-fifty in the morning Lieutenant Colonel Hanneken's men set out from their bivouac area west of the Ilu. When they arrived at the Malimbiu River, flowing into the sea at Koli Point, a scout informed them that a Japanese patrol had crossed the river, headed east, earlier that morning. Just after noon, as they halted for a rest, a large coconut tree toppled over, killing two men and injuring a captain and three enlisted men. After the mishap they pushed on toward the Metapona. The mouth of the river, like most on Guadalcanal, is separated from the sea by a sand bar, but to get to the bar from the west bank one must cross a channel about

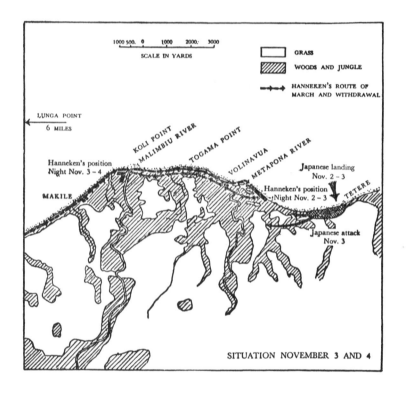

1000 500. 0 1000 2000. 3000

GRASS

WOODS AND JUNGLE

HANNEKEN'S ROUTE OF
MARCH AND WITHDRAWAL

LUNGA POINT

◀─── 6 MILES

KOLI POINT

MALIMBIU RIVER

TOGAMA POINT

VOLINAVUA

METAPONA RIVER

TETERE

Hanneken's position
Night Nov. 3 – 4

MAKILE

Japanese landing
Nov. 2 – 3

Hanneken's position
Night Nov. 2 – 3

Japanese attack
Nov. 3

SITUATION NOVEMBER 3 AND 4

METAPONA RIVER WITHDRAWAL

fifty yards wide and waist-deep. (See map.) Then the bar extends eastward for about three hundred yards to the shore on the east side. Anyone crossing over this long stretch of sand would be clearly visible as far as Berande Point. But the only feasible crossing that would afford concealment involved wading a waist-deep branch of the Metapona, then the main Metapona River, two hundred feet wide and in some places up to a man's arm pits.

Lieutenant Colonel Hanneken decided to wait until dusk, when his men could cross to the east side of the river by using the sand bar. This they did, and then the battalion took up positions at the edge of the woods along the beach, for a distance two thousand yards east from the point where the sand bar joins the beach.

There they stayed to await developments. They had not long to wait. At ten-thirty that night men in an observation post thought they saw several ships entering the bay to the east. It rained all night and visibility was poor, so they could not be sure. Then signal lights flashed from the beach about one thousand yards east of Lieutenant Colonel Hanneken's right company. The company reported that three ships — apparently a cruiser, a destroyer, and a small troop ship — were standing close in to shore on the eastern side of the bay. As the Marines watched in silence, they could hear a clatter from the ships and jabbering on the beach where the Japanese were landing under the protection of their naval guns. This landing beach extended eastward from a point a little over half a mile from the nearest Marines.

Lieutenant Colonel Hanneken promptly tried to inform Division Headquarters of this development, but the radio had broken down in the course of the long march and would not work. For more than three hours the enemy busily moved from ship to shore, then the ships were joined by another destroyer and moved off. The Marine communicators continued to try to get in touch with Division Headquarters, without success.

At dawn a patrol of eight unsuspecting Japanese trudged up the beach toward the Marines' position. When they saw men from Company F, the right flank company, the Marines fired on them and killed four. The others got away. The Japanese now knew that there were Marines scarcely a mile away from them and Lieutenant Colonel Hanneken immediately opened up with his eighty-one-millimeter mortars, laying down a heavy fire on the beach area where the Japanese had landed. He hoped, incidentally, that the mortar fire would attract the attention of Division Headquarters.

Until the middle of the morning the Japanese had not fired back at all. Lieutenant Colonel Hanneken, who had no way of judging whether the Japanese numbered in the hundreds or thousands, concluded from this inactivity that there were probably only a battalion. He decided to attack. Just then several hundred Japanese soldiers started up the beach toward the Marines' position. Machine-gun fire and continued mortar fire caused casualties among the Japanese and drove them into the woods bordering the beach. Soon heavy enemy mortar fire began hitting into F Company, on the Marines' right flank, commanded by Captain Amedo Rea. Then the Marines learned that the Japanese had succeeded in landing artillery. Shells began to whistle overhead — 4.1-inch shells we later learned.

First they fell into the sea behind the Marine mortar position, set up on the sand bar near the point where it joins the mainland, then began hitting in the Marine lines. Wounded from Company F began to come back, including their Commanding Officer. The Marines were running low on eighty-one-millimeter mortar ammunition. Still Lieutenant Colonel Hanneken had been unable to get in touch with Division Headquarters or to attract the attention of planes that flew overhead. He decided to fight a withdrawing action to the west bank of the Metapona River and make a stand there.

The sand bar was exposed to enemy observation and fire, so the Marines withdrew by the concealed but much more difficult route across the wide, deep Metapona and its tributary. First Company F and twenty-four wounded withdrew, then Company G, then the Command Group, and finally Company E. The battalion was just getting into position on the west bank when the enemy, who had apparently crossed the river upstream and worked around behind the Marines, attacked in the rear. It became apparent that the Marines must withdraw further if they were to escape the same maneuver which our own forces had so successfully executed in disposing of the Ichiki unit at the Tenaru August 21. Company G was ordered to cover the rear and Lieutenant Colonel Hanneken again tried to get a message through to Headquarters.

Back at the airfield we had heard the sound of mortars and Japanese artillery far to the east, but were at a loss to explain it. Some thought it was naval gunfire, since we knew a United States naval task force had been near-by with hopes of intercepting enemy landing forces. Because of Hanneken's complete silence, it didn't seem likely that he had engaged any Japanese forces. Planes were sent out to try to learn the origin of the sounds, but did not see any ships or any of the action that was taking place on the beach below them. It was two-forty-five in the afternoon of November 3 before Headquarters knew that the Japanese had landed east of the Metapona and that the Second Battalion, Seventh Marines, had been attacked. When Hanneken's message came in, the First Battalion, Seventh Marines was immediately ordered out to reinforce the Second Battalion at the Malimbiu, and that night they moved out to Koli Point in boats.

It was an afternoon of feverish activity inside the Marine lines around Henderson Field. The Japanese design was beginning to become apparent and steps had to be taken immediately to meet the new threat. The enemy force that landed east of the Metapona was the forerunner of a much larger force — an entire division. Those who landed the night of November 2–3 had come ahead to establish a beachhead. The others might quickly follow.

In less than three hours from the time Hanneken's message had been received at Headquarters, a large-scale movement toward the east had begun. Lieutenant Colonel Puller's First Battalion was already on its way to reinforce Hanneken. Two Army battalions were to move up to the Malimbiu River to join the Seventh Marines. Whaling's scouts were ordered to patrol inland from the mouth of the Malimbiu. Brigadier General Rupertus, Assistant Division Commander, took command of the eastern sector. Two tank companies were ordered to cross the Ilu the following morning to support operations in the east.

A battalion of seventy-five-millimeter pack howitzers — the Third Battalion, Tenth Marines (Lieutenant Colonel M. T. Curry) was sent beyond the defense perimeter to support the Seventh Marines and Brigadier General del Valle also sent his Special Weapons Battery to cover the artillery's south flank. The Ilu, swollen by rains, was running too high for trucks to cross, but Lieutenant Colonel Curry got his guns and ammunition across by hand. He also promptly ran a telephone line all the way out to Hanneken's position on the Malimbiu the night after his artillery had crossed the Ilu.

Meanwhile, units were being shifted in the western sector, beyond the Matanikau. The Third Battalion, Seventh Marines, had been relieved by an Army battalion. They became available to fill some of the gaps left in the defense perimeter by the departure of two battalions of the Seventh for the east. When Puller started out for Koli Point, a company of Pioneers and a company of Engineers were directed to move into the Seventh Marines' defensive sector south of the airfield.

While the Marine Command was hastily plugging gaps and dispatching forces to meet the new threat in the east, the Quartermaster's office called to request a 260-man working party for the morrow, to help unload ships! Such were the demands on limited strength on Guadalcanal. The Eighth Marines, under Colonel R. H. Jeschke, already a day overdue, were counted on to arrive on the 4th. There were crossed fingers at Division Headquarters that hectic afternoon. If the Eighth failed to arrive and strengthen extended lines, we would be very vulnerable to any new Japanese move.

Fortunately, they arrived, and the morning of November 4 the new regiment landed east of Lunga Lagoon. Pistol Pete opened up on the ships that brought them, and drew a devastating reply from 155-millimeter batteries and from the guns of escorting destroyers. The destroyers also delivered naval gunfire against Japanese positions east of the Metapona, blasting their beachhead and setting fires among the stores and equipment they had piled in the woods back of the beach.

The Marine Command had to make a difficult decision. Should the attack in the west be continued in view of the strength that had to be diverted to the east? There were two schools of thought. One pointed out that the Japanese would be strongly entrenched in every gully and draw west of the line we then held beyond Point Cruz. On the defensive, strongly dug in, they could be expected to resist to the last man. Our lines there were dangerously extended. There were vulnerable points along the beach. Our left flank — the landward flank — was wide open. The other school thought it important to keep the Japanese on the defensive. They supposed that the pocket of two hundred and fifty Japanese that had been cleaned out west of Point Cruz was the main point of enemy resistance east of Tassafaronga. To them it seemed vital to push the enemy back beyond the range of heavy artillery. It was important to relieve the airfield of harassing long-range artillery fire.

A situation map of American and Japanese forces on Guadalcanal at this time is a crazy-quilt of red (enemy) and blue (friendly) patches. From Cape Esperance eastward to our lines there were detachments of Japanese. South of us, along the upper reaches of the Lunga, remnants of the enemy forces defeated late in October still roamed the jungle. Our main position was a fat bulge around the airfield, with a long streamer extending toward the west beyond the Matanikau.

Toward the east of Henderson Field another series of blue patches made an arm reaching toward the Malimbiu. Then a patch of red. Twenty miles farther east, at Aola, was another blue circle on the map. The explanation for that will come later. The little islands of red and blue were set in a sea of green jungle and brown grass where enemies might pass within shouting distance, unknown to each other.

As he looked at the situation map in the Operations dugout, Lieutenant Colonel Twining used to shake his head, smile wryly, and say, 'What would the schools think of that!' The disposition of forces was hardly according to the Book.

Finally it was decided that the Second Marines, our western-most force at that time, should withdraw to a strong defensive position west of Point Cruz and dig in. The Fifth Marines returned to the defense perimeter and took up positions in the old Army sector east of Henderson Field. There was a brief flurry at Headquarters when a report came from that sector, as the switch was being effected, that a strong Japanese patrol had been sighted south of the airfield, but it turned out that an excitable sentry had seen unfamiliar troops moving into the line and at first glance mistook them for Japanese.

The newly arrived Eighth Marines were quickly put to work. Their Second Battalion (Lieutenant Colonel J. H. Cook, Jr.) was organized as a mobile reserve, ready to move at a moment's notice to any sector of the defense perimeter that might be threatened. Officers from each area were sent to the Second Battalion's bivouac area near the beach to lead them to any sector which the enemy might attack that night.

Marine and Army forces were moving up to encircle the Japanese at the Malimbiu. By evening of the 4th the Third Battalion, 164th Infantry (Lieutenant Colonel R. K. Hall), was well to the east, three to four thousand yards south of Makile. The Second Battalion, 164th Infantry (Lieutenant Colonel A. C. Tomboe), was northeast of them, preparing to cross the river forty-five hundred yards from its mouth. The Japanese were digging in on the east bank. The morning of

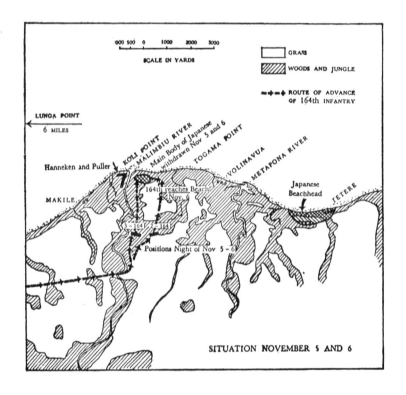

000 500 0   1000   2000   3000

SCALE IN YARDS

☐ GRASS

▨ WOODS AND JUNGLE

➡➡➡ ROUTE OF ADVANCE
OF 164th INFANTRY

LUNGA POINT

← 6 MILES

KOLI POINT

MALIMBIU RIVER

Main Body of Japanese
withdrawn Nov 5 and 6

TOGAMA POINT

Hanneken and Puller

VOLINAVUA

METAPONA RIVER

Japanese
Beachhead

JETERE

164th reaches Beach
Nov. 6

MAKILE

5 – 164 – 164

Positions Night of Nov 5 – 6

SITUATION NOVEMBER 5 AND 6

CRISIS IN NOVEMBER

the 5th the Second Battalion crossed the river, intending to move northward, determine the enemy lines, then strike. Later the Third Battalion also crossed and both battalions started moving northward, without contact. It began to look as though the main Japanese force had withdrawn to the east along the coast, to protect dumps and supplies, leaving a small rearguard at the Metapona. The First Battalion, Eighth Marines (Lieutenant Colonel M. S. Newton), had been directed to report to General Rupertus and was used for command post security and artillery security. An artillery battalion — the Third Battalion, Tenth Marines (Lieutenant Colonel M. T. Curry) — crossed the Ilu and moved toward the Malimbiu to give the Marine and Army forces in the east artillery support.

On the 6th the Americans began to come into contact with Japanese outposts. The Army battalions, now one thousand yards from the beach east of the Malimbiu, ran into a small enemy detachment, overran a machine gun, killed some Japanese, and suffered six casualties. A company of the First Battalion, Eighth Marines, had surrounded a pocket of Japanese south of the Army position. That evening the Army battalions closed in to the beach without encountering any sizable body of Japanese.

Next day the Army and Marine forces moved on east, and by nightfall the Seventh Marines were in position along the west bank of the Metapona from the mouth to a point one thousand yards inland. The two battalions of the 164th Regiment were in position about one thousand yards along the beach west of the river. During the day a destroyer had shelled the supposed Japanese positions east of the Metapona and caused several big explosions, apparently in ammunition dumps.

The Japanese Imperial Navy continued its night-time ventures into the waters off Guadalcanal. The night of November 5–6 two motor torpedo boats on patrol saw a Japanese cruiser off Koli Point, fired eight torpedoes, and sank her with at least two hits. Returning to base they saw another enemy warship, apparently a destroyer. Japanese submarines were active around the island and on the morning of the 7th torpedoed a small supply ship unloading off Lunga Lagoon and she had to be beached. That afternoon our search planes found a Japanese cruiser and ten destroyers north of Santa Ysabel, headed for Guadalcanal. A striking force of Douglas dive-bombers, Grumman Avenger torpedo planes, Airacobras, and Wildcat fighters took off from Henderson Field to attack the enemy surface force, which was escorted by many float-plane fighters, and inflicted severe damage. The cruiser suffered two torpedo hits, one hit with a thousand-pound bomb, and a near miss with a bomb. One destroyer was directly hit with a torpedo and a second destroyer took two bomb hits and two near misses. The Grummans strafed four of the destroyers. The Airacobras shot down five enemy float-biplanes and the Wildcats got seven float-Zero fighters and three float-biplanes. A Dauntless dive-bomber, out on a search mission, also shot down one Zero and two float-biplanes. Our losses in this impressive victory were four Wildcats. Despite such damage Japanese ships came back again the next night, apparently intent on reinforcing the beachhead to the east. Nine enemy warships — cruisers and destroyers — were sighted one hundred and thirty miles out at five-thirty in the afternoon, too late for a striking force to go out after them. There was nothing to stop them from coming on in to Guadalcanal but the patrol of motor torpedo boats which were our only night-time defense against the Japanese surface forces. The little boats and their gallant crews were on the job, however, and shortly before ten at night there was naval gunfire off Savo Island — the Japanese ships firing at the torpedo boats.

It was a glum night in the Marine encampment. Despite everything that had been done to meet the Japanese as soon as they landed, it looked as if there was no way to stop their ships from coming in almost any night they chose to come.

Someone who had seen the firing off Savo called the Operations Section to report. Lieutenant Colonel Twining answered the phone. 'What do you make of it?' said the voice. The Colonel was in no mood to indulge another's curiosity and replied: 'What do I make of it? I think it's a Strength through Joy trip.' Later we were cheered by news that the torpedo boats had scored one torpedo hit on a Japanese ship before they were driven off by gunfire. One P.T. boat was holed by a shell in this exchange, but none of the officers or men was injured.

General Rupertus was very ill with a tropical fever and had to return to Division Headquarters to recuperate. Brigadier General E. D. Sebree of the Army relieved him in command of the operations in the east on the 9th. In that sector the Seventh Marines and 164th Infantry continued to press eastward, closing in on the enemy east of the Metapona.

Now that the Eighth Marines had safely landed, the Marine Command decided to resume the attack in the west. It was to begin at six-thirty November 10. The Second Marines were to jump off at that time, with the Eighth Marines behind them. The offensive began as scheduled, but was short-lived. After a day and a half of fighting, the Marines beyond the Matanikau had to be withdrawn to meet a new crisis — the gravest we ever faced on Guadalcanal.

I have mentioned the principle that dictated the disposition, and limitations on use, of our ground forces from the time we landed on Guadalcanal. No large detachment needed in the defense perimeter could push forward in offensive operations beyond a point from which they could not be hastily withdrawn to reinforce the immediate defenses of the airfield in case the large concentration of enemy ships north of us should start to move. The principle is seen in operation November 11.

There were unmistakable signs that a large Japanese task force was about to move upon Guadalcanal. Our lines were greatly extended to the west and east. Now they must be shortened — and quickly. The Second and Eighth Marines were shifted back to the east side of the Matanikau to organize a defensive line up the right bank of the river and along the beach to the east. Tired Marines, who had been fighting for days in the west, meeting determined resistance in every draw, had to retrace their steps over the ground they had fought so hard to win. The withdrawal began the afternoon of the 11th, covered by artillery concentrations. General Sebree was recalled from the east and placed in command of the new defensive sector at the Matanikau. Colonel Sims of the Seventh Marines took command of the operation in the east, which continued. Beach defenses were strengthened. Then we waited for the blow that was soon to come.

As the crisis developed, the Seventh Marines and 164th Infantry continued their private war with the Japanese on the beachhead beyond the Metapona. With the storm clouds gathering over Guadalcanal, the forces in the east never knew when they might be engulfed in a torrent of enemy troops pouring ashore at the new beachhead — or, worse yet, between them and the main American position at Henderson Field.

The night of the 8th Hanneken was twenty-five hundred yards east of the Metapona, facing west. Puller was just west of the Metapona, and a 'parcel of Nips' was caught in between. The Second Battalion, 164th Infantry (Lieutenant Colonel A. C. Tomboe), then west of the Metapona, was to cross the river behind the Japanese, move northward toward the beach, and close the box of three battalions around the enemy. The other Army battalion was called back to position in the defense perimeter. The next day they began closing in. A platoon of Japanese, holding up the advance with heavy machine-gun fire, was wiped out. At last the Japanese were penned against the beach, in a clump of woods set in the grassy fields. On the 10th the Marines began firing mortars into the woods where the enemy had dug in, to drive them southward into the Army battalion. The maneuver suc-

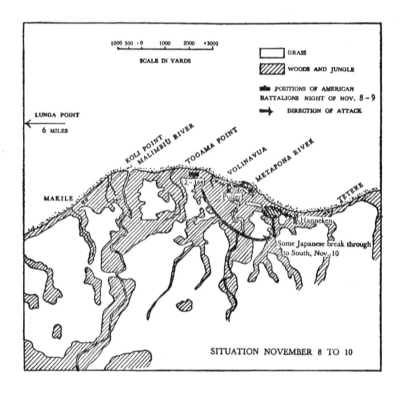

PRELUDE TO THE BATTLE OF GUADALCANAL

ceeded all too well, for the Japanese drove into the battalion south of them and some broke through the American line.

The forces under Colonel Sims mopped up enemy remnants in the Tetere area, destroyed captured arms, ammunition, and stores, then withdrew to positions west of the Metapona. Their booty included artillery pieces, fifteen tons of rice, five rubber boats, and fifty collapsible landing boats. They had killed at least three hundred and fifty Japanese. Our casualties were forty dead and one hundred and twenty wounded in action. The Japanese who escaped the trap and made for the south remained a problem for Carlson's Raiders. Their story will be told later.

In the final drive against the Japanese beachhead, Lieutenant Colonel Puller was wounded three times by shrapnel. His men report that when a doctor pinned a casualty tag on him and ordered him evacuated from the field, the Colonel shouted, 'Evacuate me, hell! Take that tag and label a bottle with it. I will remain in command.' He stayed with his men throughout the following night, and only when his wounded leg began to stiffen did he consent to be evacuated.

THE BATTLE OF GUADALCANAL: NOVEMBER 13–15

The next few days, as the Japanese had planned them, were to be mid-October all over again. A strong surface force, including battleships, would shell Henderson Field by night and knock out our air power. Then an invasion armada of transports and cargo ships, supported by surface units, would come down from the northwest, unhindered by planes from Henderson Field, and land troops, supplies, and equipment. This time, however, two divisions would be sent instead of one. This time they would land east of us as well as to the west.

The pace of events quickened November 11 and moved swiftly to a climax. No bombers had been over by daylight for more than a week, but that day we had two raids. First, a flight of Aichi type-97 dive-bombers attacked the supply ships unloading off Lunga Lagoon, without success. Four Zero fighters and one dive-bomber were shot down, and possibly two more Zeros and another dive-bomber were lost by the Japanese. We suffered heavier losses than usual — six Wildcat fighters, with two pilots saved. Two hours later twenty-five twin-engined Mitsubishi bombers came over. Our fighters shot down six, a possible eight, and the anti-aircraft batteries got another. We lost another Grumman.

The 12th started off encouragingly with the arrival of more reinforcements for the defenders of Henderson Field. As the transports, bringing two battalions of an Army infantry regiment (commanded by Colonel D. W. Hogan) and Marine replacements, unloaded off Kukum, Pistol Pete opened up and one round sent up a geyser near one of the transports. The escort destroyers turned on the offender and laid down a heavy bombardment against Japanese shore positions in the Kokumbona area. In both the morning and afternoon they shelled the enemy positions and wrecked, among other gear, twenty-five landing boats pulled up on the shore.

At two-fifteen in the afternoon came the Japanese reply. Twenty-five torpedo bombers escorted by Zeros swooped in to attack our ships. The anti-aircraft guns on the ships and shore opened up with a devastating volume of fire on the formation of Japanese planes swinging in from Tulagi and knocked down eight of them. Our fighter planes also got into them and accounted for sixteen more bombers. Only one bomber was seen escaping back toward Tulagi. The Grummans got five Zero fighters for good measure. The ships escaped damage, except that the cruiser *San Francisco* was sideswiped by a falling Japanese bomber and suffered some casualties and slight damage. We lost three Grumman Wildcats and one Airacobra in the aerial battle.

The new Army regiment came ashore, Marine replacements were assigned to units that had dwindled in size through battle casualties and disease, more artillery (105's and 155's) was landed, and needed supplies of ammunition and aviation gas were unloaded.. Our lines were shortened in the west as the Second and Eighth Marines withdrew across the Matani-kau. In the east Colonel Sims' forces had disposed of a bat-talion of Japanese and were digging in on the west bank of the Metapona. Air reinforcements arrived in the afternoon, in-cluding some Lockheed Interceptors which were making their first graceful appearance in the skies above Henderson Field. The air was tense.

As night fell the transports were sent out to sea, to escape the Japanese surface force closing in on Guadalcanal. Their escort — gallant cruisers and destroyers destined to make his-tory that night — returned to Guadalcanal after taking them to safety. Then we waited.

At one-thirty in the morning of Friday, November 13 (for three successive months the Japanese had begun attacks on the 13th), the air-raid siren wailed on Henderson Field. The horns in the tank park, the siren by the Lunga, the captured Japanese ship's bell at Headquarters, relayed the warning and men stumbled through the darkness toward their dugouts. The droning plane in the sky came closer, and we recognized it as Louis the Louse, the catapult-plane from a Japanese war-ship. He cruised about a few minutes, then dropped flares over Henderson Field. As the green flares floated down, throwing a ghostly light on faces upturned in silence to watch their descent, we all knew very well what it meant. Naval shelling would begin shortly.

But when the shelling started, it was not directed at us. Out at sea toward Savo Island the sky was filled with light and noise. The ground trembled with the salvos from big naval guns as our naval force of cruisers and destroyers tied into the much bigger Japanese force. We watched from the shore, from the coconut groves, from the coral ridges, from the jun-gle. Naval gunfire off Guadalcanal had come to seem almost commonplace to us, like bombing raids or artillery fire or the whine of snipers' bullets. But this was no commonplace battle at sea. Several days passed before we learned exactly what had happened out there, but as the sound of battle receded and we returned to our bunks to get a few hours' sleep, we were acutely aware of one important result. The Japanese had not got in to shell the airfield. Our aircraft were intact and could still take the air to meet the enemy's next stroke.

The story of the night sea battle belongs to naval history, which will tell of Rear Admiral Daniel J. Callaghan, Rear Admiral Norman Scott and their gallant officers and men who threw a little force of cruisers and destroyers against a far heavier Japanese force of battleships, cruisers, and destroyers and administered a shattering defeat. No one watching from Guadalcanal could follow the course of the battle or know which blazing or exploding ship was American or Japanese. To tense watchers on the shore it was an awesome mêlée of light and sound.

The morning search planes that took off from Henderson Field found a Japanese battleship of the Kongo class dead in the water near Savo Island with a protective cover of Zero fighters. Our fighter planes shot down eight of the enemy planes, with a loss of one Wildcat to ourselves. All day long dive-bombers and torpedo planes pumped the battleship full of high explosive. Later in the morning she got under way, making about three knots, then torpedoes and bombs left her dead in water again. Twenty-nine torpedo planes dove low to attack and eleven times their missiles struck home. Dive-bombers scored four direct hits. Five Japanese destroyers darted about her as a defensive screen. The helpless hulk was still afloat as night fell, dead in the water and abandoned by her crew. The next morning only an oil slick remained.

Except for the attacks on the crippled battleship, the day-light hours of November 13 were uneventful. No one expected the night to be quiet. At one-thirty in the morning Japanese ships returned to do what they had failed to do the night before — shell Henderson Field and knock out our aircraft. For forty-five minutes a battleship and lesser ships hurled salvo after salvo at the field, before they were driven off by torpedo boats patrolling the channel.

It had rained hard that night, the shelling had been heavy, and we wondered whether our planes —the planes that had survived the bombardment — would be able to take off. But the planes were up at dawn and put in the best day's work they were ever called upon to do.

A Japanese invasion force had started to move upon Guadalcanal by the familiar route between New Georgia and Santa Ysabel Islands. A battleship, two heavy cruisers, and four destroyers made up one force, only one hundred and fifty miles away. By mid-morning they had been joined by six more destroyers and twelve troop transports and cargo ships. Out to the west, one hundred and forty miles away, there was another column of two light cruisers and five destroyers, evidently part of the force that had bombarded us the night before, for they were speeding away from Guadalcanal.

The previous night's shelling had dug some craters in the fighter strip, but they were quickly filled. One dive-bomber had been destroyed by shell splinters and two Grumman Wildcats were burned up, but all the rest of our planes were intact or quickly reparable. Seventeen Grummans had been hit by shell splinters, but most were in the air by the end of the day.

Major J. Sailer, leading a flight of Marine planes in a search for the ships that had shelled us, took off at dawn. They found the cruisers and destroyers, then one hundred and forty miles from Guadalcanal, and attacked them. Four squadrons of naval aircraft (one scouting squadron, one bombing squadron, and two torpedo squadrons) had arrived from U.S.S. Enterprise to reinforce the Marine squadrons on Henderson Field. Avenger torpedo planes put three torpedoes into the first cruiser and Dauntless dive-bombers scored two hits on the second cruiser with thousand-pound bombs.

The transport force was spotted at ten-thirty and thereafter, for the rest of the day, planes shuttled back and forth from Henderson Field with orders to 'hit the transports.' They hit

them hard. First, Major Sailer led all available Marine dive-
bombers, escorted by Marine Wildcat fighters, on a striking
mission. When they returned to Henderson Field to rearm
and refuel, the Navy Squadrons of Scout bombers, torpedo
planes, and fighters continued the attack. The Marine and
Navy flights alternated all day long. It was an anxious day
for the Marine ground forces on Guadalcanal. If that number
of transports was able to reach the island and put ashore thousands of men and large amounts of equipment and supplies,
the fate of Henderson Field would be unpredictable. Those
Japanese ships moving down from the northwest, brimming
with men and supplies, represented the enemy's biggest —
and we somehow sensed, final — gamble in his efforts to drive
us off Guadalcanal.

Spirits rose by the hour as reports came in from Air Operations. One after another of the Japanese troop-carriers was
hit. Their escorting warships abandoned them to their fate
and by late afternoon they were milling about helplessly,
burning, ripped with holes, settling in the water only eighty
miles from us, near the southern end of Santa Ysabel. By the
time the last striking force from Henderson Field returned to
base as darkness settled over the Solomons, five of the transports had been sunk, three were burning and dead in the
water, and of the four still under way, two had been hit by
bombs. Those that could make any way were trying desperately to close in to Santa Ysabel to save what they could of the
men and equipment on board. The mighty invasion force
had been routed.

In one of the most remarkable aerial actions of the war,
planes operating from Henderson Field had, in two days,
administered the *coup de grâce* to a damaged battleship, had
seriously damaged two cruisers, had sunk or left sinking eight
transport ships, and the next day were to sink four cargo ships.
Five Marine squadrons, four Navy squadrons, and one Army
squadron, of dive-bombers, torpedo planes, and fighters,
shared in this triumph. All aviation units on Henderson

Field were then under the command of Brigadier General Louis E. Woods. All bombing planes were grouped under the tactical command of Lieutenant Colonel Albert D. Cooley. This decisive victory for Colonel Cooley's Bomber Command had been accomplished with a loss of nine men — five pilots and four gunners.

One of the pilots lost in the battle was Lieutenant Colonel Harold W. Bauer, then in command of the Fighter Squadrons on Henderson Field, whose plane was shot down November 14 as he escorted the bombers on their last striking mission against the Japanese invading force.

He and Captain Joseph Foss had swooped low to strafe the Japanese transports after the bombers had dived. As they were skimming the water away from the ships, Zeros attacked them. Captain Foss was chasing one Japanese fighter when he saw Lieutenant Colonel Bauer speeding past in the opposite direction with a Zero on his tail. Foss shot down his victim, then turned to see what had happened to Bauer. Below him he saw an oil slick spreading out in a circle, and in the center was a figure. He dived low and saw Bauer swimming. He tried to drop the rubber boat from his own plane, but the release would not work, and a faulty radio prevented him from notifying Henderson Field of Bauer's location. No one could be sent to pick up Bauer until Foss got back to the field. Major Joseph Renner, a close friend of Bauer's, immediately volunteered to take up the 'duck' (Grumman amphibian) to rescue Bauer. More time was lost as the 'duck' was warmed up and a flight of B–26's came in to land as Major Renner was trying to take off. By the time he could get out to the Russell Islands where Bauer was last seen, it was too dark to spot anything. For half an hour he circled the area, hoping to see a signal from Bauer, but the only lights he saw on the dark sea and islands below were the flames from five blazing Japanese ships. For four days Major Renner continued his search, flying low over all the islands in and near the Russells, without success.

Lieutenant Colonel Bauer's achievements won him the Congressional Medal of Honor. Twice, on visits to Guadalcanal in September and October, he had volunteered to take up a fighter plane as Japanese air raiders approached. In his first volunteer flight he shot down a bomber, and in the second he shot down four Zero fighters and left a fifth smoking badly. His most remarkable performance, already noted, was when he alone had engaged a squadron of Japanese dive-bombers which attacked the destroyer *U.S.S. Macfarland*, October 16, as he was leading air reinforcements to Henderson Field and shot down four before he ran out of ammunition.

That night the battle at sea resumed. A United States surface task force, including two battleships, steamed into the straits and at eleven-thirty began blasting at the remaining Japanese ships that were again closing in on Guadalcanal under cover of darkness. For more than half an hour we heard the sound of battle. The giants of both sides were engaged and sixteen-inch and fourteen-inch guns thundered out toward Savo. Our force under Rear Admiral Lee pursued the Japanese out toward the northwest, inflicting heavy damage. One battleship or battle cruiser, three large cruisers, and one destroyer were sunk. Another battleship was hit many times with sixteen-inch and five-inch shells and a cruiser and destroyer were left burning.

Despite the heavy losses they had taken, the Japanese succeeded in getting a transport and three cargo ships to Guadalcanal. Early in the morning the ships approached the coast between Kokumbona and Cape Esperance. None survived long. Our 155-millimeter guns and the five-inch shore batteries of the Third Defense Battalion opened up on the nearest ship, off Kokumbona, and set it afire. Dive-bombers set the others afire, and by the middle of the morning all were beached and blazing. In the afternoon a destroyer came over from Tulagi, shelled the ships, and raked the shoreline where the Japanese had been landing their men and supplies. Huge fires burned along the beach for hours.

The crisis was over. In three days and nights of sea and air fighting the Japanese had lost twenty-eight ships.

United States naval forces and aircraft operating from Henderson Field had sunk one battleship, a second battleship or heavy cruiser, three heavy cruisers, three 'large' cruisers (not further described in Navy Department Communiqués), two light cruisers, six destroyers, eight transports, and four cargo transports. Ten other Japanese combatant ships had been damaged — two battleships, a cruiser, and seven destroyers.

In contrast to the shattering losses inflicted on the Japanese, our Navy lost only two light cruisers and seven destroyers, with some damage to other ships. At last, more than three months after the beginning of the Solomons campaign, the Japanese Navy had suffered such a heavy blow that they would hesitate again to try to take Guadalcanal.

Of the thousands of men — probably at least thirty thousand — destined to land on Guadalcanal and attack Henderson Field, comparatively few had reached the island. Japanese air activity had been conspicuously light. Except for the air raids on the 11th and 12th, aimed at our shipping, the enemy had made no daylight air attacks against Guadalcanal throughout the battle. Our own strength was growing daily as more and more planes appeared on Henderson Field. Almost every day cargo ships or transports came in to bring more supplies, equipment, and reinforcements. Soon the soldiers coming ashore at Lunga Lagoon and Kukum could be considered as relieving forces rather than reinforcements. The First Marine Division, Reinforced, would soon be relieved.

PART THREE

Chapter 10

Thirty Days in the Jungle:
Carlson's Raiders

THE NIGHT when Lieutenant Colonel Hanneken's Marines crouched on the beach east of the Metapona and watched Japanese ships slip in and unload where blinking lights directed, other signal fires burned on the coast of Guadalcanal.

The previous day, November 2, a party of Marines had shoved off from the dock at Lunga Lagoon to go down the coastline, east to Aola, where a new airfield was to be built. There the group of Marines and scouts were to prepare the beach for an American landing party, lighting bonfires after midnight of the 2d to mark the limits of the beach where Higgins boats could bring in their loads of men and supplies from an American surface force due to arrive in the early morning hours.

They lighted their fires in a driving rain and waited. A few miles west of them a similar party of Japanese waited in the darkness for their own landing force. The Japanese landed that night, but the Americans did not. From the beach at Aola the flames leapt up through the rain as the Japanese were busily unloading east of the Metapona. Fortunately, the enemy did not see the Marines' signal fires, or perhaps they saw them, but did not know what to make of them.

In any case, the fires burned out without drawing enemy fire.

The next night, during the early hours of November 4, the fires were lighted again. This time the American ships arrived, bringing two companies of the Second Raider Battalion under Lieutenant Colonel Evans F. Carlson, who were to secure the beachhead and cover the landing of naval construction workers and engineering equipment for work on the proposed airfield. After daybreak the Army units who were to guard the area after the Raiders withdrew began landing, and all day long the men, supplies, and equipment came ashore.

The Raiders had expected to leave with the ships after completing their mission of securing the beachhead during the original landing. The Japanese landing near the Metapona, however, gave them another mission. They received orders to push through the jungle to the west and help destroy the Japanese beachhead party. Four more companies of the battalion started for Guadalcanal to reinforce them.

November 6 the Raiders set out from Aola. They struck off through the jungle on a trail along the foothills, west to the Bokokimbo River about ten miles from Aola, and then headed north for the village of Reko. Across the river they surprised a foraging party of Japanese who had just killed a pig and were about to carve up their morsel. They killed two in the group of Japanese, who fired one volley and fled. The Raiders continued on to the Kema, scene of the First Raiders' landing when they had raided the Japanese beachhead at Tasimboko two months earlier. There the two companies divided, one going to the village of Tasimboko where they picked up food sent by Higgins boat from Aola, the other one pushing on to Tina.

November 9 the two companies of Raiders rejoined at Tina and advanced on to Bino on the Balesuna River, four miles from the coast. They had not yet had any major contact with the enemy. Lieutenant Colonel Carlson decided to use Bino as a base for future operations, since that was the westernmost village still occupied by natives. The village was, moreover, south of the pocket of Japanese now enveloped by the Seventh Marines and 164th Infantry, which the Raiders were to help mop up. The Raiders used Tetere as a beachhead for bringing in food from Aola.

November 11 the Raiders began to come into contact with the enemy. Part of the Japanese force trapped against the beach east of the Metapona had escaped through the ring of Marine and Army troops. As four Raider patrols fanned out from Bino on the 11th, they met the enemy detachments that had escaped. The southernmost patrol — Company C — ran into the main force about two miles from Asamana, a village on the Metapona four miles from its mouth. The company had crossed a grassy plain and just as they entered a patch of woods bordering the field, the Japanese opened up on them with machine guns, twenty-millimeter guns, rifles, and mortars. Company C lost five killed and three wounded in this clash. They quickly notified Lieutenant Colonel Carlson of the contact.

The Colonel ordered Company E, then two miles north of Asamana on the Metapona, to cross to the west bank of the river, move south, and hit the Japanese from the west. Company D was directed to move south along the east bank of the river and strike the enemy from the northwest. They, too, had to cross a grassy field and were hit as they entered the woods, losing two killed and three wounded. Meanwhile, Company E under Captain Washburn moved up the west bank of the Metapona, and just as they reached Asamana, surprised two companies of Japanese who were crossing the river from east to west. Some of the Japanese were stripped, swimming and bathing in the river. Others were wading across and passing supplies and equipment to the other side. As the Raiders came up and fired into the Japanese, enemy outposts opened up from good positions. A machine gun in the fork of a banyan tree was particularly effective and succeeded in pinning the Raiders down. Then Japanese forces began a flanking maneuver to get behind Captain Washburn's company. He withdrew to reorganize. The first attack had been led by the first platoon under Lieutenant Evans C. Carlson, the Colonel's son. When the Raiders withdrew, the Japanese apparently thought the attack was over and again began crossing the river.

Company E returned, however, with a fresh platoon — the second platoon under Lieutenant C. E. Early — in the lead. This time they knocked out the machine gun in the banyan tree, but as the Marines fired on the enemy soldiers in the river, the Japanese again began a flanking movement from two directions. As one force tried to work to the west of Washburn's company, six machine guns opened up on the Marines from the opposite bank. Washburn knew that Companies C and F were engaged two miles east of him, but the only line of withdrawal open to him was through a narrow gully to the north. The Raiders retired by this route, covered by a gunner at a machine gun who lost his life protecting the withdrawal of his company. The Raiders had killed one hundred and twenty Japanese at the river crossing.

When Lieutenant Colonel Carlson directed Companies D and E to move against the enemy engaged with Company C, he also had sent one platoon from Company B, his base security, directly to Company C as reinforcement. He also had recalled Company F from Tetere. When Company F arrived at Bino, Lieutenant Colonel Carlson moved with it to the scene of Company C's engagement to co-ordinate a concerted attack. The attack was executed by Company F and the platoon from Company B as darkness was falling. Aside from a few snipers, it was found that the enemy had evacuated to the south.

Leaving Company F on the scene of the action with orders to pick up the trail at daylight, Lieutenant Colonel Carlson returned to Bino with the rest of his force. Companies D and E had already arrived. The next morning (November 12) he led Companies B and E back to the scene of Company C's engagement. From Captain Schwerin (Company F) Colonel Carlson learned that the force he was covering had moved south for about three miles and crossed the Metapona to the west.

Company F was directed to return to Bino and relieve Company C as base security. Colonel Carlson then led Companies B and E to Asamana, where Washburn had dealt the enemy such a severe blow the preceding day. Here excellent positions for about a battalion were found on both sides of the river. Also notices in Japanese were found pinned on trees directing where various companies were to go. While Lieutenant Colonel Carlson was looking around, his outguards shot two enemy messengers, one entering from the east and the other from the west. He decided that this was the rendezvous and disposed his companies in a defensive position from which they could cover by observation and fire the grassy fields which lay beyond the narrow strip of bush which bordered the river. Augmented by Company C, which arrived the night of the 12th, the Raiders occupied these positions for two days and two nights. During the first eighteen hours they shot twenty-five messengers and stragglers who attempted to enter the position. To quote Colonel Carlson: 'It was like shooting ducks from a blind.' He reported this success to Headquarters and added 'still killing [strays].'

On the morning of the second day (November 13) it was discovered that the enemy force which had crossed the river below Asamana was in the woods to the south of Asamana, while the remnants of the force hit by Captain Washburn lay in the woods to the west and north. These forces began to get uneasy, probably because their messages had miscarried. They attempted to enter Asamana several times during the day, but their movements were never co-ordinated. The Raiders simply waited until the advance elements of a group approached within a hundred yards of their position, then opened fire on them with machine guns while throwing mortars back on the main body.

At one point a Marine lookout reported the remarkable news that a forest was moving toward the Raiders' position. Through field glasses Colonel Carlson saw that indeed Birnam Wood was moving to Dunsinane. A company of Japanese, in mass formation, was marching across a field of grass wearing cloaks of foliage and twigs. When within easy range the Raiders opened on the 'forest' with mortars and watched it break up into 'trees' which scattered in all directions.

On November 14, all being quiet on his front, Colonel Carlson returned to Bino with the three companies. During the two days at Asamana this group had accounted for one hundred and sixteen known Japanese dead without the loss of a man.

It was on the following day (November 14) that a scout reported the location of a small enemy base in a defile five miles south of Bino and west of the Balesuna River. A detachment of Company F under Captain Schwerin was sent to deal with it. The defile was so narrow that only three men could enter at a time. Waiting until the enemy sentry had been recalled for 'chow,' Captain Schwerin led an assault which resulted in the annihilation of the fifteen men in the enemy group and the capture of considerable arms, ammunition, and supplies without the loss of a man. Included in the captured materiel were the personal effects of Major General Kawaguchi, who had commanded the Japanese force that attacked Henderson Field in the Battle of the Ridge.

The First Battalion, Tenth Marines, a battalion of seventy-five-millimeter pack howitzers commanded by Lieutenant Colonel P. M. Rixey, supported Carlson in his operations against the Japanese around Asamana. The artillery had moved up with the Seventh Marines and 164th Infantry as they closed in on the enemy east of the Metapona. As Carlson's Raiders spotted 'pockets of Nips,' they requested artillery concentrations on those areas. The team of Raiders and artillery killed many and drove the rest farther inland.

Lieutenant Colonel Carlson returned to Division Headquarters for conferences when his men had cleaned out Asamana and had taken it over. At Headquarters it was decided that he should continue in pursuit of enemy remnants, make a wide swing around our position to the south, and seek out detachments of Japanese known to be camping far up the Lunga and destroy their field guns. These little detachments were, for the most part, survivors of the enemy's futile and costly attempts to take Henderson Field from the south late in October. He was also directed to locate the trail used by the enemy to shuttle troops from the west to the east side at the division position at Henderson Field.

The Raiders continued to push through the jungle and hills, taking a general southwesterly course. The going became harder and harder as steep coral ridges and dense jungle replaced the flat land and occasional grassy fields near the coast. November 25 patrols found a large amount of equipment abandoned by the Japanese two and a half miles south of the airfield near the Lunga. By the 29th they had pushed far inland to a point where the Tenaru and Lunga Rivers are separated only by a steep, narrow ridge. Reconnaissance indicated that a trail near this point was the main Japanese track from west to east behind our defense perimeter.

The Raiders started across the ridge. The sides were steep and treacherous and the Marines had to use ropes climbing up and down the cliffs. As they started down, it began to rain and slippery mud added to their troubles. They found their reward, however, on the other side, for when they had worked their way down to the Lunga they found, as they had hoped, the main Japanese base.

It was a bivouac area large enough for a regiment, with three distinct positions for battalions. In the first the Raiders found several field pieces for which they had been looking. A second encampment was also deserted, except for a few stragglers. Two trails led up the river, one along the bank and the other angling away from the river. Colonel Carlson, who was with the point, directed that a squad be sent up each trail.

He followed the squad which struck off toward the interior and which was led by Corporal John Yancey. It climbed a ridge which tapered off toward the river and on the top Colonel Carlson paused to consider the situation, for the point was getting well ahead of the main body, the bulk of which was still coming over the ridge. The rain was beating down in torrents. Suddenly, to quote Colonel Carlson, 'all hell broke out ahead.' Bursts of automatic fire were punctuated by yells of 'Hi, Raider,' from Raiders identifying their location so as not to fire into each other.

Yancey had run into a third bivouac area, one which was operating as an active enemy base and was occupied by about one hundred men. As Yancey said, it got 'spookier and spookier' as he moved silently through the jungle seeing no one. He called softly, 'Hi, Stinky,' to another man in the squad he knew was near-by — and saw four Japanese jump up. He swept them with automatic fire. His Captain (Schwerin) called through the jungle: 'What's up?' 'I've flushed a covey,' replied Yancey. 'Send up a squad.'

Actually Yancey had only six men with him, but these men acted with precision and speed. Each selected a sector of the enemy bivouac and dashed into it with automatic weapon blazing. The enemy was caught at a disadvantage, for most of his weapons were stacked against trees in the center of the bivouac area. In half an hour Yancey and his band had accounted for about seventy-five and the balance had fled to the surrounding bush. Additional Raiders were available to assist Yancey, but Colonel Carlson decided not to send them in so long as Yancey was proceeding successfully, for fear of increasing the probability of casualties from our own fire. It was obvious from the sound of the explosions that our men were doing most of the firing. This base proved to contain an artillery detachment and a field hospital. It was heavily stocked with food and contained large quantities of weapons and supplies.

On the following day a company was sent in to mop up the

adjacent jungle area and twenty-three more Japanese were killed. One of our men was killed by a sniper, our only casualty in this engagement on the upper Lunga. Patrols also scouted the main trail to the southwest, killing ten stragglers. There was no indication of a major movement from the west via this trail, and Colonel Carlson so reported to General Vandegrift. The Division Commander directed him to return with his battalion to the airfield area.

The battalion was now bivouacked immediately south of Mambulo (Mount Austen), the hill which dominates Henderson Field on the southwest and which at this time was still held by the enemy. In returning to the Lunga area, Carlson decided to send the three companies which had been out the longest back by way of the Tenaru River and to take the three strongest companies over Mambulo. This would bring him out near the mouth of the Matanikau and would enable him to gather useful information concerning the enemy disposition on Mambulo. For success he banked heavily on surprise.

The movement began on the morning of December 3. On the preceding day a reconnaissance patrol had learned that at the top of the mountain (fifteen hundred feet) there was a central hub from which radiated a spider web of ridges. The Japanese had dug entrenchments for a very strong position around the top of the hub. Colonel Carlson's first objective was to occupy that position as quickly as possible. With this in view he pushed his advance guard up the precipitous slope. At the point near the crest Japanese footprints were observed on the trail. The Colonel drew these to the attention of Lieutenant Jack Miller, who commanded the point. A few minutes after Lieutenant Miller gained the 'hub,' a strong enemy combat patrol was observed approaching along one of the ridges from the east. As it neared the crest, it apparently became suspicious and deployed. This was the signal for the Raiders to open fire.

Carlson started a double envelopment of the enemy force, but presently it became apparent that a double envelopment by the enemy was creeping around our flanks. The Colonel then sent a platoon wide around each flank with orders to encircle. When the latter troops got into position, they closed on the enemy with yells of 'Hi, Raider,' exterminating him. That night the Raiders made a 'dry' camp in the enemy position, no water being available. Our casualties consisted of four wounded. One of these died in the following day during the trek down the mountain.

At daylight the Raiders began their movement down the north side of the mountain, carrying their wounded. One of the wounded men was Gunnery Sergeant Mahakian, who had been wounded in the right wrist during the Makin raid. Here on Mambulo he had been shot through the *left* wrist, the bullet striking his wrist watch and spreading the pieces through the arm.

The point had proceeded only five or six hundred yards down the trail when it was ambushed and the leading man was killed. A double envelopment succeeded in cleaning up the ambush, but at the cost of two additional men. Each Japanese held a cleverly concealed position and stood his ground until discovered and killed.

The balance of the trip was made without incident, though, to quote the Raiders, 'We smelled Japs all the way down the mountain.' Colonel Carlson firmly believed the Japanese were present in considerable force, but allowed his command to pass through because of the strength exhibited by the Raiders in the two engagements on the mountain. In the middle of the afternoon the column entered the Division lines near the Matanikau. After dispatching the wounded to the hospital the companies moved by marching to their old bivouac on the Tenaru beyond the east flank of the Division. On the following day the entire battalion entered a 'rest' area on the beach to await transportation back to its base.

During the month it had spent in the jungle the battalion had tramped one hundred and fifty miles and had fought engagements of some sort practically daily. The known enemy dead for whom they had accounted numbered four hundred and eighty-eight, and their own casualties had been seventeen killed and seventeen wounded. They captured and destroyed large quantities of weapons, ammunition, food, and medical supplies as well as three field pieces. Even more important was the information provided the Division Commander, for now Major General Vandegrift and Major General Patch, his Army successor, could rest assured that no major enemy movement from west to east behind Mount Austen (Mambulo) was afoot.

Most significant, though, was the demonstration of the ability of American troops, properly trained and indoctrinated, to operate independent of established supply lines in the jungle. In the thirty engagements it fought, the battalion had been surprised only twice. On the other occasions it gained complete surprise over the enemy. This fact, plus its skill in jungle fighting and its tremendous fire power, explain the low casualties we sustained in comparison to those of the enemy. The heroes of Makin Island had added another exceptional feat of arms to their history.

OTHER PATROL ACTIONS

Every day Marine patrols operated in the jungle beyond the defense perimeter. Such routine activity, taking men over difficult terrain in constant danger of enemy ambush, was a constant test of alertness and endurance. Less spectacular than the pitched battles that broke out periodically between relatively large forces, patrol activity was characteristic of the jungle fighting that lasted throughout the Guadalcanal campaign.

Two patrol actions late in November were particularly successful. They illustrate the high state of combat efficiency which the Marines had reached after their weeks of experience in the Solomons. Both involved surprise of unsuspecting enemy groups. Both called for silent movement, perfect coordination, and well-timed action.

November 22 a patrol of fifty-five men from Company F of the First Marines, under Second Lieutenant Gordon Maples, surprised about two hundred Japanese in a bivouac near the top of Grassy Knoll, and killed almost half of them with Marine casualties of only two wounded. A few days earlier a Marine patrol had run into an ambush on the hill and Lieutenant Maples' group was sent to mop up the enemy detachment.

The patrol's approach to Grassy Knoll led them up the Lunga through very rough country of jungle and steep ridges. As they came near to Grassy Knoll, ten men were sent round to the eastern slope of the hill, to cut off a possible Japanese withdrawal in that direction, while the main body of the patrol made its way up the western slope to the summit. Another group of thirty-five Marines took up a position at the bottom of the hill on the eastern side. The first night out, Lieutenant Maples' patrol bivouacked near the top of Grassy Knoll about a quarter of a mile from the main enemy bivouac area.

In the morning the Marines attacked. While one group covered the left flank, the main body took positions just below the summit on the side where the Japanese were encamped. The enemy was completely surprised. He had posted no sentries and the Japanese soldiers were chattering and rattling their mess gear as they prepared for breakfast, completely unaware that the Marines were closing in. Many were unarmed and far from their weapons.

Then, on Lieutenant Maples' signal, the Marines rushed down the side of the hill, all weapons firing, and took a heavy toll of the panic-stricken Japanese. About thirty fell in the initial assault. Some of the Japanese reorganized after their flight into the woods and tried to outflank Maples' group. They ran into his flank guards and fifty or sixty more fell to Marine bullets and grenades. By the time the Japanese, who had outnumbered the Marines five to one when the action began, had sufficiently recovered to set up machine guns, the

Marine patrol was withdrawing. They came out of the skirmish almost unscathed.   Every man returned from the patrol
and only two were wounded.

Lieutenant Maples' raid on the camp and his complete success in surprising the Japanese was typical of many patrol
experiences on Guadalcanal. During the early months of the
war the Japanese had built up a reputation of being peerless
jungle fighters, able to move through terrain where others
could not move, silent and stealthy, clever at infiltration, patient and tireless.   On Guadalcanal, for the first time in the
war of the Pacific islands, the Japanese found themselves faced
with fighters who could move as silently as they, who could be
as patient, and who could live in the jungle as well. Through
losses of fifty to one, thirty to one, twenty to one, they came to
learn the nature of the enemy that opposed them.

When they moved into the southeastern Solomons in the
late spring and early summer of 1942, the Japanese had set up
observation posts at vantage-points where they could observe
ship movements through the islands. One of these was established at Cape Astrolabe, on the northwestern tip of Malaita
Island. Late in November First Lieutenant James W. Crain
and forty men, from the Third Battalion, Second Marines,
then stationed on Tulagi, were sent to Malaita to wipe out the
Japanese lookout station. Major John M. Mather, a former
trader on Malaita who had joined the Australian Army when
the Solomons were overrun, and had been attached to Lieutenant Colonel Buckley's Intelligence Section after the Marines occupied Henderson Field, had gone to Malaita earlier to
reconnoiter the Japanese position. Taking care that his
presence on the island should not become known, lest renegade
natives inform the Japanese and put them on the alert, Major
Mather directed the work of scouts who gathered information
for maps of the Japanese camp on the tip of the island. Lying
in the bush, the scouts thoroughly learned the routine of the
enemy post — when they got up in the morning, when they
ate, when they changed sentries.   One scout also cut a trail

leading to the camp, for the use of the Marines who would come to destroy the observation post.

In a night trip from Tulagi November 2–3, the Marine patrol under Lieutenant Crain went to Malaita and landed at Auki, miles from their objective. The next day they marched twelve miles to the village of Fauban where they bivouacked. The patrol was divided into teams of six men each, who spent a day rehearsing their parts in the attack to come, taking up positions around an imaginary enemy camp.

After the rehearsal the Marines marched by night toward the Cape Astrolabe. They arrived at the Japanese camp just before dawn and silently took up their positions around the area, surrounding it on three sides. The sea cut off escape on the fourth side.

They had learned from the scouts that the Japanese gathered in the mess hall, one of four shacks with open sides, for breakfast at seven o'clock, and the plan of attack called for the Marines' lying doggo in the brush until all the enemy soldiers were together at breakfast. One team of Marines wriggled along the ground to positions very close to the mess hall. The Japanese moved toward the shack for breakfast. Still the Marines held their fire, waiting for those who were washing and brushing their teeth to join the others, but only fourteen went into the mess hall. Then, as two got up from the table to leave, Lieutenant Crain gave the signal to fire. Fire from automatic weapons sprayed the mess hall, killing everyone in it and some others near-by. The surprise was complete, and not a shot was returned.

Nineteen of the twenty-two Japanese in the camp were killed. Two, badly wounded, succeeding in getting into the bush, and one wounded prisoner was brought back to Tulagi. The Marines suffered no casualties at all. They not only wiped out the soldiers in the post, but recovered the Japanese radio set intact and brought it back to Guadalcanal.

Chapter 11

Departure from Guadalcanal

FIRST MARINE DIVISION LEAVES GUADALCANAL

A FTER THE SHATTERING DEFEAT of the Japanese in the middle of November, Guadalcanal grew quieter. Regiments which had borne the brunt of the fighting for more than three months were drawn back from the only active sector, in the west, and were replaced by newer arrivals on the island. The Eighth Marines under Colonel R. H. Jeschke, who had arrived November 4, took over the line of the Matanikau. An infantry regiment of the United States Army, commanded by Colonel D. W. Hogan, was placed along the ridges back of the Eighth Marines.

A western sector, consisting of all forces west of the original defense perimeter, was organized under the command of Brigadier General E. D. Sebree, Assistant Division Commander of the America Division, which was moving up to Guadalcanal in increasing numbers. Brigadier General William H. Rupertus, Jr., Assistant Division Commander of the First Marine Division, assumed command of forces inside the defense perimeter around Henderson Field. Major General Vandegrift, in effect, was commanding a Corps rather than a Division. By the middle of November the forces under his command in the Guadalcanal-Tulagi area had grown to one complete Marine Division, two reinforced regiments of another Marine Division, two Army regiments, Army artillery units, a Marine Raider Battalion, and elements of two Marine Defense Battalions.

Ground activity in the latter half of November was confined to patrolling by all units, the thirty-day expedition of the Raiders, and to constant pressure against the Japanese beyond the Matanikau. The enemy's remaining strength, concentrated in the region between the Matanikau and Kokumbona, was steadily pounded by Marine and Army units which pushed out to Point Cruz. The Second and Eighth Marines and the two Army regiments then on Guadalcanal were all engaged, at different times in November, in maintaining the pressure in the west. The Eleventh Marines harassed the enemy in that sector with sporadic artillery fire, day and night, and attack planes droned back and forth over Japanese positions at all hours.

The American forces, however, were not yet ready to undertake an offensive to drive the Japanese remnants off the island. The new Army units that began coming in late in November were not reinforcements. They were coming in to relieve the First Marine Division.

Brigadier General E. D. Sebree had arrived on Guadalcanal November 2 and soon other members of the Staff of the America Division came to the island. Major General Alexander M. Patch, Division Commander, arrived on the 19th. As Army staff officers moved in with the Marine staff sections, watching their procedure and learning the local situation, the Marines' thoughts turned more and more to preparations to leave the island.

In the lull which followed the sinking of Japan's invasion armada, enemy aerial activity ceased except for harassing raids by small groups of bombers at night. At the end of the month naval activity flared up again, and for a time it looked as though the Japanese were building up to another major attempt to recapture Henderson Field. Two engagements with Japanese surface craft — one by a United States naval task force and one by aircraft based on Henderson Field — resulted in heavy ship losses to the enemy, and the new offensive, if it was meant to be one, died aborning.

The surface engagement occurred the night of November 30–December 1. Japanese troop transports, escorted by destroyers, including some large ones which possibly were cruisers, approached Guadalcanal that night. A force of United States cruisers and destroyers moved up to the channel between Guadalcanal and Florida to meet them. The American force found some enemy ships already near the beach west of Lunga Point and opened fire. In the engagement that followed, according to the Navy communiqué, nine enemy ships were sunk — two large destroyers (or cruisers), four destroyers, two troop transports, and one cargo ship. We lost the heavy cruiser *Northampton* and other ships suffered damage.

The Japanese came back in force three days later. They were spotted the afternoon of the 3d as two heavy cruisers, two light cruisers, and six destroyers were speeding toward Guadalcanal. Dauntless dive-bombers, Avenger torpedo planes, escorted by Airacobras and Wildcats, went out from Henderson Field to meet them. The planes found them one hundred and fifty miles from Guadalcanal, still pressing on toward the island. At dusk they attacked and when they turned to head back to Guadalcanal they left behind them four crippled Japanese ships. One cruiser had taken two direct hits by thousand-pound bombs, another cruiser had suffered one bomb hit, a large destroyer had been hit twice by torpedoes, and two possible torpedo hits were scored on a second destroyer. Float-biplane fighters, probably based on Rekata Bay, tried to protect the Japanese surface force, but ten of them were shot down by the Grumman Wildcats and Airacobras. Our losses were one Wildcat, one Avenger, and one Dauntless.

During this period the Japanese were building up their air bases in the northeastern Solomons. For the first time Munda became a familiar name. Working under the concealment of coconut trees at Munda Point on the southern side of the west end of New Georgia, the Japanese were hastily building the runway which was to become the objective of the next United States attack in the Solomons seven months later. The outlines of the runway began to show through the umbrella of coconut fronds. It meant that the Japanese were using the opportunity provided by the long Guadalcanal campaign to add yet another barrier to the American advance against their Pacific defense perimeter.

We, too, were strengthening our air base on Guadalcanal. Work was pushed on a second fighter strip west of the Lunga River. Preliminary work on another airfield at Aola had shown that it would be a long, difficult task to construct an adequate runway in the rough wooded country there, and the forces which had been landed to work in and defend that area were transferred to the broad grassy plains south of Koli Point where strips could be quickly and easily developed.

More and more planes crowded Henderson Field. Almost every day supply ships and transports were unloading off Lunga Lagoon and at Koli Point. Inside the defense perimeter there was a new bustle of activity as men and supplies moved ashore.

Finally a day long awaited arrived. After several postponements, transports arrived to take from the island the Fifth Marines, the first units of the First Marine Division scheduled to leave. It was December 9, and at dawn the officers and men of the Fifth Marines and reinforcing units began moving to the beach.

To the west lay a beached supply ship which had been torpedoed a few days before. To the east, beyond the Tenaru, another torpedoed supply ship had been run up on the beach a month earlier. Both vessels had been attacked by Japanese submarines which somehow slipped through the screen of destroyers and escaped the eyes of pilots patrolling overhead. We half-expected another torpedo to crash into one of the transports that stood as such attractive targets in the channel as they took on their loads of Marines.

The embarkation, however, proceeded without interruption. Twice during the day the sirens wailed on land and general quarters sounded on the ships as Japanese planes came within a few miles of Guadalcanal, but fighters from Henderson Field drove them off.

By the middle of the afternoon we were under way, headed for the southeast. Back in the west, beyond the Matanikau, we could see a pall of smoke from bombs and artillery hanging over the ridges and jungle between the Matanikau and Kokumbona. A cloud of dust rose over Henderson Field. Bombers and fighters circled overhead, and some streaked off toward Kokumbona to add to the destruction in the Japanese positions. There the battle would continue for six weeks, until finally a team of Army and Marine units drove westward to sweep the area clean of the enemy, and the Army fought on to Cape Esperance to end all organized resistance.

As we passed Koli Point and Togama Point, an officer came up to me and pointed to the next tree-covered spit of land jutting out into the sea which concealed the rest of the island lying beyond. 'Is that the end of the island?' he asked hopefully. 'No, sir, that's Taivu Point. We have about forty miles to go yet.' He shook his head and turned away. Probably few were unhappy to see the last of Guadalcanal. Yet it stood in great beauty in that clear tropical afternoon. Only from the sea can you appreciate the island's real beauty. There you see the palm-fringed shores, the ridges rising behind, and green mountains towering still farther back. We lined the rails for a last look as the short tropical twilight turned to night. 'The smoking lamp is out,' came over the ship's public address system. 'No lights will be shown on the weather decks.'

Once again we were at sea. Now our only worries were the submarines, and for some foolish reason we felt that, having passed those four months on Guadalcanal without disaster, nothing now would happen to interfere with our safe with-drawal to a quiet spot. We would see cities and lights and women again. George was going to get a rest.

RETROSPECT

It was a tired, ragged, weather-beaten outfit of Marines that lined the rails of the transports that evening to have a last look at the island where they had fought and worked for more than four months. Their dress was an odd assortment of green dungarees and dirty khaki. Some had shirts cut off at the sleeves and trousers cut off at the knees, some had no shirts at all, some had clothes ripped and torn, and all had clothes stained by the sweat and muck of Guadalcanal. Socks had become a luxury and many had long ago rotted away. Field shoes — 'boondockers' — were run down at the heels, tied up with patched and knotted shoe laces or bits of string.

Everyone who could find one had made a dash for the showers as soon as he boarded his transport, but it would be a long time before the dirt of Guadalcanal would be thoroughly washed off bodies and out of clothes. There is another kind of dirt in the Solomons that would never leave them. It is the dirt of death, the stench of bodies quickly rotting in the sun on a tropical battlefield, which so sticks in the nostrils that he who smells it can never feel clean.

Rather surprisingly, there was little elation in the faces of the Marines who lined the rails. There was only an unaccus-tomed attitude of ease, with an apparent feeling of content-ment at the thought that at last they were going to get a rest they had suffered much to earn. There had been a time, in the first weeks after our original landing, when they had won-dered when they would push on to new conquests. They had been eager to move on northward, farther into the enemy-held Solomons. Now they thought of rest and recuperation. As the weeks had passed on Guadalcanal — the weeks of pound-ing by the enemy, of heat and dirt and sweat — they came to realize they would not soon be able to lead off another offensive in the islands of the Pacific. A far worse ailment than the 'combat fatigue' that tired men's bodies and minds, and a far worse enemy than the Japanese, had stricken them. The bronzed muscled backs were deceptive — within those bodies malarial parasites were teeming. The numbers of those who burned with malaria fever and collapsed from the sapping power of the disease grew from day to day. Thousands were incapacitated.

These men, who had landed on Guadalcanal and Tulagi as green troops four months earlier, now were battle-hardened veterans. Boys in their teens could tell grisly tales. They had learned all the tricks of jungle warfare, they had been pounded for months as few men in the history of war have been pounded, they had seen their buddies stricken down at their sides, and they had learned the loneliness of fighting in a far Pacific island. But they had taken the measure of the enemy, and, if they respected him, they did not fear him. After four months of Guadalcanal, they wore an air of assurance and self-confidence. It was assurance without cockiness and self-confidence without swagger. These men knew they had made the name Guadalcanal one for the enemy to fear and they felt the confidence that comes only with such knowledge.

The Guadalcanal campaign had not been on a large scale compared with the huge operations which final victory in the Pacific and in Europe would entail. The island was one small sector in a front line extending thousands of miles through the Pacific and Asia, a front line broken by vast expanses of water where the land fronts were small and scattered.

As the only active sector in the South Pacific except for New Guinea, however, Guadalcanal had been the magnet for powerful Japanese forces and a sink-hole for Japanese strength. Even if Guadalcanal had been a place of no importance, the Japanese would have reacted violently to the sudden seizure of an airfield they had almost completed for their own use.

Considerations of face, if no others, would have ensured a determined Japanese counter-attack. But Guadalcanal was a place of importance in its own right, important to both belligerents as a defensive and offensive base, and the Japanese risked much strength in ships, planes, men, and material in their vain efforts to recapture Henderson Field.

The American people, anxiously watching the battle from the homeland, had begun to wonder whether this would be typical of the war against Japan. Would there be the same long, grueling struggle for each of Japan's island outposts? Would it take years for our forces to inch toward the island heart of the new Japanese Empire?

In a way the struggle for Guadalcanal *was* typical. Throughout the islands of the Pacific our men would have to fight in the same type of jungle terrain, sloughing through mud in tropical torrents or sweating under a merciless sun. There would be the same long lines of communication to maintain, growing even longer as we approached our ultimate objective. Landings and later actions on land would call for the same type of tactics, perfected in the Guadalcanal laboratory.

Few people, however, seemed to realize that the Guadalcanal venture would differ from later offensive actions in one respect of great importance. The battle there dragged on for six months because the Japanese were able to launch powerful counter-attacks. Our offensive was undertaken with limited means, at a time when Japan was free to throw great forces against the island outpost — forces which threatened at times to overwhelm our relatively weak defenses. As United Nations power in the Pacific grew, as we gained strength to attack Japan's defense perimeter at many points, the enemy's ability to counter-attack would correspondingly diminish. A prolonged struggle for one position, such as that for Henderson Field, was unlikely to occur again.

Of the larger strategy of the war, which led to the original attack on Guadalcanal, with limited means employed according to hastily made plans, I cannot speak, for I know nothing of it. The high councils which decided upon the venture will doubtless make the reasons known in their own good time. I can only say that those to whom fell the honor to initiate that first United States offensive in the Pacific entered upon their task and carried it out with enthusiasm and zeal. Their success against great odds, against an enemy hitherto unbeaten, quite properly has made 'Guadalcanal' a symbolic name and given it a unique place in our military history.

As their distinguished Commanding Officer, Major General Vandegrift, turned over his command on Guadalcanal, he paid tribute to the men who had served so ably under his command. The General's personal bravery and eagerness to share the dangers of his men had made him a familiar figure at the front line in the fighting on Guadalcanal. His men knew him, not just as a name back at the Command Post, but as a commander who led them in person. His bravery, his sure judgment in the most difficult situations, his *expertise* in the science of war, won for him the great distinction of the Congressional Medal of Honor.

The General's letter to his men, written on the occasion of his relinquishing his command to Major General Alexander M. Patch, is the sincere tribute of an officer who through four difficult months had watched with keen appreciation the gallant, and sometimes desperate, fight of the men who served under him. He, better than anyone else, knew what they had gone through and what they had accomplished, and he better than they foresaw the day when they would again go into action, not as the inexperienced men who had the honor to lead off the United States' first offensive in the Pacific, but as skilled and toughened veterans whose deeds on Guadalcanal had made the name of their Corps a symbol of death and fear to the enemy.

December 7, 1942

In relinquishing command in this area, I hope that in some small measure I can convey to you my feeling of pride in your magnificent accomplishments and my thanks for the unbounded loyalty, limitless self-sacrifice, and high courage which have made those accomplishments possible.

To the soldiers and marines who have faced the enemy in the fierceness of night combat; to the pilots, Army, Navy, and Marine, whose unbelievable achievements have made the name 'Guadalcanal' a synonym for death and disaster in the language of our enemy; to those who have labored and sweated within the lines at all manner of prodigious and vital tasks; to the men of the torpedo boat command slashing at the enemy in night sortie; to our small band of devoted allies who have contributed so vastly in proportion to their numbers; to the surface forces of the Navy associated with us in signal triumphs of their own, I say that at all times you have faced without flinching the worst that the enemy could do to us and have thrown back the best that he could send against us.

It may well be that this modest operation, begun four months ago today, has, through your efforts, been successful in thwarting the larger aims of our enemy in the Pacific. The fight for the Solomons is not yet won, but 'tide what may,' I know that you, as brave men and men of good will, will hold your heads high and prevail in the future as you have in the past.

(Signed)   A. A. VANDEGRIFT

Major General, U.S. Marine Corps

THE END

APPENDIX

THE SECRETARY OF THE NAVY

WASHINGTON

4 February 1943

CITED IN THE NAME OF

THE PRESIDENT OF THE UNITED STATES

THE FIRST MARINE DIVISION, REINFORCED

UNDER COMMAND OF

MAJOR GENERAL ALEXANDER A. VANDEGRIFT, U.S.M.C.

CITATION:

The officers and enlisted men of the First Marine Division, Reinforced, on August 7 to 9, 1942, demonstrated outstanding gallantry and determination in successfully executing forced landing assaults against a number of strongly defended Japanese positions on Tulagi, Gavutu, Tanambogo, Florida and Guadalcanal, British Solomon Islands, completely routing all the enemy forces and seizing a most valuable base and airfield within the enemy zone of operations in the South Pacific Ocean. From the above period until 9 December, 1942, this Reinforced Division not only held their important strategic positions despite determined and repeated Japanese naval, air and land attacks, but by a series of offensive operations against strong enemy resistance drove the Japanese from the proximity of the airfield and inflicted great losses on them by land and air attacks. The courage and determination displayed in these operations were of an inspiring order.

(Signed)   FRANK KNOX

Secretary of the Navy

UNIT COMMENDATIONS FROM

THE COMMANDING GENERAL

FIRST MARINE DIVISION

1. The Commanding General desires to transmit to all hands here on Guadalcanal the good news that has reached us from Tulagi. Our comrades there have added the name of a splendid victory to the long roll of battle honor of the Corps. Striking from the sea they assaulted and conquered a series of organized positions defended in great strength by a wily and determined opponent. The fight was carried to the enemy at all times and in all places and he was driven from every place he held by the resolute attack of men who were not afraid to die. God favors the bold and the strong of heart; the Commanding General is grateful to inform you that casualties, while severe, were less than at first believed and by no means disproportionate to the results achieved. We salute the officers and men of our division who carried through the Tulagi operations to so brilliant a conclusion.

A. A. VANDEGRIFT
Major General, U.S. Marine Corps
Commanding

COMMENDATION FOR RESULTS OF
BATTLE OF THE TENARU RIVER

1. The Commanding General desires that all personnel of the Division be informed concerning the results of the Battle of the Tenaru River which commenced at 0200 August 21 and was terminated at nightfall of that date.

2. The 1st Marines and supporting units, when their defensive position west of the Tenaru River, north coast of Guadalcanal, Solomon Islands, was assaulted under cover of darkness by a well trained, well equipped enemy landing force of about 700 men whose mission was to seize the airport west of the river, defended their position with such zeal and determination that the enemy was unable to effect a penetration of the position in spite of repeated efforts throughout the night. The 1st Marines, counter-attacking at daybreak with an envelopment which caught the enemy in the rear and on the flank, thus cutting off his withdrawal and pushing him from inland in the direction of the sea, virtually annihilated his force and achieved a victory fully commensurate with the military traditions of our Corps. The Commanding General conveys to the officers and men who carried through this outstanding operation the salute of all officers and men of the Division.

A. A. VANDEGRIFT
Major General, U.S. Marine Corps
Commanding

1. The Commanding General desires that all personnel of the 1st Division and attached units be apprised of outstanding efforts made by and the conspicuous successes attained by VSB–232, VF–223, VS–5 and 67th Fighting Squadron (U.S.A.), all of which were stationed at Guadalcanal, Solomon Islands during all or a portion of the 10-day period from 21 to 30 August, 1942.

2. During this period one or more of the above-named units have contacted the enemy on the sea or in the air eight times. Sustaining losses to themselves which were far below what might be expected in view of the results obtained they have destroyed 16 enemy twin-engine bombers, 5 single-engine bombers, 39 Zero Fighters and 3 destroyers in addition to which they have hit and probably destroyed one cruiser, two destroyers and 2 transports.

3. Operating under difficulties from an unfinished advance air base with limited facilities for upkeep and repair these units have without regard for the cost sought out the enemy at every opportunity and have engaged him with such aggressiveness and skill as to contribute conspicuously to the success of the allied cause in the Solomon Island Area.

4. The Commanding General takes pleasure in conveying to the officers and men of the above-named units in behalf of the officers and men of the 1st Division appreciation and felicitations for their outstanding performance of duty.

A. A. VANDEGRIFT

Major General, U.S. Marine Corps
Commanding

1. The Commanding General desires to commend the outstanding efforts of the First Raider Battalion, the Parachute Battalion, and the Eleventh Marines during the enemy attack on the First Division positions on Guadalcanal Island on the night of September 13–14, 1942.

2. On that night the First Raider Battalion with the First Parachute Battalion attached, having been assigned the mission of occupying and defending a key position along a ridge located about one thousand (1000) yards south of the Guadalcanal air field had scarcely moved into the position when the enemy launched an attack on it and broke through the front lines. The situation of forward units having become untenable, a skillful withdrawal to the reserve position was effected.

3. During the period from 1930 on the 13th to 0600 on the 14th the enemy launched a series of ferocious assaults on the reserve position, each culminating in fierce hand to hand combat in which both attacker and defender employed bayonets, rifles, pistols, grenades and knives. The Parachute Battalion, hastily reorganized into two companies after its withdrawal from the main line of resistance, counter-attacked the enemy advancing on the left of the reserve position to extend that position to the left and to straighten the line then being held by the Battalion Reserve. This counter-attack was carried out successfully in that the enemy was forced to withdraw into the edge of the woods fronting the reserve position, his flanking movement which had threatened the whole position having been halted. During this courageous attack the Parachute Troops suffered casualties estimated at 40%.

248

4. Throughout the night the Eleventh Marines supported the Raiders and Parachutists by nine hours of almost constant artillery fire of the greatest accuracy and effectiveness, and greatly assisted them in standing off the attacks of the enemy. The morning of the 14th found the enemy retreating and the reinforced Raider Battalion in complete control of the field of battle.

5. Almost without exception the officers and men engaged in this action proved themselves to be among the best fighting troops that any service could hope to have, and in extending to them the salutation of the officers and men of the Division the Commanding General wishes to state that he considers it a privilege and an honor to have had troops of this calibre attached to his command.

A. A. VANDEGRIFT

3RD BATTALION, 164TH INFANTRY, COMMENDATION OF,
FOR OPERATIONS AGAINST THE ENEMY ON 24, 25 AND
26 OCTOBER, 1942

1. The Commanding General commends the 3rd Battalion, 164th Infantry, U.S. Army, for the effectiveness of its operations against the enemy on 24, 25 and 26 October, 1942. The 1st Battalion, 7th Marines occupying a defensive sector of a width of 2500 yards situated to the south of the positions of the 1st Marine Division (reinforced) on Lunga Point, Guadalcanal, British Solomon Islands, having been attacked by a numerically superior enemy force at about 1000, 23 October, 1942, the 3rd Battalion, 164th Infantry, then in Regimental Reserve, was ordered to reinforce the line.   Moving by a forced march at night through rain and over difficult and unfamiliar terrain it arrived in time to prevent a serious penetration of the position and by reinforcing the 1st Battalion, 7th Marines throughout its sector, made possible the repulse of continued enemy attacks throughout the night.   The following day, having been assigned the left half of the sector formerly occupied by the 1st Battalion, 7th Marines, the 3rd Battalion, 164th Infantry so occupied and prepared the position that when the main effort of another enemy attack was directed at it on the night of 24 and 25 October, 1942, it was able to hold the position without serious loss to its own personnel, although heavy casualties were inflicted upon the enemy forces.   The 1st Division is proud to have serving with it another unit which has stood the test of battle and demonstrated an overwhelming superiority over the enemy.

A. A. VANDEGRIFT

1. The Commanding General commends the 11th Marines for the remarkable effectiveness of fire delivered in support of the 3rd Battalion, 1st Marines, during an attempted tank assault upon its position at the mouth of the Matanikau River, Guadalcanal, British Solomon Islands, during the night of 23 October, 1942. The fire of the 11th Regiment which was delivered promptly on call is directly credited with the disabling of three 15-ton tanks and with the virtual annihilation of a unit of the enemy forces approximating a battalion in size. The repeatedly demonstrated effectiveness of the fires of the 11th Marines is a tribute to the technical proficiency and devotion to duty on the part of the Regimental Commander, Brigadier General Pedro A. del Valle and the officers and men of his regiment.

A. A. VANDEGRIFT

1. The Commanding General commends the 1st Battalion, 7th Marines for its determined and vigorous defense against an attack conducted by numerically superior enemy forces on' the night of 23–24 October, 1942. The 1st Battalion occupying a defensive sector of a width of about 2500 yards situated on the south line of the 1st Division position on Lunga Point, Guadalcanal, British Solomon Islands, was attacked at about 1000 by an enemy force of a strength estimated at 3000 men. The 1st Battalion assisted by effective artillery fire from the 11th Marines successfully maintained its lines against determined enemy assaults until 0330 when it was reinforced throughout the position by the 3rd Battalion, 164th Infantry. Together with that Battalion, the successful defense was continued throughout the night inflicting heavy losses upon the opposing enemy troops. The high combat effectiveness demonstrated by the 1st Battalion, 7th Marines is a tribute to the courage, devotion to duty and high professional attainments of its Commanding Officer, Lieutenant Colonel Lewis B. Puller and to the Company Commanders, Captain Charles W. Kelly, Jr., Captain Regan Fuller, Captain Robert H. Haggerty, Captain Marshall W. Moore and Captain Robert J. Rodgers.

A. A. VANDEGRIFT

1. The Commanding General commends the 2nd Battalion, 7th Marines for operations against the enemy on 24, 25 and 26 October, 1942. Having been ordered on 24 October, 1942 to occupy and defend a ridge line running generally in an easterly direction from a point on the Matanikau River, Guadalcanal, British Solomon Islands, about 1000 yards from the north coast of the island, the 2nd Battalion moved into position through a heavy enemy artillery barrage. On the 25th the Battalion was subjected to further heavy bombardment by hostile artillery so that considerable losses had been suffered by the Battalion prior to any attack by hostile infantry. At 0300, 26 October, 1942, the position of the 2nd Battalion was assaulted by an enemy force estimated at one battalion. After furious hand to hand fighting the enemy was able to effect a penetration on the left of the position by 0500. At this critical moment the 2nd Battalion demonstrated a degree of fighting morale that is considered worthy of commendation. At 0540 it counter-attacked the ridge at the point of the break-through and at 0600 it had restored the situation. The success of this counter-attack insured the success of the entire action and the hostile force withdrew shortly thereafter leaving approximately half its number dead on the field of battle.

A. A. VANDEGRIFT

1. The Commanding General commends the 3rd Battalion, 1st Marines for noteworthy performance of duty during the period 9 October, 1942 to 1 November, 1942. On 9 October, 1942, occupying an outlying defensive position on the east bank of the Matanikau River, Guadalcanal, British Solomon Islands, and extending to the south of the mouth thereof, the 3rd Battalion so organized the position as to make it impregnable to enemy attacks which followed shortly thereafter. On 21 October, 1942, the 3rd Battalion after having been subjected to heavy enemy mortar and artillery fire, sighted and with the support of one section, Battery 'B,' 1st Special Weapons Battalion, knocked out one 15-ton tank as it approached their position. On 23 October, 1942, after an extensive preparation by hostile artillery, mortars and machine gun fire, the 3rd Battalion with the support of one section, Battery 'B,' Special Weapons Battalion, one platoon, Battery 'C,' Special Weapons Battalion and with the fire support of the 11th Marines, halted the advance of and completely disabled 9 hostile 15-ton tanks as well as accompanying infantry. On the 24th light attacks by hostile forces were repulsed by infantry action. The Commanding General commends the officers and men of the 3rd Battalion for the fine soldierly qualities demonstrated by all personnel of that Battalion during a hazardous and difficult period of operations.

A. A. VANDEGRIFT

OFFICERS AND MEN OF

FIRST MARINE DIVISION AND

ATTACHED MARINE UNITS

DECORATED FOR ACTS

PERFORMED ON GUADALCANAL

AUGUST 7 — DECEMBER 9, 1942

N. & M. C. MEDAL

TODD, John S., Second Lieutenant
CATES, John B., Staff Sergeant
TOMPKINS, Irving J., Staff Sergeant
GARNER, George M., Technical Sergeant
ROYAL, William W., Corporal
LAMOUREUX, Wesley D., Master Technical Sergeant

PERSONNEL OF MEDICAL CORPS
U.S. NAVY AND NAVAL RESERVE
DECORATED FOR ACTS
PERFORMED ON GUADALCANAL
WHILE ATTACHED TO UNITS OF
FIRST MARINE DIVISION

NAVY CROSS

COLEMAN, Karl Burton, Pharmacist's Mate Third Class
EILERS, Delbert Dale, Pharmacist's Mate First Class
JARRETT, Thirl E., Lieutenant (M.C.) U.S.N.
JOY, Daniel Albert, Pharmacist's Mate Second Class
MCLARNEY, Edward P., Lieutenant (M.C.) U.S.N.
MARSH, Wilbur Lee, Pharmacist's Mate First Class
MATHIS, Lloyd Thomas, Pharmacist's Mate First Class
PARKER, Thaddeus, Hospital Attendant First Class
POTTER, Albern Marshall, Jr., Pharmacist's Mate Second
Class
PRATT, Theodore C., Lieutenant Commander (M.C.)
U.S.N.R.
RINGNESS, Henry R., Lieutenant (M.C.) U.S.N.
ROEBUCK, Gerald Edward, Pharmacist's Mate Third
Class

LEGION OF MERIT

KNOWLTON, Don S., Commander (M.C.) U.S.N.R.

SILVER STAR

ARNOLD, John Alvin, Pharmacist's Mate Second Class

ARRINGTON, Gerald Thomas, Pharmacist's Mate Second Class

BATEASE, John Charles, Hospital Attendant First Class

BROWN, Jay Arthur, Pharmacist's Mate First Class

CARIMI, Sam Joseph, Pharmacist's Mate Third Class

CARPENTER, Cecil Leonard, Pharmacist's Mate Second Class

CLEVELAND, Alfred Winson, Pharmacist's Mate Second Class

COLLINS, Edward Furman, Hospital Attendant Second Class

DAVIS, Obed Loyal, Pharmacist's Mate First Class

DURANT, Kenneth William, Pharmacist's Mate Third Class

EILERS, Delbert Dale, Pharmacist's Mate First Class

FECHTER, John Worthley, Chief Pharmacist's Mate

FITZGERALD, Sidney J., Jr., Pharmacist's Mate Third Class

FRAMENT, Paul Stanley, Pharmacist's Mate Third Class

GARRETT, Richard James, Pharmacist's Mate Third Class

GODBEY, John R., Lieutenant (M.C.) U.S.N.R.

HAGGARD, Wesley Burton, Pharmacist's Mate First Class

HENDERSON, Richard Gordon, Pharmacist's Mate Third Class

KERPER, Griffin Hart, Pharmacist's Mate First Class

KECK, Everett B., Lieutenant Commander (M.C.) U.S.N.R.

LADUE, George Orson, Pharmacist's Mate Second Class

LIDDLE, William Porter, Jr., Pharmacist's Mate Third Class

McFANN, Harold, Jr., Pharmacist's Mate Third Class

MAIDA, Joe Cyril, Pharmacist's Mate Third Class

MURRAH, George Clifton, Jr., Pharmacist's Mate First Class

OWENS, James Warren, Pharmacist's Mate First Class

PRESTON, Leroy Newton, Jr., Pharmacist's Mate Third Class

SAPHIER, Jacques C., Lieutenant (j.g.) (M.C.) U.S.N.R.

SCHRAUDT, Carl Tucker, Pharmacist's Mate Third Class

SMITH, Robert Lee, Pharmacist's Mate Third Class

SUTHERLAND, Joseph Andrew, Pharmacist's Mate First Class

TEDFORD, Orville Franklin, Pharmacist's Mate Second Class

TODAK, Alfred Joseph, Pharmacist's Mate First Class

URY, Jimmy Ray, Pharmacist's Mate Second Class

WALKER, Russell H., Lieutenant (M.C.) U.S.N.

WILSON, Dale Emerson, Pharmacist's Mate First Class

YOUNG, Johnny Wilbur, Pharmacist's Mate Second Class

DISTINGUISHED SERVICE MEDAL

FISKE, Charles L., Lieutenant Colonel (A) *

HAYES, Charles H., Lieutenant Colonel (A)

THOMAS, Gerald C., Colonel

WOODS, Louis E., Brigadier General (A)

* (A) indicates aviation personnel.

LEGION OF MERIT

CATES, Clifton B., Colonel
DAVIS, James N. M., Captain
DEL VALLE, Pedro A., Brigadier General
JACK, Samuel S., Lieutenant Colonel (A)
JOHNSON, Chandler W., Lieutenant Colonel
KNIEJA, Edward J., Private First Class (A)
MORET, Paul, Lieutenant Colonel (A)
SANDERSON, Lawson H. M., Colonel (A)
SCOLLIN, Raymond C., Lieutenant Colonel (A)
SIMS, Amor L., Colonel
TWINING, Merrill B., Lieutenant Colonel

MEDAL OF HONOR

BAILEY, Kenneth D., Major
BASILONE, John, Sergeant
BAUER, Harold W., Lieutenant Colonel (A)
EDSON, Merritt A., Colonel
FOSS, Joseph J., Captain (A)
GALER, Robert E., Major (A)
PAIGE, Mitchell, Platoon Sergeant
SMITH, John L., Major (A)
VANDEGRIFT, Alexander A., Major General

GREAT BRITAIN
DISTINGUISHED SERVICE ORDER

EDSON, Merritt A., Colonel
GALER, Robert E., Major (A)
SMITH, John L., Major (A)

CONSPICUOUS GALLANTRY MEDAL

GOSS, Angus, Marine Gunner
RAYSBROOK, Robert D., Sergeant

SILVER STAR (NAVY)

ALO, George E., Platoon Sergeant
ALVIS, Logan V., Corporal
AMERINE, Richard R., Second Lieutenant (A)
ANDERSON, Clarence G., Corporal (A)
ARNDT, Charles C., Sergeant
ARNOLD, James W., Corporal
AUGUSTYNOWICZ, Fred, Private First Class

BAILEY, Kenneth D., Major
BAILEY, Roy C., First Sergeant
BARNES, George S., Staff Sergeant (A)
BARNES, Roy L., Private
BARR, Woodrow W., Private First Class

BARRETT, Charles D., Jr., Second Lieutenant
BATTEN, Linoard M., Corporal
BAUER, Francis J., Corporal
BEASLEY, Charles J., Captain
BEHLAND, Wesley C., Private First Class
BELET, Robert A., Technical Sergeant
BENNER, Stanley G., Second Lieutenant
BENNETT, Sam D., Jr., Private
BLACK, Charles O., Private First Class (A)
BLAIR, Freeman B., Private
BLALOCK, James G., Master Gunnery Sergeant
BLOTTER, Michael E., Jr., Private First Class
BONNAUD, Daniel, Private First Class (A)
BOUTELLE, Herman H., Staff Sergeant (A)
BRUSH, Charles H., Jr., Captain
BUFF, Howard F., Staff Sergeant (also GOLD STAR)
BURNETTE, Robert W., First Lieutenant
BURRIS, Thurman B., Private First Class

CAMMARATA, Gus J., Private
CAMPBELL, Stuart, Private
CARLSON, Evans C., First Lieutenant
CARMACK, Lawrence E., Corporal
CARPELLOTTI, Louis J., Private First Class
CATALE, Joseph J., Private First Class
CHAMBERS, Justice M., Major
CHENOWETH, Robert J., Corporal (Aviation)
CHITLIK, Edward, Private First Class
CHUDIO, John, Private First Class
CIANCI, Joseph J., Sergeant
COBB, Charles T., Second Lieutenant
COGSWELL, Charles L., Major
COGSWELL, Theodore, Corporal

CONLAN, George I., Corporal
CONNOR, Harry S., Captain
COULTER, Robert L., Corporal
COX, David C., Second Lieutenant
CRAIG, Robert J., Private First Class
CRANDALL, Budington W., Private First Class
CROFT, Orin, Corporal
CROSBY, David H., Jr., Second Lieutenant
CURRIN, Ralph H., Captain

DALRYMPLE, Robert S., Private
DAVIS, Pete P., Private
DAVIS, Quentin R., Private
DE BOER, Henry J., Jr., Private First Class
DE LONG, Earl R., Corporal
DE PASQUALE, Albert F., Private First Class
DIETERICH, Charles W., Jr., Private First Class
DILLARD, Robert H., Captain
DIMICK, Arthur J. J., Corporal
DITTA, Louis G., Captain
DIX, Henry J., Private
DOBBINS, Ernest T., Corporal
DOYLE, John B., Jr., Second Lieutenant (also GOLD STAR)
DRAKE, Francis E., Jr., Private First Class
DUCY, William V., Corporal
DUSSAULT, Thomas W., Corporal
DYAR, Francis J., Private First Class

EARLY, Cleland E., First Lieutenant
EDWARDS, Ray K., Corporal
ELY, Walter R., Jr., Sergeant (A)
ELLENBERGER, Jack H., Jr., Private First Class
EVANS, Cecil H., Private

FERGUSON, Lawrence M., Jr., Corporal
FISCHER, William H., Staff Sergeant
FLESHMAN, Howard L., Private
FLYNN, Lawrence H., Corporal
FOLEY, Ernest P., Major
FORD, Ralph R., Technical Sergeant (A)
FULLER, Regan, Captain

GARY, Albert Von K., Captain
GATELY, John J., Second Lieutenant
GATES, John H., Private First Class
GEISSINGER, Harold J., Private First Class
GIDDENS, Joe, Private First Class
GIERHART, George B., Second Lieutenant
GILLIGAN, John J., Jr., Private
GLOVER, Jessie R., Platoon Sergeant
GOBLE, Joseph O., Sergeant
GOLDBLATT, Julius E., Second Lieutenant
GOLDING, Raymond P., Private First Class
GOODMAN, Howard K., First Lieutenant
GRAUSGRUBER, Ernest A., Private
GRIFFIN, Robert K., Private
GRZECZKOWSKI, Frank V., Jr., Corporal
GYATT, Edward E., Private

HAGGERTY, Robert H., Captain
HANCOCK, James W., Sergeant
HANSEN, Teddy L., Second Lieutenant
HEATER, Donald L., Private First Class
HEATH, Volstead, Corporal
HELLER, Leonard R., Second Lieutenant
HENSON, Everett C., Gunnery Sergeant
HERROD, Ted B., Corporal

HINES, Cloyd V., Corporal

HIRSCH, Sam, Private

HITT, Wade H., Captain

HOLLAND, John W., Second Lieutenant

HOOKER, Hurshall W., Private

HORTON, James W., Second Lieutenant

HOWARD, Edwin A., Corporal

HUBBARD, Charles S., Jr., Private

HUBBS, Carlton C., Private

HUNTER, Ralph R., Corporal

HUTTON, Clayton W., Gunnery Sergeant

IVERSON, Daniel, Jr., Captain (A)

JACHYM, John J., Second Lieutenant

JACOBSON, James P., First Lieutenant

JENKINS, Charles H., Platoon Sergeant

JOHNSON, Albert, Corporal

JOHNSON, F. L., Master Technical Sergeant (A)

JOHNSON, George A., Private

JOHNSON, Louis E., Private

JOHNSTON, Lewis E., Private First Class

JOLLEY, Hugh M., Master Gunnery Sergeant

JOYCE, John J., Jr., Sergeant

KAPLAN, Stanley, Private

KAUFMAN, James W., Sergeant (also GOLD STAR in lieu
    of second Silver Star)

KELLY, George R., Private First Class

KELLY, Richard J., Private First Class

KENTFIELD, Mark D., Private

KING, Charles R., Private First Class

KOBASIAR, Steven, Private

KOLARIK, John, Jr., Private First Class
KOSANOVICH, Milo, Private
KOZLOWSKI, Edward K., Private

LACOY, Joseph R., Private
LAUBER, Eugene W., Private
LARSON, Everett F., Private First Class
LAWTON, Leonard G., First Lieutenant
LEARY, John J., Corporal
LEAVY, James P., Private
LEIDEL, Hugh O., Second Lieutenant
LEROY, James T., Private First Class
LIBBY, Norbert E., Private First Class (A)
LICHTMAN, Alfred M., Captain
LOCKE, Albert C., Private First Class
LOHMILLER, George R., Sergeant
LONG, Edward F., Private First Class (A)
LUKE, Alexander J., Platoon Sergeant
LUTCHKUS, George F., Corporal
LYNN, James T., Private First Class
LYONS, Rondell, Private First Class

McAVOY, George B., Private
McCLANAHAN, James F., Second Lieutenant
McCLINCHY, James J., Private
McCOLLUM, Warren H., Corporal
McCRARY, James W., Jr., Private First Class (A)
McCULLOCH, Gordon R., Second Lieutenant
MACDONALD, Dermott H., Master Technical Sergeant
McGAHERN, William J., Private First Class
McLAIN, Lonnie H., Gunnery Sergeant
MAGHAKIAN, Victor, Platoon Sergeant
MAITLAND, Thomas F., Second Lieutenant

MALONE, Titus, Supply Sergeant
MANUEL, Maurice J., Private First Class
MAROTTA, Alexander R., Private First Class
MARTIN, Roy S., Staff Sergeant
MILANOWSKI, Hubert D., Private
MILLS, Justin G., Second Lieutenant
MITCHELL, Oliver, Second Lieutenant (A)
MONTE, Arthur J., Private
MOORE, Marshall W., Captain
MOORE, Paul, Jr., Second Lieutenant
MOORE, Thomas F., Jr., Second Lieutenant
MORTON, M. P., Private First Class (A)
MULCAHY, Joseph J., Corporal

NARTER, Guy G., Major
NEES, Charles M., Major
NELSON, Earl W., Private
NELSON, Robert W., Staff Sergeant
NEUFFER, Robert P., Captain
NICKEL, Thomas F., Private

O'HALLORAN, James S., Major
OLLIFF, James A., Corporal
OSWALD, Kenneth E., Corporal
OWENS, Homer L., Sergeant

PAINE, Robert I., Private
PEREGRINE, Marion T., Private
PETRIE, Clarence E., Private First Class
PLANTIER, George S., Second Lieutenant
POLLARD, Thomas D., Sergeant
PORT, Robert M., Second Lieutenant
POWELL, Mack, Corporal

PROCTER, Donald, Corporal
PUTNAM, Robert J., Captain

RADIGAN, Richard A., Private First Class
RAMPULLA, Andrew, Private
RATZA, Edmond J., Private First Class
REESE, Foy M., Private First Class
REEVES, Charles L., Private First Class
REID, Wallace J., Corporal (A)
REILLY, Joseph J., Corporal
REYNOLDS, McCoy, Private
RIGGLE, Robert D., Private First Class
ROBINSON, Jack C., Private First Class
ROBINSON, John N., Private
RODGERS, Robert J., Captain
ROSE, Donald V., Second Lieutenant (A)
ROUGH, Carlton R., Private First Class
ROWE, John E., Private First Class
ROZGA, Walter J., Corporal
RUSSELL, Charles B., Corporal
RUTH, John G., Platoon Sergeant
RYDER, Astle A., Second Lieutenant

SANDERS, Verbon C., Private First Class
SEIDEN, Bernard, Private First Class
SHAW, Richard L., Corporal
SILEO, Nicholas, Private First Class
SKIPPER, Homer H., Sergeant
SLOCUM, Donald J., Private
SMITH, Casimir A., Private First Class
SMITH, Homer F., Private First Class
SMITH, James, Sergeant
SNEDEKER, Edward W., Lieutenant Colonel

SNYDER, Lester R., Private First Class
SNYDER, Morris E., Corporal
STAFFORD, Richard Y., Captain
STANKUS, John S., Private First Class
STEVENSON, Nikolai S., First Lieutenant
STOKES, David A., Private First Class
STONE, James B., Private First Class
STOVER, William H. J., Private First Class
STRUNK, Jack N., Private
SVEC, Leonard A., Sergeant (A)

TABER, David P., Private First Class
TALBERT, Wayne K., Private First Class
TASSONE, Frank F., Private First Class
TAYLOR, Lawrence C., Second Lieutenant (A)
TEERELA, Rudolph S., Sergeant Major
TERZI, Joseph A., Second Lieutenant
THAMES, Franklin P., Staff Sergeant (A)
THOMAS, Robert H., Corporal
THOMPSON, Walter D., Jr., Private First Class
TRAW, London L., Platoon Sergeant
TRIPLETT, Orban P., Staff Sergeant (A)

UMSHLER, Warren H., Private First Class (A)

VAN BELLE, Joseph A., Private First Class (A)
VASCONCELLOS, William S., Captain
VAUGHT, Edward E., Private
VOLAN, Stuart J., Private First Class

WAGNER, Carroll M., Corporal
WAGNER, Leonard K., Staff Sergeant (A)
WALT, Lewis W., Captain

WARDLOW, John C., Private
WASHBURN, Richard T., Captain
WASHICK, Alexander, Corporal
WATERS, John R., Sergeant
WATSON, Thomas A., Second Lieutenant
WELSH, Fred L., Private
WIGGINS, Lloyd G., Private
WILLIAMS, Lloyd O., Second Lieutenant
WILLMAN, Oliver J., Corporal (A)
WOLFF, Charles L., Corporal
WOODBURY, Levi, Second Lieutenant

YOUNG, James K., Sergeant Major

DISTINGUISHED FLYING CROSS

ACKERMAN, Ralph P., Technical Sergeant
ARMISTEAD, Kirk, Major
ASHCROFT, Wortham S., First Lieutenant

BANGERT, Douglas A., First Lieutenant
BATE, Oscar M., Jr., First Lieutenant
BRUSHERT, Jack L., Second Lieutenant

CAMPBELL, William B., Second Lieutenant
CAMPBELL, William T., First Lieutenant
CONLEY, Robert F., Second Lieutenant

D'ARCY, Robert M., Second Lieutenant
DOOLEY, George E., Captain

EADES, Edward L., Corporal
EAKIN, Carl F., Jr., Second Lieutenant
ECK, Walter A., Second Lieutenant
ELLISON, William McL., Second Lieutenant

FOSS, Joseph J., Captain
FREEMAN, William B., Second Lieutenant

GARRABRANT, Clifford D., Staff Sergeant
GILLESPIE, Samuel T., Second Lieutenant

HAMILTON, Henry B., Marine Gunner
HAYTER, William C., First Lieutenant
HENDERSON, John S., Second Lieutenant
HISE, Henry W., Second Lieutenant
HOLLOWELL, George L., Second Lieutenant
HOOD, Harlen E., Second Lieutenant
HULL, John O., Second Lieutenant

IRWIN, Darrel D., Captain

JOHANNSEN, Robert W., Second Lieutenant
JONES, John M., Second Lieutenant

KENDRICK, Charles, Second Lieutenant
KENNEDY, Matthew H., Second Lieutenant
KUNZ, Charles M., Second Lieutenant

MCCAFFERTY, Donald E., Second Lieutenant
MCSHANE, Bernard, Second Lieutenant
MANGRUM, Richard C., Lieutenant Colonel
MOORE, Clarence H., Second Lieutenant

NICOLAY, Stanley S., Captain

PARRISH, William P., Second Lieutenant
PATTERSON, Robert M., First Lieutenant
PHILLIPS, Hyde, Second Lieutenant
POOL, Lionel N., First Lieutenant

RICHARD, Robert H., Major
ROBERTSHAW, Louis B., Major
ROUSH, Martin B., Second Lieutenant

SHEPARD, John E., Second Lieutenant
SMITH, Lucius S., III, Second Lieutenant

WATERMAN, Joseph M., Jr., Second Lieutenant
WETHE, Wallace G., Second Lieutenant

NAVY CROSS

AHRENS, Edward H., Private First Class
ARNOLD, Herman F., Private First Class
ATWOOD, Arthur J., Private First Class
AUMAN, Joseph M., Private

BALDINUS, Lawrence, Second Lieutenant (A)
BALDUCK, Remi A., Corporal
BARNES, William, Private First Class
BARTHOLOMEW, Arthur F. D., First Sergeant
BODT, Walter J., Corporal
BRAITMEYER, Nelson, Platoon Sergeant
BROWN, Fletcher L., Jr., Major (A)
BROWN, Robert S., Major
BURAK, Walter J., Corporal

CARL, Marion E., Captain (A)
CARLSON, Evans F., Lieutenant Colonel (GOLD STAR)
CASE, Leo B., First Lieutenant
CHAMPAGNE, Joseph D. R., Private First Class
COCKRELL, Alvin C., Jr., First Lieutenant
CODREA, George, Second Lieutenant
CONKLIN, George E.
CONOLEY, Odell M., Major
COOK, Andrew F., Jr., Second Lieutenant
COOLEY, Albert D., Lieutenant Colonel (A)
CORZINE, Jimmy W., Private First Class
CRAM, Jack R., Major (A)
CRESSWELL, Lenard B., Lieutenant Colonel
CRUMPTON, Billie J., Private

DIAMOND, Le Roy, Corporal
DOBBIN, John F., Major (A)
DORSOGNA, Edmund J., Private First Class
DUNN, Harry, Jr., Private
DWORNITSKI, Nicholas, Corporal

FEDORAK, Michael P., Private First Class
FOX, Myles C., First Lieutenant
FRYBARGER, Raymond, Jr., Private First Class

GAY, Roy M., Sergeant
GEIGER, Roy S., Major General (A)
GRAZIER, George H., Private
GRIFFITH, Samuel B., II, Lieutenant Colonel

HACKER, Elmer, Private First Class
HARRISON, Lawrence A., Platoon Sergeant
HERNDON, Raymon W., Private First Class

HILLS, Clifford C., Platoon Sergeant
HILSKY, Robert J., Private
HUDSPETH, Daniel W., Sergeant
HUNT, Wilfred A., Private First Class

JACOBS, Whitney W., Private

KEITH, Willard W., Jr., Captain
KEY, Eugene, M., First Lieutenant
KIMMEL, Charles J., Second Lieutenant
KOPS, Stanley D., Platoon Sergeant

LEBLANC, Joseph G., Corporal
LESLIE, Dale M., Second Lieutenant (A)
LOEFFEL, Glen B., Second Lieutenant (A)
LONGAZEL, Michael, Platoon Sergeant

MCILHENNY, Walter S., First Lieutenant
MCKELVY, William N., Jr., Lieutenant Colonel
MCLENNAN, Noyes, Second Lieutenant (A)
MALANOWSKI, Anthony P., Jr., Platoon Sergeant
MANGRUM, Richard C., Lieutenant Colonel (A)
MAPLES, Gordon, Second Lieutenant
MATHER, Thomas C., Second Lieutenant
MEAD, George H., Jr., Second Lieutenant
MELNITSKY, Edward, Corporal
MIELKE, John W., Private
MOORE, Paul, Jr., Second Lieutenant
MORRELL, Rivers J., Jr., Major (A)
MORRIS, Emmett R., Private First Class
MOWERY, Earl J., Sergeant
MURPHY, John J., Jr., Private First Class

PARKER, Raymond D., Private
PETTUS, Francis C., Sergeant
PIASECZNY, William L., Private First Class
POLLOCK, Edwin A., Lieutenant Colonel
POND, Zenneth A., Second Lieutenant (A)
PULLER, Lewis B., Lieutenant Colonel (GOLD STAR in
    lieu of third Navy Cross)

RAYSBROOK, Robert D., Sergeant
REYNOLDS, Terrence J., Jr., Corporal
RIVERS, John, Private
RUPERTUS, William H., Brigadier General

SAILER, Joseph, Jr., Major (A)
SANDS, James E., Private
SANGUEDOLCE, Silvio, Sergeant
SCHMID, Albert A., Private
SCHNEIDER, Robert G., Private
SCHWERIN, William E., Captain
SHEPPARD, Charles M., Private First Class
SIMMONDS, Wesley P., Private First Class
STARK, Jerome J., First Sergeant
STERLING, Barney, Private First Class
STEVENSON, William D., Captain
SUGARMAN, Jack, Private First Class
SULLIVAN, Richard E., Second Lieutenant

VANDEGRIFT, Alexander A., Major General

WELLS, Erskine W., Captain
WEST, Theodore G., Private
WILLIAMS, Robert H., Lieutenant Colonel
WILLOX, Nicholas A., Private

WOLVINGTON, William H., Corporal

YAKSICH, John T., Private
YANCEY, John, Corporal

AIR MEDAL

ANDERSEN, Darrell A., Technical Sergeant
BEAR, Robert J., Second Lieutenant
BLUMENSTEIN, John H., Second Lieutenant
BROOKS, William V., Second Lieutenant
BYRD, Virgil S., Sergeant
CREMER, Robert L., Second Lieutenant
DEWEY, John L., Technical Sergeant
GENTRY, Wayne R., Second Lieutenant
HARTLEY, Dean S., Jr., Second Lieutenant
HOFFMAN, Albert, Technical Sergeant
HORTON, Richard B., Corporal
KIRBY, Robert C., Corporal
KNAPP, William J., Jr., Second Lieutenant
MACIAS, Lewis P., Corporal
METZ, Adam A., Marine Gunner
NAUMAN, Melvin R., Second Lieutenant
PROSSER, Bruce, Captain
SANDRETTO, Amedeo, Second Lieutenant
VAUPELL, Robert W., First Lieutenant
WALTER, Howard L., Second Lieutenant
ZUBER, John W., Second Lieutenant

Index

277